Research and Practice in Applied Linguist

General Editors: **Christopher N. Candlin** a
ment, Macquarie University, Australia.

All books in this series are written by leading researchers and teachers in Applied
Linguistics, with broad international experience. They are designed for the MA
or PhD student in Applied Linguistics, TESOL or similar subject areas and for the
language professional keen to extend their research experience.

Titles include:

Francesca Bargiela-Chiappini, Catherine Nickerson and Brigitte Planken
BUSINESS DISCOURSE

Sandra Beatriz Hale
COMMUNITY INTERPRETING

Geoff Hall
LITERATURE IN LANGUAGE EDUCATION

Richard Kiely and Pauline Rea-Dickins
PROGRAM EVALUATION IN LANGUAGE EDUCATION

Virginia Samuda and Martin Bygate
TASKS IN SECOND LANGUAGE LEARNING

Cyril J. Weir
LANGUAGE TESTING AND VALIDATION

Tony Wright
CLASSROOM MANAGEMENT IN LANGUAGE EDUCATION

Forthcoming titles:

Dick Allwright and Judith Hanks
THE DEVELOPING LEARNER

Anne Burns
LITERACIES

David Butt and Annabelle Lukin
GRAMMAR

Alison Ferguson and Elizabeth Armstrong
COMUNICATIONS DISORDERS

Lynn Flowerdew
CORPORA AND LANGUAGE EDUCATION

Sandra Gollin and David R. Hall
LANGUAGE FOR SPECIFIC PURPOSES

Regine Hampel and Marie-Noelle Lamy
ONLINE COMMUNICATION IN LANGUAGE LEARNING AND TEACHING

Marilyn Martin-Jones
BILINGUALISM

Martha Pennington
PRONUNCIATION

Norbert Schmitt
VOCABULARY

Helen Spencer-Oatey and Peter Franklin
INTERCULTURAL INTERACTION

Devon Woods and Emese Bukor
INSTRUCTIONAL STRATEGIES AND PROCESSES IN LANGUAGE EDUCATION

Research and Practice in Applied Linguistics
Series Standing Order ISBN 1–4039–1184–3 hardcover
Series Standing Order ISBN 1–4039–1185–1 paperback
(*outside North America only*)

You can receive future titles in this series as they are published by placing a standing order. Please contact your bookseller or, in case of difficulty, write to us at the address below with your name and address, the title of the series and one of the ISBNs quoted above.

Customer Services Department, Macmillan Distribution Ltd, Houndmills, Basingstoke, Hampshire RG21 6XS, England

Community Interpreting

Sandra Beatriz Hale

University of Western Sydney

First published 2007 by
PALGRAVE MACMILLAN
Houndmills, Basingstoke, Hampshire RG21 6XS and
175 Fifth Avenue, New York, N.Y. 10010
Companies and representatives throughout the world

PALGRAVE MACMILLAN is the global academic imprint of the Palgrave Macmillan division of St. Martin's Press, LLC and of Palgrave Macmillan Ltd. Macmillan® is a registered trademark in the United States, United Kingdom and other countries. Palgrave is a registered trademark in the European Union and other countries.

ISBN-13: 978–1–4039–4068–1 hardback
ISBN-10: 1–4039–4068–1 hardback
ISBN-13: 978–1–4039–4069–8 paperback
ISBN-10: 1–4039–4069–X paperback

This book is printed on paper suitable for recycling and made from fully managed and sustained forest sources. Logging, pulping and manufacturing processes are expected to conform to the environmental regulations of the country of origin.

A catalogue record for this book is available from the British Library.

A catalog record for this book is available from the Library of Congress.

10   9   8   7   6   5   4   3   2   1
16   15   14   13   12   11   10   09   08   07

Printed and bound in Great Britain by
Antony Rowe Ltd, Chippenham and Eastbourne

To my baby, James Lucas

Contents

List of Tables   xi

List of Figures   xii

General Editors' Preface   xiii

Acknowledgements   xv

Part I   Key Concepts and Research Issues

**1   Overview of the Field of Interpreting and Main
Theoretical Concepts**   **3**

1.1   Introduction: What is interpreting? Interpreting as
process   3

1.2   The differences between Interpreting and Translation   8

1.2.1   A continuum of translational activities   13

1.3   The interpreting process   14

1.3.1   Comprehension   14

1.3.2   Conversion   21

1.3.3   Delivery   24

1.4   What is Community Interpreting?   25

1.4.1   Controversy over its label   27

1.5   Differences between Conference and Community
Interpreting   31

**2   Interdisciplinarity: Community Interpreting in the
Medical Context**   **34**

2.1   Introduction   34

2.2   Interpreting in medical settings   36

2.2.1   Communication in doctor–patient interaction   36

2.2.2   The significance of questioning style in
achieving effective communication   37

2.2.3   Patients' compliance with treatment   40

2.3   Treating patients through interpreters   40

2.3.1   The controversy about interpreter roles in the
medical setting   41

2.3.2   Examples of what has been described as the
'mediator', 'visible' or 'involved' interpreter   48

		2.3.3	The case for the trained, faithful medical interpreter	57
		2.3.4	Health care providers and interpreters working as a professional team	61
	2.4	Summary		62

3 Interdisciplinarity: Community Interpreting in the Legal Context **64**
	3.1	Introduction		64
	3.2	Police interviews and interrogations		65
		3.2.1	The right to an interpreter in a police interview	68
		3.2.2	Interpreting in the police context	71
		3.2.3	Discourse issues	73
		3.2.4	Interpreting the caution	77
	3.3	Lawyer–client interactions		79
	3.4	Tribunal hearings		82
		3.4.1	Refugee hearings	83
		3.4.2	Special considerations necessary when evaluating asylum seekers' claims	86
		3.4.3	Interpreters in the refugee hearing	87
	3.5	Courtroom hearings and trials		90
		3.5.1	The language of the courtroom	90
		3.5.2	Interpreters in the courtroom	91

Part II   Practical Applications

4 Analysing the Interpreter's Code of Ethics **101**
	4.1	Introduction: practising interpreters' views about the code of ethics		101
	4.2	The aims of a code of ethics and controversies surrounding it		103
	4.3	Comparison of codes of ethics from around the world		107
		4.3.1	Accuracy	109
		4.3.2	Impartiality	117
		4.3.3	Role	124
	4.4	Ethical dilemmas		129
	4.5	Summary		134

5 The Practitioners' Voices: Views, Perceptions and Expectations from Legal, Medical and Interpreting Practitioners **137**
| | 5.1 | Introduction | | 137 |
| | 5.2 | Sources of challenges faced by interpreters | | 138 |

	5.2.1	Interpreting-related issues	138
	5.2.2	Context-related issues	144
	5.2.3	Participant-related issues	145
	5.2.4	System-related issues	161
5.3	Conclusion		162

6 Community Interpreting Training — **163**

6.1	Introduction		163
6.2	Lack of recognition for the need for training		164
6.3	The need for compulsory pre-service training		166
6.4	Community Interpreting courses		167
6.5	Challenges faced by course designers and educators		169
	6.5.1	The educators' voices	169
6.6	Content and methodologies of Community Interpreting courses		177
	6.6.1	A discourse-based approach to interpreter training	184
	6.6.2	An integrated training framework	185
6.7	Conclusions		193

Part III Research into Community Interpreting

7 Main Traditions and Approaches in Community Interpreting Research — **197**

7.1	Introduction		197
7.2	Summary of research studies in Community Interpreting		200
7.3	Methods used in Community Interpreting research		203
	7.3.1	Approaches to research into Community Interpreting	204
	7.3.2	Discourse analysis	204
	7.3.3	Ethnographic studies	215
	7.3.4	Survey research	219
	7.3.5	Experimental studies	221

8 Conducting Research in Community Interpreting — **225**

8.1	Introduction		225
8.2	Steps to conducting research		225
	8.2.1	Interest in a topic	226
	8.2.2	Reading and reviewing the literature	227
	8.2.3	Defining the research question or questions	228
	8.2.4	Building hypotheses	228

	8.2.5	Deciding on the approach and the sources of data to be collected	229
	8.2.6	Conducting ethical research	232
	8.2.7	Deciding on the methods of analysis to be employed	233
	8.2.8	Writing up and disseminating the results	235
8.3		Sample research projects	236

Part IV   Further Resources in Community Interpreting

9	**Key Resources**			**261**
	9.1	Bibliographies		261
	9.2	Journals		262
	9.3	Useful teaching and learning resources		264
	9.4	Professional development programmes and courses		265
		9.4.1	Formal Community Interpreting courses	265
		9.4.2	Short Community Interpreting courses	266
		9.4.3	Specialist formal Legal Interpreting courses	267
		9.4.4	Short specialist Legal Interpreting courses	268
		9.4.5	Specialist formal Medical Interpreting courses	268
		9.4.6	Short specialist Medical Interpreting courses	269
	9.5	Professional associations and other related professional bodies		269
	9.6	Codes of ethics		270
	9.7	Email lists and bulletin boards		271
	9.8	Web-based glossaries		272
		9.8.1	Medical	272
		9.8.2	Legal	273
		9.8.3	General topics	273
	9.9	Useful research resources		274
	9.10	Other useful websites		275

Notes	276
References	280
Index	297

List of Tables

1.1	Interpreting modes	10
1.2	Factors involved in the conversion process	22
1.3	Factors influencing style of delivery	25
1.4	The main differences between Conference Interpreting and Community Interpreting	32
3.1	Main legal domains in the English-speaking world	66
4.1	Respondent profiles	102
4.2	Frequency of main aspects included in the codes of ethics	108
4.3	Entries on accuracy	109
4.4	Entries on impartiality	118
4.5	Entries on role	125
4.6	Descriptions of role	128
5.1	Question: Do you trust interpreters?	150
5.2	Explanations of the interpreter's role provided by service providers	155
5.3	Questions interpreters consider should be addressed by research	159
6.1	Participants' profiles	170
6.2	Relevant methodologies used to teach Community Interpreting competencies	179
6.3	An integrated training framework	186

List of Figures

1.1   Continuum of different types of translation activities   9
1.2   Interpreting approaches   22
5.1   Challenges faced by the community interpreter   138

General Editors' Preface

Research and Practice in Applied Linguistics is an international book series from Palgrave Macmillan which brings together leading researchers and teachers in Applied Linguistics to provide readers with the knowledge and tools they need to undertake their own practice-related research. Books in the series are designed for students and researchers in Applied Linguistics, TESOL, Language Education and related subject areas, and for language professionals keen to extend their research experience.

Every book in this innovative series is designed to be user-friendly, with clear illustrations and accessible style. The quotations and definitions of key concepts that punctuate the main text are intended to ensure that many, often competing, voices are heard. Each book presents a concise historical and conceptual overview of its chosen field, identifying many lines of enquiry and findings, but also gaps and disagreements. It provides readers with an overall framework for further examination of how research and practice inform each other, and how practitioners can develop their own problem-based research.

The focus throughout is on exploring the relationship between research and practice in Applied Linguistics. How far can research provide answers to the questions and issues that arise in practice? Can research questions that arise and are examined in very specific circumstances be informed by, and inform, the global body of research and practice? What different kinds of information can be obtained from different research methodologies? How should we make a selection between the options available, and how far are different methods compatible with each other? How can the results of research be turned into practical action?

The books in this series identify some of the key researchable areas in the field and provide workable examples of research projects, backed up by details of appropriate research tools and resources. Case studies and exemplars of research and practice are drawn on throughout the books. References to key institutions, individual research lists, journals and professional organizations provide starting points for gathering information and embarking on research. The books also include annotated lists of key works in the field for further study.

The overall objective of the series is to illustrate the message that in Applied Linguistics there can be no good professional practice that isn't based on good research, and there can be no good research that isn't informed by practice.

Christopher N. Candlin and David R. Hall
Macquarie University, Sydney

Acknowledgements

First, I would like to thank the editors of this series, and in particular Christopher Candlin for his extensive knowledge of the literature and his ability to comment insightfully on almost every aspect of the typescript.

I also thank my research assistants, Elizabeth Friedman, Ana Isabel Lozada and Cecilia Alal, who helped with the collection and analysis of the data for the surveys of the legal, medical and interpreting practitioners. My thanks go to all those interpreters, lawyers, medical practitioners and interpreter educators who replied to our questionnaires or participated in the focus group discussions.

I am grateful to Jill Lake, commissioning editor at Palgrave Macmillan, for extending the deadline due to the birth of my third baby.

Finally, I would like to thank my husband, Adrian, and my beautiful daughters, Débora and Elena, for their understanding and support, and my mother, Ethel, for her help in looking after my baby, James, since his birth in May 2006, so that I could complete this book.

Part I
Key Concepts and Research Issues

1
Overview of the Field of Interpreting and Main Theoretical Concepts

This chapter:

- Explores the definitions and aims of the act of translation[1] as proposed by different authors.
- Introduces the controversy over the concepts of faithfulness, accuracy and equivalence.
- Describes the differences between translation (written) and interpreting (oral).
- Compares and contrasts the different translation activities, from the written, to the hybridity between written and oral, to the wholly oral.
- Analyses the different orientations of different translation tasks, from the more target audience-oriented to the more source text-oriented.
- Describes the different steps to the interpreting process.
- Defines community interpreting.
- Outlines the differences between community interpreting and conference interpreting.

1.1 Introduction: What is interpreting? Interpreting as process

Interpreting has traditionally been regarded as a branch of Translation. A number of authors have provided different definitions of translation as a conversion process from one language to another, in either the written or the spoken mode. More specifically, interpreting refers to the translation of the spoken word and Translation to the translation of the written word.

Quotes 1.1–1.4 highlight different aspects of the translation process as the overarching term for both written and oral translation. There are, of course, many other definitions of written translation which will not be discussed here, as this book is about community interpreting. However, the following discussion about translation encompasses the general principles of message transfer from one language to another.

Rabin provides a succinct definition where such a process involves the reproduction of the meaning of a message which was originally delivered in another language:

Quote 1.1   Rabin's definition of translation

Translation is a process by which a spoken or written utterance takes place in one language which is intended and presumed to convey the same meaning as a previously existing utterance in another language.

(Rabin, 1958: 123)

This definition highlights the intention and expectation of the translation process: the translation has the intention of conveying the same meaning as the original utterance, and such a goal is presumed by others. Those who read translations assume that they are reading a faithful representation of the author's original.

House is specific about the aim of translation, which is to achieve a pragmatic equivalence at the expense of semantic equivalence. Semantic equivalence relates to the context-free meaning of an utterance, whereas pragmatic equivalence is concerned with the meaning of utterances in context, taking into account the communicative intention and the relationship between the participants of the communicative event.

Quote 1.2   House's definition of translation

In translation, it is always necessary to aim at equivalence of pragmatic meaning, if necessary at the expense of semantic equivalence. Pragmatic meaning thus overrides semantic meaning. We may therefore consider a translation to be primarily a pragmatic reconstruction of its source text.

(House, 1977: 28)

Wadensjö avoids referring to reproduction of meaning or intentions and highlights the role of the translator/interpreter by proposing that such a mediator is in essence speaking and writing on behalf of another author of an utterance. This definition does not imply a need to remain faithful to the original, but implies that the translator will create his or her own version of the message.

Quote 1.3   Wadensjö's definition of translation

An act of translating is in practice performed by a specific 'I', speaking or writing on behalf of a substantial other.

(Wadensjö, 1998: 41)

Pöchhacker highlights the process and the product of oral translation, namely interpreting. He points to the fact that interpreting involves the process of translating an utterance in the source language that is heard only once and producing an utterance in the target language that cannot be edited after it has been uttered. He also avoids making any reference to the need for fidelity of the meaning of the message.

Quote 1.4   Pöchhacker's definition of interpreting

Interpreting is a form of Translation in which a first and final rendition in another language is produced on the basis of a one-time presentation of an utterance in a source language.

(Pöchhacker, 2004a)

As can be seen, opinion is divided as to whether the target or translated text should be a faithful rendition of the source or original text, or at least on how important the concept of faithfulness is to the main goal of the translation process. Throughout the history of translation studies, there have been strong arguments proposing different degrees of 'faithfulness' to the original text, and by inference different definitions of the meaning of 'fidelity'. These range from the need to be as literal as possible to the original at one extreme, to the virtual disregard of the source text at the other. Grades of these two extremes appear in between. Hermans (1995) comments that the early concept of 'fidelity' in translation was later replaced by the concept of 'equivalence', which has in turn been rejected by some in favour of 'norms'. One could argue that these are all variations of a single theme and share a common goal. It is not the concepts that change, but the understanding of how they are applied and what they represent according to a number of factors. Most theories contribute to the understanding of the process in some way and all have some merit when they are applied to practice. The theory, orientation or priority that is adopted will depend on a number of factors surrounding the translation task, such as the text type, the purpose of the source text, the purpose or mandate of the translation and the circumstances that surround its production. No one theory is all-encompassing. As Holmes comments, definitions of translation that propose only one view 'are in reality no more than codifications of time, place and/or text type-bound norms' (1978: 101). Toury (1980) calls the different factors that surround a translation task, translational norms. These determine the decisions made by the translator and the type of equivalence that is to ensue: 'it is the norms that determine the (type and extent of) equivalence manifested by actual translations' (Toury, 1995: 61). Such a theory of translation norms does not contradict or render the aim for faithfulness or equivalence invalid, but rather complements and clarifies it.

Concept 1.1   What is the meaning of equivalence?

Although some argue against the use of the term 'equivalence' to describe the core of translation, it is useful to describe the goal of translation activity. We read of formal and textual equivalence (Catford, 1965), dynamic equivalence (Nida, 1964) and semantic and pragmatic equivalence (House, 1977, Koller 1995), which describe the main orientations in translation. If translation is to be distinguished from autonomous text production, then there needs to be a way of referring to such an activity. 'Between the resultant text in L2 (the target – language text) and the source text in L1 (the source-language text) there exists a relationship, which can be designated as a translational, or equivalence relationship' (Koller, 1995: 196). Equivalence is therefore seen as the term that best describes the relationship between the source and the target texts. Different types of equivalence may be appropriate at different times or at least useful in the process of achieving the optimum product, depending on its aim.

Wadensjö (1998) states that interpreters understand that when they are interpreting they are not only translating between two languages, they are performing activities on behalf of others, such as persuading, agreeing, lying, explaining, etc. I see no difference between the act of interpreting and the act of performing speech acts on behalf of others, as long as those speech acts were originated by those others. Translation should never be misunderstood for a word-matching exercise, but it cannot be completely detached from the source text from which it originates. As Hatim explains, from a relevance theoretical perspective, 'translation proper involves the representation of what someone else has thought or said. Furthermore, translations are intended to achieve relevance, not alone as communication in their own right, but by standing in for some original' (2001: 40). Wadensjö (1998) argues that approaches that look at equivalence from one language to another and attempt to match the original speaker's intentions are flawed because they are looking at the interaction as monological rather than dialogical. A monologue has one author for the entire text, whereas a dialogue is dynamically produced contemporaneously by a number of authors. In a dialogic view, 'an utterance is a link up in a chain of utterances' (Wadensjö, 1998: 43). However, each turn in a dialogue is produced by a speaker who is responsible for those words and who intends to express some meaning, which needs to be reflected in its translation.

The differences of opinion that are described above may simply be attributed to a confusion about the working definitions of the terms 'faithful', 'equivalent' and 'accurate'. If by these words what is meant is a literal translation – that is, a target text that is equivalent at all levels of the language hierarchy (lexical, syntactic, semantic and pragmatic) – then such a requirement is largely unachievable. If, however, as has been argued (House, 1977; Alcaraz, 1996; Hale, 1996, 2004; Nord, 1997), equivalence is viewed from a pragmatic perspective, it is an achievable end. This implies understanding the meaning of the utterance beyond the literal meaning of the words, understanding the speaker's intentions in context, taking into account the participants and the situation, and then assessing the likely reaction of the listeners to the utterance. It also involves understanding the appropriateness of the utterance according to the different cultural conventions that are linked to the languages in question. After having analysed the original utterance in detail, the interpreter will perform a mental process which will essentially pose the following questions: how would the original utterance (in the given context, with the given participants) be appropriately phrased in the target language and culture in order to reflect the author's intention and achieve a similar reaction in the listeners as the original might have? There is no doubt that the interpreter's understanding of the original intention and of the original impact on him- or herself are subjective. It is to this subjective interpretation of the source utterance that an interpreter has an obligation to be faithful. Nothing more can objectively be asked. As Hervey and colleagues state, 'It seems obvious, then, that if good translation is defined in terms of "equivalence", this is not an *objective* equivalence, because the translator remains ultimately the only arbiter of the imagined effects of both the ST and the TT' (1995: 14). It is also clear that such subjectivities will be minimised the more familiar the interpreter is with the languages and cultures in question, the participants, the situation, the context and the setting.

1.2   The differences between Interpreting and Translation

Although Interpreting and Translation have much in common, the differences between them are great. The first, obvious, difference is that one is expressed in written form (Translation) and the other in oral form (Interpreting), and for this reason, the translation process includes a number of steps that are not available to the interpreter. Translators have the complete text in front of them, which they will read and thoroughly analyse as a first step. The relevant research will take place at this initial comprehension stage to facilitate understanding. The amount of research necessary will depend on the type of text. Technical texts will require a different type of preparation from general or literary texts. The translator will also need to research parallel texts in the other language, to compare styles, terminology and appropriate thematic structures. The conversion process will then take place, followed by the production of the text in the target language, with a number of drafts preceding the final version. The translator has access to numerous resources when preparing the translation and these are becoming increasingly sophisticated with very important aids, such as translation memory software packages, which complement a translator's long-term memory. Interpreters, on the other hand, need to deal with the oral text as it is presented to them, without the opportunity to consult references, previous interpreting assignments (except through the use of their own memory) or correct and edit their final product. The role of both short- and long-term memory is crucial in their work. Conference interpreters, as a general rule, are provided with material to research and papers to prepare before their work commences. In this respect, it can be argued that Conference Interpreting has more in common with translation than Community Interpreting. The hybridity and overlap between different types of translation activities are illustrated in Figure 1.1, where they are placed in a continuum, with written translation at one extreme and Community Interpreting at the other. In Community Interpreting, interpreters are given very little information about their future assignment, either for reasons of confidentiality or insufficient knowledge about the purpose of the interaction. For example, in the case of a first-time visit to a lawyer, only the lay client will have any knowledge about the purpose of the visit. However, in a case where there is a long brief, such a brief is unfortunately not provided to the interpreter as

```
←---T --------SubT --------ST --------SI --------CI --------DI --------(Ch)---→
Target audience-oriented------------------------------------→ Author/speaker-oriented
Monologic-------------------------------------------------→ Dialogic
More time to prepare---------------------------------------→ No time to prepare
Text availability------------------------------------------→ No text availability
```

Figure 1.1   Continuum of different types of translation activities

T: Translation, SubT: Subtitling, ST: Sight translation, SI: Simultaneous interpreting, CI: Long consecutive interpreting, DI: Dialogue interpreting, Ch: *Chuchotage*.

background material on the grounds of confidentiality, notwithstanding the interpreter's obligation to confidentiality under their code of ethics (cf. chapter 4). Community interpreters are therefore required to have extensive knowledge of the social and institutional settings in which they work, so that they are prepared to deal with new 'texts' at every assignment. When community interpreters are experienced in working in different settings, there is naturally an element of predictability that aids them in the comprehension and delivery stages.

One less obvious difference between interpreting and translation (depending on the text type) is the amount of licence a translator as opposed to an interpreter is able to enjoy. A translator is able to assess the readership and the purpose of the text and adapt the translation to suit the audience. Many translations can be said to be complete cultural adaptations of the original. This is particularly true in the translation of advertising, which requires many cultural adaptations for it to sell the particular product successfully in another language. Such adaptations can include a complete restructuring of the text, the use of different images, the omission of whole paragraphs and the addition of others, and so on. Such licence is also used in literary and other types of translation, such as in the translation of community brochures. A poorly written community brochure will require the translator to improve on its expression and clarity for a better understanding of the aim of the text by the target audience. This may not be the case with a legal document, for example, where due to its binding nature, it may require a specific format, formulaic sentences and specialised terms in order to ensure its validity. As a general rule, however, translation is target audience-oriented, whereas, as a general rule, interpreting tends to be more source text-oriented, although this depends greatly on the type of interpreting.

The monologic types of interpreting (See Table 1.1), such as simultaneous and long consecutive interpreting, have as their main objective to convey the propositional content in the clearest, most accessible way. For this reason, it is widely accepted that text condensing is a necessary

Table 1.1 Interpreting modes

Interpreting mode	Definition of mode	Context where it is used	Interactional type
Simultaneous (with use of equipment)	The interpreter listens to the speaker through headphones and begins interpreting a few seconds after the commencement of each utterance	Conferences, international meetings	Monologic
Simultaneous whispering or *chuchotage* (no equipment)	As above. However, the interpreter is not aided by equipment and relies on the acoustics of the room in order to hear what is being said	Courtrooms, psychiatric consultations, informal meetings where more than one person in the same language need interpreting services	Monologic
Long consecutive	The speaker delivers a speech in segments of up to five minutes each while the interpreter takes notes. The interpreter then renders each segment in turn in the target language	Small conferences, information sessions, informal meetings	Monologic
Dialogue (short consecutive)	The interpreter interprets a dialogue between two people who speak different languages. Each turn is relatively short, and is determined by the previous turn.	Interviews, consultations, courtroom	Dialogic

and desirable strategy in simultaneous and long consecutive interpreting (Herbert, 1952; Dam, 1993). Text condensing involves the omission of non-content features, such as hesitations, discourse markers, repetitions and backtrackings, to produce a smoother rendition for the audience.

This strategy also allows simultaneous interpreters to avail themselves of more time to keep up with the speaker, if necessary, or the consecutive interpreter, to avoid taking unnecessary notes. This practice is logical in light of the monologic nature of written translation and of these two types of interpreting, where there is no interaction between the author of the text and its reader/listener, be it the source text or the translated text. On the other hand, dialogue interpreting is more source speaker-oriented because there is interaction between the speakers and the opportunity for repair or clarification. The speakers are responsible for their speech and able to clarify misunderstandings or rectify mistakes. This opportunity for immediate clarification is not available to translators (who have no contact with the author of the text) or simultaneous interpreters working in a booth (who are physically removed from the speakers). In dialogue interpreting the interpretation is speaker-oriented because the interpreter's aim is to empower the speakers to communicate with each other by removing the language barrier through the medium of interpreting. The dialogue interpreter attempts to reproduce the original intention (illocutionary point) (Austin, 1962) and illocutionary force (Searle, 1975) to achieve the reaction in the listener that the original would have achieved if the message had been understood in its original language (perlocutionary act) (Austin, 1962). Hale (2004) conducted experiments which demonstrated that such a goal is possible when features additional to propositional content, such as markers of register variation, hesitations, discourse markers, repetitions and backtracking, are maintained in the target language rendition. These features are important cues that help reveal the speaker's attitudes, commitment to the truth of their utterance, level of education and even social and regional membership. If the interpreter aims to maintain such features, then the speakers will be given the opportunity to react to the message as it is presented to them, rather than receive a censored or edited version from the interpreter. The requirement to maintain stylistic features in the interpreter's rendition is crucial in certain settings, such as the courtroom or a medical consultation. In these settings demeanour and discourse style, which form the manner in which a testimony is presented or a condition described, are essential in the evaluation of witness character or a patient's diagnosis (cf. Davidson, 2000; Hale 2004). Apart from the consequences that will ensue from making substantial changes to the original, it would be impossible for the interpreter to change an oral text to the same extent as a translator, because the complete text is not available all at once, but is presented piecemeal.

The type of translation that would most closely resemble dialogue interpreting is literary translation, which requires the translation of dialogue. When the translator translates the dialogues of different characters, the characters' individual styles must be retained to allow for the identification of the different voices. Similarly, in dialogue interpreting, the speakers need to retain their individuality through the interpreted rendition. The principal difference between these two types of dialogue is, of course, that the translated dialogue is static and the translation will not change the subsequent turns. In dialogue interpreting, the interpreter's renditions of each speaker's turn will determine the next turn, and hence the dialogue is dynamically created by three participants, rather than by two.

Concept 1.2 The triadic construction of text

As Wadensjö states, 'meanings conveyed by language use are conceptualized and co-constructed *between* speaker and hearer(s) *in interaction*' (1998: 41).

In a dialogue, each turn from one speaker will prompt a response or a reaction from the other speaker. In a dialogue interpreting situation, each turn is processed through the interpreter, who, even when attempting to be fully accurate to the original, is a different person from the other interlocutors and will inevitably bring to the interaction his or her own person – a third participant. Different interpreters will produce different renditions, choosing different words, different syntax, different nuances, which may trigger different reactions in the participants, the significance of which is yet to be determined.

In a study of Russian/English police interpreting, Krouglov (1999: 295) found that a key phrase allegedly uttered by a suspect received three different interpretations by three different interpreters working at different times. These were: 'I'll kill you', 'I'll get you' and 'I'll stitch you up'. All are accurate renditions of the original, taking into account that the interpreters did not know the context of the utterance. The police were fortunately alerted to this and no case was made on the basis of the differences. In an analysis of dialogue interpreting, Mason and Stewart highlight a number of interpreter-induced misunderstandings due to their inability to produce pragmatically equivalent renditions. They state that 'what is striking about these particular triadic exchanges is the degree to which the intervention of the interpreter subtly affects the pragmatics of the interventions of the other two speakers and thus modifies the unfolding relationship between the principal participants (2001: 67–8). With these caveats in mind, the interpreter's aim remains to attempt to reduce the differences between the original and the interpreted versions by matching, as far as possible, the illocutionary point and force, thus producing a similar perlocutionary act (the reaction in the hearer). Like actors in a play who will interpret and represent the same scripts in their own way, according to their personal understanding of the role, attempting to be faithful to the playwright's intentions, interpreters reproduce the original script in their own, individual ways, also attempting to be faithful to their understanding of the original author's message. The more they know about the author, about the topic, about the discourse strategies and styles of that particular setting, the closer their understanding of the source message will be to the author's own understanding. It is not unusual for interpreters to reach a synchronicity with the speakers and even pre-empt what they are about to say.

1.2.1 A continuum of translational activities

There are two types of translation activity that fall between interpreting and translation: sight translation and subtitling. Sight translation requires interpreters to simultaneously interpret orally a written text that is in front of them. In this activity, the interpreter has access to the whole text and is able to read it once before beginning. The interpreter will then orally translate into the target language as they read the text in the source language. Unlike interpreting *per se*, sight translation consists of a written source text and an oral target text.

Subtitling can be described as the opposite of sight translation: the source text is oral and the target text is written. Although the source text is oral, it is recorded and can be stopped and reviewed. This type of activity is constrained by the number of characters permitted per caption. However, subtitlers are able to work at their own pace and consult references, which the interpreter doing a sight translation cannot do.

What emerges is a continuum between different types of translation activities, as represented in Figure 1.1. At one end of the continuum we find translators working by themselves to analyse a full written text that has been written by an author who is often unknown to them, with time to prepare and with the main aim of catering to the target audience. Such an activity is monologic, with no interaction between the author and reader of the text. At the other end of the continuum we find the interactive, dialogic activity of dialogue interpreting. In this activity the speakers are producing text contemporaneously; the interpreter receives the text piecemeal because the full text is yet to be created turn by turn, and therefore has no time to stop, read what has been said, analyse it and then reproduce it, as a translator would. The interpreter's rendition is also contemporaneous, unrehearsed and aided only by the context (Hatim and Mason, 1990). The other activities, such as subtitling, sight translation, simultaneous interpreting and long consecutive interpreting, fall in between. It could be argued that there is less time to prepare in simultaneous interpreting than short consecutive interpreting. However, when discussing simultaneous interpreting, I refer to the activity performed in the context of Conference Interpreting, where the interpreter is – or should be – provided with preparation material beforehand. The simultaneous interpreting performed in the context of Community Interpreting, often referred to as *chuchotage* or whispering interpreting, can be more demanding, in that there is no access to the text, it is performed in a straining soft voice (*sotto voce*), by only one interpreter and with very few breaks.

1.3   The interpreting process

The three main steps of the interpreting process are comprehension, conversion and delivery. Each needs to be analysed in its own right in order to understand the complexity of the process.

1.3.1   Comprehension

Concept 1.3   Is mutual understanding in communication possible?

'Communication is itself miscommunication' (Coupland et al., 1991: 3). Coupland and colleagues argue that communication among participants is impossible, that all interaction creates miscommunication. S ome have argued that no two people ever understand words in exactly the same way. The anthropologist and linguist Edward S apir proposed that 'no two languages are ever sufficiently similar to be considered as representing the same social reality. The worlds in which different societies live are distinct worlds, not merely the same world with different labels attached' (1949: 162). Arrojo (1998), following a deconstructionist paradigm, argues that texts do not hold stable meanings that can be transferred across languages, and that translations become reinterpretations of previous reinterpretations. How, then, is mutual monolingual communication possible? And how is translation possible?

Understanding each other in conversation involves a complex set of issues, which become even more complicated when two languages and two cultures are involved. As Pöchhacker states:

> It is now an established fact that comprehension is not a passive, receptive process but depends crucially on what is already known. Processing new information thus requires the active construction of some form of mental representation integrating the input with various kinds of pre-existing knowledge – lexical, syntactic, pragmatic, encyclopaedic, etc. (Pöchhacker, 2004a: 119)

Despite such complexity, for the most part humans manage to understand each other's meanings and, on the whole, interpreters and translators are capable of reproducing those meanings accurately. After all, most of the world's theories and philosophies have been made widely available only through the medium of translation, and their contents are attributed to their authors, not to their translators. Schegloff states that 'talk in interaction is built for understanding, and on the whole effortless understanding' (1987: 202).

Concept 1.4   The principle of charity

Davidson (1984) proposed the 'principle of charity', which talks of a 'bridgehead' of commonality across languages. His principle proposes that all humans share some common ground by virtue of being human. The more common ground we share, the easier our understanding of each other's meanings will be. Therefore, although mutual understanding can be a complex enterprise, it is nevertheless a feasible one, and by extension, so is the act of translation. As Smirnov comments, 'overdosing on such ideas as "untranslatability" or "inadequacy of human communication" may not be particularly conducive to successful training of translators and interpreters, including their chances of developing a self-image as professionals' (1997: 214).

Paraphrasing Bakhtin (1979), Foley (1997: 15) states that 'any present meaning is always a reframing of the past, reworking things from past histories into the present relationship'. Grice (1975) spoke of a cooperative principle (CP) which governs effective conversation between two participants. In such a principle, the responsibility for understanding is shared by both parties. Four maxims apply to the CP: quantity (say only as much as needed to be understood), quality (speak the truth), relevance (be relevant) and manner (be clear). When people have a dialogue with each other, they assume that the other participants are abiding by such maxims. In this way, they can deduce the pragmatic meaning of the utterance from the literal, semantic meaning of what has been said. Maxims can be deliberately flouted by speakers to achieve rhetorical purposes. For example, the maxim of quality (telling the truth) needs to flouted to achieve sarcasm or irony, or to utter figures of speech or common expressions that use exaggeration. The maxims of quantity, quality and manner may be incompatible with the maxims of politeness, and hence may need to be flouted. Speakers who share the same pragmatic conventions will usually understand them in the way they were intended. However, when their intention is not clearly understood by the hearer, they can cause communication breakdown. If misunderstandings occur between speakers who share the same language, culture and past common histories, how much greater the potential for misunderstanding is when different languages and cultures come into contact. Here is where the mediation of the interpreter is crucial, as the interpreter will share common ground with both speakers. As Foley acknowledges, 'translation requires deft interpretive handling of all aspects of language... it is a world of significance, bound in contextualized, communicative, cultural and linguistic practices' (1997: 175). The interpreter/translator, who is conversant with both worlds, becomes the medium by which communication is made possible between the two. The main issue to contemplate at this stage is the crucial necessity for the interpreter to understand before they can start to interpret. Being aware of the possible sources of misunderstanding can to some extent improve the chances of comprehension.

Concept 1.5   Sources of misunderstanding

We can divide the sources of misunderstanding into those that are discourse-internal and those that are discourse-external (House et al., 2003). Bazzanella and Damiano's (1999: 819) propose a taxonomy of discourse-internal sources of misunderstanding which includes all levels of language, from the phonetic to the pragmatic. This implies that there is potential for misunderstanding in any part of the discourse: incorrect pronunciation, an unknown lexical item, a marked syntactic order, an incoherent utterance, an indirect speech act or pragmatic implicature – all can be sources of misunderstanding which are expressed through the discourse. However, background knowledge of the topic, shared knowledge with the speaker and contextual cues will greatly determine whether the hearer understands the discourse or not.

In the interpreting process the following will minimise the potential sources of misunderstanding and facilitate the comprehension process:

1. At the discourse-internal level
   From the interpreter:

   - a thorough knowledge of the two languages involved.

   From the speaker:

   - coherence of discourse style,
   - a willingness to be understood,
   - unambiguous expression.

2. At the discourse-external level
   From the interpreter:

   - an understanding of the discourse roles in the interaction,
   - an understanding of the social roles attributed to the participants,
   - an understanding of the context of the situation,
   - an understanding of the setting,
   - an understanding of the relevant cultures,
   - a knowledge of the subject matter,
   - common or shared knowledge with the speakers.

   From the setting:

   - good physical conditions which will not hinder hearing or concentration.

   From the speakers:

   - an understanding of the interpreter's role,
   - an understanding of the interpreter's needs.

We can see that there are more points under the discourse-external category than under the discourse-internal category. This is because discourse-external factors will impinge on the understanding of the discourse itself. How much an interpreter understands the 'language' of the speaker will be determined by how many of the extra linguistic requirements that interpreter meets. Once again, referring to Grice's

(1975) cooperative principle, we assume that the speakers want to be understood and will be partly responsible for the hearer's comprehension ability.

The following examples from interpreted data illustrate how misunderstanding occurs due to different sources.

Example 1.1   Guilty or not guilty?

1. Magistrate: How do you plead, guilty or not guilty?
2. Interpreter: ¿*'Usted se declara culpable o no culpable?*
3. (Do you declare yourself guilty or not guilty?)
4. Witness: *Sí, sí.*
5. Interpreter: Yes, yes.
6. Magistrate: How do you plead guilty or not guilty?
7. Interpreter: ¿*Es culpable o no?* (Are you guilty or not?)
8. Witness: Yeah.
9. Interpreter. Yes, yes.
10. Magistrate: Well that is not a plea. Do I take it that when you say yes you are admitting the offence?
11. Interpreter: *Señor, cuando usted me dice que sí* ¿*está admitiendo que cometió ese delito?* (Mr X, when you tell me yes, are you admitting that you committed that crime?)
12. Witness: Yes.
13. Interpreter: Yes.

(Extract from a NSW Local Court mention)

Example 1.1 is one of a misunderstanding between the magistrate, the witness and the interpreter due to discourse-external sources. The magistrate's original question is 'Do you plead guilty or not guilty?' (line 1). This is a legal speech act[2] which requires an answer that adheres to the appropriate felicity conditions[3] for it to be valid. The answer needs to be either 'guilty' or 'not guilty'; any indirect speech act such as 'yes' or 'I didn't mean it' or 'I won't do it again' does not constitute a plea, as stated by the magistrate in line 10. The interpreter interprets the question accurately, using the pragmatic approach (lines 2 and 3). The use of the word *'declarar'* (declare) shows a knowledge of the appropriate legal register in Spanish. The witness no doubt understands the language used, but does not understand the requirements of the institution. The source of the misunderstanding is not discourse-internal. He therefore simply answers with a 'yes', meaning, 'yes, I'm guilty'. The magistrate repeats the question in the same form. Here, however, the interpreter deviates from her accurate rendition of the same question, and possibly assuming that the witness did not understand the legal register (discourse-internal source), attempts to clarify the question by asking a different question that does not belong to the legal register and will not elicit the legally required answer: 'Are you guilty or not?' The witness's answer to this is coherent with the question: 'yes', meaning 'yes, I am'. The interpreter's attempt to help has the opposite effect of reinforcing the witness's misunderstanding. We can surmise that the interpreter here has misunderstood the purpose of the original question (discourse-external source), albeit the words used were understood. This is most probably due to an ignorance of the requirements of the law – a lack of knowledge of the setting. In previous work on court interpreting (Hale, 2004), Hale found that a major source of difficulty for interpreters, manifested in poor interpretations, was the interpreters' lack of knowledge of the setting, of the specific legal or strategic ways language is used in the courtroom, which in turn led to misunderstandings. This reinforces the assertion that knowledge of two languages alone is insufficient to interpret accurately.

Miguélez (2001) reports the findings of causes of comprehension difficulty for interpreters who had to interpret expert witness evidence simultaneously. She found that, although there was some specialised terminology in the testimonies, technical jargon was not one of the main sources of difficulty. Especially challenging was the occurrence of grammatical or structural irregularities, false starts and embeddings, and what Miguélez refers to as 'semantic ambiguities' or 'total loss of coherence'. An example from her data is given in Example 1.2.

Example 1.2

I checked the speedometer reading from the general reading to the decimal indicator at the end of the reading from one point to the next and then in sequence and then got at the mileage by subtraction.

(Miguélez, 2001: 18)

Miguélez cites this as a case where the interpreter 'has no choice but to render an ongoing interpretation of what she/he hears as it is virtually impossible spontaneously to correct or improve the quality of spoken language when cohesion and coherence are so totally lacking' (2001: 18). Such examples fit in the discourse-internal category, where the source of misunderstanding lies in the speaker's inability to express him- or herself coherently. In situations such as this, it is not the interpreter's responsibility to clarify the utterance. Rather, the interpreter has no choice but to maintain the incoherence in the interpreted rendition.

Mason and Stewart (2001) quote from the O. J. Simpson trial instances where the interpreter's renditions fail to achieve a pragmatic equivalence, resulting in misunderstanding between the witness and the lawyer, as Example 1.3 shows.

Example 1.3

Att: And you've been here 27 years, correct?
Int: +++
W: *Haga la cuen/vine en 69. Haga la cuenta.*
(Calcula/I came in 69. Calculate)
Int: I came in '69, YOU figure it out. (*laughter in courtroom*)
Att: Okay. Why don't YOU tell me, how long you've been here.

(Mason and S tewart, 2001: 60)

Mason and Stewart aptly comment that the witness's remark was not intended to be impolite, as the interpreter's rendition was. The use of the imperative in Spanish is not regarded as a sign of impoliteness as it might be in English. The possible reasons for the inappropriate interpretation are: first, the interpreter's misunderstanding of the original intention; second, the interpreter's unawareness of the impolite tone of her interpretation in English; or third, the interpreter's inability to produce a pragmatically equivalent utterance under pressure. A more appropriate interpretation would have been something like 'Can you help me work it out' or, as Mason and Stewart suggest, 'Could you work it out for me?' (2001: 61). The interpreter's inaccurate rendition (incorrect illocutionary point and force) caused the attorney to misunderstand its intention, and he reacted (perlocutionary act) with an equally impolite response.

The cause of the misunderstanding illustrated in Example 1.4 is discourse-external, an unawareness of the context of the situation.

Example 1.4

Question: Do you see where... there is a couch a rectangle for a couch, do you
see that?

Interpreter: *Y, ¿hay una especie de cama o sillón rectangular ahí marcado?*(And,
there is a type of bed or rectangular lounge marked there?)

(Extract from a NSW Local Court hearing)

The misunderstanding in Example 1.4 is reflected in the interpreter's
hedging when interpreting the word 'couch', as 'a type of bed or rectangular lounge'. The word 'couch' was accurately interpreted as *sillón*,
taken out of context. In the context of a doctor's surgery, as was the
case here, the correct interpretation in Spanish is *camilla*, a rendition
the interpreter produces later in the hearing, when the context becomes
clear.

1.3.2 Conversion

Concept 1.6

The translation choices interpreters make during the conversion phase of the
process are linked to their theoretical approach to interpreting.

The conversion phase is the mental translation process. This is where
the interpreter needs to make strategic mental choices to decide what
is the most appropriate and most accurate rendition in the target
language. A constraining difficulty found at this phase in interpreting,
and which is not found in translation, is the need to act in real
time, with little opportunity to contemplate the choices. A whole
range of issues will contribute to the characterisation of this phase (see
Table 1.2).

Factors 1 and 2 are self-explanatory and have been discussed by others.
Factor 3, however, is one that (to my knowledge) has never been explicitly linked to this phase of the interpreting process. I propose that the
choices interpreters make during the conversion process are inextricably linked to the approach they adopt to their interpreting, which may
rely on their natural intuition or on careful, informed study. There are
three general approaches that can be taken by the interpreter which are

Table 1.2   Factors involved in the conversion process

1. Knowledge of the target language	This includes not only a thorough knowledge of the grammar, but also knowledge of the appropriate lexicon, registers and pragmatic conventions.
2. Interpreting skills	These are acquired through training and/or experience. A bilingual person may understand perfectly well what was said by the source speaker (phase 1 of the process), but will not be able to convert the utterance into the target language if unequipped with the appropriate interpreting skills. Technical skills required include: • note-taking, • mastery of the different modes of interpreting (short consecutive, long consecutive, simultaneous, sight translation), • situational management (knowing when and how to interrupt, take turns, seating arrangements), • the ability to deconstruct and reconstruct the message quickly, • the ability to make difficult, complex choices under pressure, • the ability to concentrate, listen and make use of long- and short- term memory.
3. A theoretical underpinning approach	A conscious understanding of the reasons behind each choice.

linked to the levels of language and to whether the translation process is viewed as top-down or bottom-up, as illustrated in Figure 1.2.

Those who take a bottom-up view argue that languages can be matched by substituting equivalent words and will interpret at the word level, producing a literal rendition. I argue that only very incompetent bilinguals and absolute beginners adopt this approach, as it is

Language level	Interpreting product	Approach
DISCOURSE LEVEL	Pragmatic	Top-down
SENTENCE LEVEL	Semantic	
WORD LEVEL	Literal	Bottom-up

Figure 1.2   Interpreting approaches

extremely difficult to translate literally consistently. By literal, I mean matching every word in the same order, for example: 'By God went-I to house brother-me and hit-I sister-me telephone' (*Wallahi ruH-t bayt ab-ii wa Darab-t ukhtii tilifuun*) is a literal translation from Arabic, which adequately translated would read: 'I'm telling you, I went to my brother's house and phoned my sister' (Campbell, 2001: 1). Similarly, 'No give-I more' is a literal translation of the Spanish *No doy más*, which adequately translated would read, 'I'm dead tired'.

There are some instances where a literal translation will make sense semantically and even pragmatically, but these are rare.

Most untrained, 'natural' interpreters, to use Harris and Sherwood's (1978) term, or novice interpreters, take a middle approach, aiming for translation at the sentence level and producing a semantic rendition. By this I mean a rendition that is grammatical in the target language, conveys a message that on the surface, and out of context, may appear to be correct, but that fails to capture the original intention, its illocutionary point and force. This is what Thomas (1983) called 'pragmalinguistic transfer'.

Quote 1.5   Pragmalinguistic transfer

...the inappropriate transfer of speech act strategies from one language to another, or the transferring from the mother tongue to the target language, of utterances which are semantically/syntactically equivalent, but which, because of different 'interpretative bias' tend to convey a different pragmatic force in the target language.

(Thomas, 1983: 101)

Only the most competent interpreters will convert the message pragmatically, taking the top-down approach, understanding the text as discourse rather than as words or sentences strung together.

Mason and Stewart (2001: 58), in discussing the performance of an interpreter in the O. J. Simpson trial, comment that 'the requirement to translate literally tends to dissuade interpreters from adding, for example, hedges or particles to convey pragmatic implicature', yet they concede that such an assumption is not validated by the data they present, as the interpreter in question does not interpret literally. As most community interpreters are untrained bilinguals, it is unlikely that an external mandate to interpret literally will guide their rendition; rather, it is a lack of training and a lack of competence. Interpreters do not usually interpret according to what lawyers tell them they should do, but according to what they think is the best choice at the time, or what comes to mind first. The better trained, the more thoughtful, the more prepared, the more experienced the interpreter is, the closer she or he will get to achieving a discourse-based interpreted rendition of the original. Jacobsen argues that fully authorised and trained interpreters in Denmark will interpret pragmatically in spite of their code of ethics, which 'instructs them to deliver absolute verbatim versions of originals' (Jacobsen, 2002: 282). This is an important issue, which is examined more fully in chapter 4 when I discuss codes of ethics. It is only when interpreters are insecure that they will produce renditions that are syntactically and semantically very close to the original, producing renditions that are pragmatically inaccurate (cf. Gile, 1998). The main question posed by the interpreter in the conversion phase is: 'How would I express this utterance in the target language in this situation, with these participants to achieve a similar reaction in the listener?'

1.3.3   Delivery

The delivery phase comprises the end-product, the verbal output after the previous two phases have been completed. The style of the delivery will depend on the type and mode of interpreting and on the purpose of the interaction, as shown in Table 1.3.

As Table 1.3 shows, three modes – simultaneous, whispering simultaneous into the minority language, long consecutive – focus on the propositional content of the original. The main purpose of the interpretation is to transmit the propositional content of the original to the target audience in the most coherent and succinct way. Such an aim will be reflected in the interpreter's delivery. The constraints of these modes will also force the interpreter to paraphrase and omit non-content discourse features. The other two modes – dialogue and whispering simultaneous into the mainstream language – focus on both content and form. Such a focus is due to the demands and expectations of the settings and the purpose of the encounter. The difference between whispering simultaneous interpreting into the minority language and into the mainstream language is also related to the different aims of the two activities. When the interpreter interprets simultaneously for a defendant in the back of the courtroom, the purpose is for defendants to hear their case in their own language. When the interpreter interprets simultaneously for a psychiatrist in a mental health consultation, the purpose is to enable the physician to extract information from which to carry out a diagnosis. Such a diagnosis is based on both the content and the presentational

Table 1.3 Factors influencing style of delivery

Mode	Setting	Focus	Style	Register
Simultaneous	Conference	Propositional content	Coherent, omission of non-content features, repetition, backtracking	Formal
Whispering simultaneous into minority language	Community (in particular the courtroom)	Propositional content	Coherent, omission of non-content features, repetition, backtracking	Formal
Long (classic) consecutive	Conference Community	Propositional content	Coherent, omission of non-content features, repetition, backtracking	Formal
Short consecutive (dialogue)	Community (especially in the courtroom)	Propositional content and style of speech	As original	Formal and informal
Whispering simultaneous into mainstream language	Community (especially mental health sessions)	Propositional content and style of speech	As original	Informal

style of the patient's speech. Similarly, when the interpreter interprets a dialogue, it is not only the content of the utterances that is crucial in the interaction, but also the manner in which these utterances are expressed, which denote much meaning intended by the speakers. Extra-linguistic features such as tone, intonation and register are important components of the interactive discourse (cf. Hale, 2002).

* * *

Having discussed translation and interpreting in general, the discussion will now shift to Community Interpreting specifically.

1.4   What is Community Interpreting?

Community Interpreting takes the interpreter into the most private spheres of human life. It does not take place at negotiations about major international political decisions or conferences on recent scientific discoveries; it takes place in settings where the most intimate and significant issues of everyday individuals are discussed: a doctor's surgery, a social worker's or a lawyer's office, a gaol, a police station or courtroom. These are only a few examples of settings where community interpreters work and where they are made privy to confidential information that would never have been available to them except in their capacity as an interpreter. The assurance that interpreters will abide by a strict code of ethics, which, among other things, ensures accuracy, confidentiality and impartiality (cf. chapter 4), is important in being accorded such trust. One would imagine it difficult for anyone willingly to allow a stranger into such intimate situations unless they were assured of these ethical obligations. Whether interpreters abide by them is explored later in this chapter and in chapter 4 in connection with the professional codes of ethics.

The magnitude of the community interpreter's responsibility can only be understood when realising that their work is crucial for the lives of innumerable people who would be unable to communicate without their services. According to Garber, 'the circumstances in which community interpreters practise carry even more risk and more responsibility than conference interpreting' (2000: 19). Smirnov compares community interpreting with the more lucrative business interpreting and concludes that community interpreting is 'superior in [its] "humanitarian" (social) significance' (1997: 213). Unlike international gatherings, where for many delegates speaking their national language represents a political, symbolic statement rather than a necessity (see Viaggio, 2004), in Community Interpreting settings the participants would simply not be able to communicate without the services of an interpreter. This makes the interpreter a crucial link between the two interlocutors. The need for competent, ethical community interpreters is therefore paramount. As Smirnov states, 'Sadly enough it is not the life of an interpreter, but that of his client that may become a price paid for a poor rendition' (1997: 215). Garber agrees that the consequences of incompetent interpreting in the community setting can be great and proposes that 'standards must be high enough to ensure that the risk to the client is not increased because of inaccurate or unethical interpretation' (2000: 17). The demands placed on the community interpreter are high, yet there are no consistent standards for their practice or any formal requirement for adequate training around the world, as the job of the community interpreter continues to be misunderstood and undermined by many. As Mikkelson states, community interpreting is 'the least prestigious and most misunderstood branch of the interpreting profession' (1996: 124). According to

Gentile and colleagues, even conference interpreters misunderstand Community Interpreting, not regarding it as 'an area of interpreting in its own right, but rather as a residual arm of language work at best, or multilingual welfare work (often with a charity air) at worst' (1996: 8-9). Gehrke goes as far as to suggest that Community Interpreting 'represents a combination of two separate professions: interpreting and social work' (1993: 420). Gentile et al. (1996) speculate that this confusion may be related to its historical development (which grew from the outset of the twentieth-century welfare migrant state) and to the participants involved in the interactions. They believe that the status of the participants in the communicative event influences the status of the interpreter. Since conference interpreters interpret for international figures, their own status is elevated. Community interpreters interpret for participants of differing status, but are normally identified with the migrant or refugee, who tends to be a powerless participant. Roberts (1997) argues that the low status of Community Interpreting is self-perpetuating, with words such as 'assistance' and 'service' being common in definitions of Community Interpreting, but uncommon in definitions of Conference or Business Interpreting. Hale (2005) argues that such low status emanates mainly from four interconnected causes: the disorganised and unstructured state of the industry; the absence of mandatory university education; the lack of a strong professional identity; and the general unawareness of the complexity of the task. Such unawareness is reflected not only in the monolingual participants' attitudes, but also in the attitude of many who act as interpreters, with their usual statement 'I'm just the interpreter' when referring to themselves.

1.4.1 Controversy over its label

The lack of consensus over the term Community Interpreting has led to controversy about the appropriateness of having any type of classification for the different types of interpreting at all. Gentile (1997) and Roberts (1997) argue against classification, advocating the single term 'Interpreting' to avoid divisiveness. Such a view is reinforced by Mikkelson (1996: 126), who comments that different sectors of the interpreting profession have tried to distance themselves from others deemed to be less prestigious – for example, conference interpreters from community interpreters and court interpreters from ad hoc interpreters – resulting in a weakening of the profession. Nevertheless, classifications and labels do exist and will probably never cease to exist.

As Snell-Hornby states, 'the tendency to categorise is innate in man and essential to all scientific development' (1988: 26).

Quote 1.6   Alexieva on types of interpreting

Today, translator- and interpreter-mediated encounters vary tremendously in terms of their settings, modes, relationship among participants and other factors, posing a major challenge to the theory, practice and didactics of interpreting in particular.

(Alexieva, 1997: 153)

Because there are such significant differences between the different types of interpreting, categorising facilitates the study and understanding of the different genres. Some have tried to classify interpreting in terms of mode – for example, simultaneous interpreting versus consecutive interpreting (Slevsky, 1982 in Alexieva, 1997) – others in terms of context and situation, and others in much more detailed typologies (see Alexieva, 1997). The two main classifications are Conference Interpreting and Community Interpreting (cf. Mason, 2000), which derive their differences mostly from the context and situation, with Business Interpreting sometimes seen as a distinct third category.

The term Community Interpreting has been used with slightly different meanings around the world. In some countries the term refers to ad hoc, unpaid interpreting conducted by volunteers (Dueñas González et al., 1991); in some it refers to the health and welfare sectors only (Pöchhacker, 1999); in others it is used more broadly to include all types of interpreting other than Conference Interpreting (Roberts, 1997; Ozolins, 1998); and in countries such as Denmark, they are still struggling to find a term that suits their language and situation.[4] Other labels that have been used are 'escort interpreting' (Mikkelson, nd), 'public service interpreting' (Valero Garcés, 2003a), 'cultural interpreting', 'ad hoc interpreting' (Roberts, 1997), 'community-based interpreting' (Chesher et al., 2003), 'dialogue interpreting' (Mason, 2001) and 'liaison interpreting' (Gentile et al., 1996; Erasmus, 2000).

Quotes 1.7–1.9 provide different understandings of the meaning of Community Interpreting. Mikkelson classifies it in relation to the people the services are rendered for – the 'residents of a community'. She distinguishes these participants from those who would normally be the recipients of Conference Interpreting (e.g. diplomats and conference delegates), and from business people.

Quote 1.7   Mikkelson's definition of Community Interpreting

... community interpreters provide services for *residents of a community*, as opposed to diplomats, conference delegates, or professionals travelling abroad to conduct business...

(Mikkelson, 1996: 126-7, original emphasis)

Gentile and colleagues use the term 'Liaison Interpreting' rather than Community Interpreting and define it in relation to the language directionality of the activity. In their definition they include Business Interpreting, which was rejected by Mikkelson (1996) and by Smirnov (1997). Harris also used the terms 'Liaison' or 'Escort' Interpreting to refer exclusively to the 'type of interpreting done when accompanying visitors, diplomats and businessmen to meetings and negotiations' (Harris, 1983: 5).

Quote 1.8   Gentile, Ozolins and Vasilakakos's definition of Liaison Interpreting

Liaison interpreting is the name given to the genre of interpreting where the interpreting is performed in two language directions by the same person.

(Gentile et al., 1996: 17)

Pöchhacker defines Community Interpreting in relation to the setting, placing it in the realm of institutional, public service settings. Such specificity excludes other types of interpreting performed by community interpreters that do not fall under this category, such as damages cases, private doctor's consultations, interviews with bank managers, to name just a few. He makes the important point that the term 'community' refers to both the mainstream and the minority communities, which can include ethnic, aboriginal or hearing-impaired communities.

Quote 1.9   Pöchhacker's definition of Community Interpreting

In the most general sense, community interpreting refers to interpreting in institutional settings of a given society in which public service providers and

---

Quote 1.9   (Continued)

individual clients do not speak the same language...community interpreting facilitates communication within a social entity (society) that includes culturally different sub-groups. Hence, the qualifier 'community' refers to both the (mainstream) society as such as its constituent sub-community (ethnic or indigenous community, linguistic minority etc.)...

(Pöchhacker, 1999: 126-7)

The many different stages of development of the profession around the world make it difficult to find one detailed definition to suit all countries. In Australia, the term Community Interpreting has been used since the 1970s (Chesher, 1997) to refer to interpreting that takes place among members of that country's community, as opposed to Conference Interpreting, which takes place between delegates from different countries in a conference setting. It is worth noting, however, that the term is very rarely used by interpreters to refer to themselves. A recent discussion on the AUSIT[5] e-bulletin demonstrated a lack of consensus among practising interpreters. Interpreters generally simply refer to themselves as interpreters working in different contexts. The following example from Belgium presents us with a useful insight. In Belgium it was decided that separate descriptions of interpreting types would not be used, as this stigmatised Community Interpreting. Instead, they refer to the activity as 'interpreting' followed by the setting: interpreting in conferences, interpreting in the courts, and so on (Miguélez, 2003).

This book will adopt 'Community Interpreting' as the overarching term for the type of interpreting that takes place within one country's own community, and between residents of that country, as opposed to Conference Interpreting, which takes place between delegates who are residents of different countries, in the context of an international conference or meeting. Although Community Interpreting is the blanket term, clear differences determined by the context will be highlighted. The two main specialisations that fall under the umbrella term Community Interpreting are medical interpreting and legal interpreting. The other types that take place under the name of Community Interpreting are too diverse to warrant specialised names. These include welfare, immigration, education, to name just a few. Sign Language and Aboriginal Language interpreting, although with specific particularities not shared by other languages, also fall under the umbrella term of Community Interpreting.

1.5 Differences between Conference and Community Interpreting

The main distinction in the field of interpreting has traditionally been between what is commonly known as Conference Interpreting and Community Interpreting. It is generally assumed that the main difference between these two types lies in the mode, with Conference Interpreting conducted in the simultaneous mode and Community Interpreting in the consecutive mode. Although it can be safely stated that most Conference Interpreting is conducted in the simultaneous mode with the aid of equipment, community interpreters must use all modes: consecutive, simultaneous and sight translation (Nicholls, 1992). Gentile and colleagues cite the following factors as belonging to Liaison Interpreting and which distinguish it from Conference Interpreting:

> the physical proximity of the interpreter and clients; an information gap between the clients; a likely status differential between the clients; the necessity to interpret into both language directions; working as an individual and not as part of a team. (Gentile et al., 1996: 18)

Level of formality is another difference. The register normally used in Conference Interpreting settings is formal or semi-formal, whereas in Community Interpreting it varies according to participant and text type, ranging from the very formal (e.g. reading of a charge) to the very informal (e.g. a defendant using expletives).

Table 1.4 sets out the main differences between the two genres, although, as Alexieva states 'the boundaries between these phenomena are likely to remain fluid and... we cannot expect to delineate clear-cut categories' (1997: 156).

The most obvious differences between Conference and Community Interpreting have been discussed by others, and relate to mode of delivery, level of formality, status, participants and proxemics (see Gentile et al., 1996). Mikkelson (nd: 2) proposes that one major difference between Conference and Community Interpreting is the way each activity is perceived by the clients and interpreters themselves (see Hale, 2005 for a discussion on the relationship between perception and the construction of professional identity). One very important difference that has not been discussed (to my knowledge) is the various consequences of the interpreting intervention. Without any intention to undermine the role of the conference interpreter, the significance of achieving the highest level of accuracy in Community Interpreting is

Table 1.4 The main differences between Conference Interpreting and
Community Interpreting

	Conference Interpreting	**Community Interpreting**
Register	Generally formal, although informal registers, mainly in the form of idioms and jokes, are common	Ranges from the very formal to the very informal
Language directionality	Mostly unidirectional	Bidirectional
Proxemics	Generally isolated in a booth, away from the speakers	Close proximity to speakers, which allows them to be more involved in the interaction
Mode	Generally simultaneous with the aid of equipment, although consecutive is sometimes used	Short consecutive (dialogue), long consecutive, simultaneous (whispering), sight translation
Consequences of inaccurate rendition	Medium	High
Level of accuracy required	Medium	High
Participants	Of the same professional status	Mostly of differing status
Number of interpreters	Two (working as a team)	One (working alone)

much greater than in Conference Interpreting. Whereas in most conferences the interpreter's purpose is to enable delegates to understand the content of papers presented by the speakers, if the interpreter misses or distorts a point, the papers will usually be published and confusing issues clarified. In political negotiations, the role of the interpreter is more crucial, where tone and affect are also important elements of the message. However, in such circumstances it is common for most delegates to speak a common language and use their mother tongue only as a political statement rather than as a necessity. It is also not uncommon for the major decisions to have been made already in the margins of the plenary meetings and in the absence of interpreters. In Community Interpreting the participants' need for the services of the interpreter is real, as they would simply not be able to communicate without them. The situations they are in – a police interview, a court case or a medical consultation – require precision in the interpretation, since inaccuracy can have major ramifications on the outcome of a case or on the treatment of an illness. There is no other opportunity to read what the speakers have said or even to notice that an error or misunderstanding has occurred. The other difference between the two genres is the meaning of accuracy. While in Conference Interpreting the content is the most important aspect, regardless of form or manner (Shlesinger 2000:7), in Community Interpreting manner is just as important (Tebble, 1999; Berk-Seligson, 1990/2002; Hale, 2004). This suggests that the onus on the community interpreter to perform a high quality job is much greater than a conference interpreter because of what is at stake. Yet community interpreters, with much greater demands than conference interpreters, receive much lower pay and have little status as professionals.

Further reading

Carr, Roberts, Dufour and Steyn (1997). A selection of papers from the first international conference on Community Interpreting which marked an historic event in the discipline. The papers present different perspectives, practices and research results from around the world.

Gentile, Ozolins and Vasilakakos (1996). This is one of the first manuals on Community Interpreting and provides a practical overview of the field in Australia.

Pöchhacker (2004). This book provides an excellent overview of the whole field of Interpreting Studies, with some specific references to Community or Public Service Interpreting.

2

Interdisciplinarity: Community Interpreting in the Medical Context

This chapter:

- Outlines the main issues surrounding interpreting in the medical setting.
- Highlights the importance of language in this setting and the need for interpreters to take this into account when deciding how to interpret.
- Discusses the different suggested roles of the interpreter in the medical setting.
- Analyses the consequences of such roles on the outcome of the medical events.

2.1 Introduction

Quote 2.1   Gentile et al.'s definition of Liaison Intepreting

Liaison interpreting is a profession where, like medicine, teaching and the law, the client's welfare is usually affected *directly*. This is not only because most liaison interpreting takes place in the context of other professions such as medicine, teaching and the law, but also because interpreting has its own particular kinds of knowledge, skills and practices which require particular ethical considerations. Liaison interpreting is, then, subject to ethical considerations both along the lines of any other profession and along lines of its own. And because liaison interpreting takes place in the context of so many other professional institutional settings, ethical conflicts often arise for the interpreter.

(Gentile et al., 1996: 57)

Interpreters work with other professionals in the delivery of their services. There is often misunderstanding about each other's tasks, roles, needs and expectations. Untrained interpreters may not understand the reasoning behind procedures, specific questions or mode of delivery in different settings, as well as the significance of the lay person's responses in allowing the primary service providers to perform their duties adequately. On the other hand, professionals working with interpreters rarely understand the complexity of the task and the interpreter's needs in producing an accurate rendition. Professional interpreters have a responsibility to acquire the necessary language and interpreting skills, to gain an understanding of the settings in which they work and their requirements, of the purposes for which language is used in each of these settings, and to abide by a code of ethics. However, few training opportunities exist, pay and working conditions are poor, and the lack of understanding of the interpreter's role and others' lack of appreciation of the task place pressures on interpreters which make it difficult for them to perform at a professional level. Even the best qualified and most competent professional interpreters will have difficulty interpreting accurately if they are not provided with adequate conditions. These relate to the provision of preparation material prior to the interpreting event, appropriate physical facilities, adequate breaks to avoid fatigue and the correct management of turns during the event. Confident interpreters can go a long way in asserting their needs to those who speak through them, by explaining the procedures of speaking through interpreters, controlling the length of the speakers' turns, arranging the seating in the most effective way, asking for breaks when needed and requesting background information in order to prepare for the job. However, confidence comes with competence, status and a strong professional identity, and these characteristics are normally a natural consequence of pre-service compulsory university training (cf. Hale, 2005). Professionals who have had to acquire a university degree in order to practise tend not to treat the interpreter as an equal if the interpreter has not been educated at university level. Such a situation reinforces the perception that interpreting is an unskilled task that requires no training. This perception is also reflected in low pay and poor working conditions. Kuo and Fagan (1999), two medical practitioners, argue that in order to save on limited financial resources in medical settings in the United States, family and friends should be used as interpreters. They base their conclusion on a survey they conducted among patients and residents asking them to rate their level of satisfaction with family and friends acting as interpreters as compared to staff interpreters. Family and friends received a 62 per cent satisfaction rate from the residents and an 85.1 per cent rate from the patients. Staff interpreters received a 98 per cent satisfaction rate from the residents and a 92.4 per cent satisfaction rate from the patients. Although the rate was higher from both residents and patients for the staff interpreters, Kuo and Fagan argue that the rate for family and friends was high enough not to warrant the expense of a staff interpreter. This disregards the need for specialist skills, assuming that any lay bilingual can do the job – an assumption reinforced by the fact that the majority of staff hospital interpreters in the United States have little or no training at all. It is difficult to imagine anyone suggesting that the work of surgeons should be performed by nurses to save on limited resources, because it is clear that in order to perform surgery, specialist training is required. However, it is not clear that in order to interpret adequately, training is also required. Until that becomes clear, professional interpreters will continue to be dismissed as redundant. It is also not clear to other professionals that poor, inaccurate interpreting will impinge on their ability to perform their own duties. Education is needed for interpreters and for those who speak through them in order to achieve optimum results (cf. Isaacs, 2002; Tebble, 2003).

2.2   Interpreting in medical settings

Medical settings include private practice, hospital settings and consultations with other health care professionals, such as speech pathologists, dieticians or physiotherapists. Interpreters working in this field are often referred to as medical interpreters or health care interpreters. The focus of the research into medical communication has mostly been on doctor–patient interactions (Candlin and Candlin, 2003). Interpreters are involved in the consultation between the health care professional and the patient; therefore, research into medical discourse is of utmost relevance to their work. Just as it is crucial for interpreters to understand the purpose behind language use in the courtroom in order to avoid interfering unnecessarily with the process (see chapter 3), so it is important for them to understand the significant role language plays in a medical consultation and other related health settings. Such an understanding will help the interpreter to make informed decisions in the course of their work.

2.2.1   Communication in doctor–patient interaction

Successful health care provision depends largely on successful communication between the health care provider and the patient, with language playing a central role. Successful communication relies on a number of factors, among which are the health care provider's ability to ask appropriate questions in the most effective way; to listen attentively and empathetically to all a patient has to say, not only to what directly relates to the questions posed, including indirect clues that may lead to further understanding of the patient's problem (Cordella, 2004; Vásquez and Javier, 1991); and to build up a positive and collaborative relationship with the patient (Candib, 1995; Ong et al., 1995; Ferguson and Candib, 2002; Zoppi and Epstein, 2002). When interpreters are involved in medical consultations, they are required to interpret the health care provider's questions and the patient's answers. It is therefore crucial that interpreters understand the significance of questioning style and the importance of patients' answers, not only in providing direct information in response to questions, but also in providing clues for the health care provider.

2.2.2 The significance of questioning style in achieving effective communication

Questioning style and technique have been prominent in the literature about successful doctor–patient interaction. Cambridge states that 'the patient may well present symptoms unrelated to the real problems, and the diagnostic skill of the doctor relies heavily on skilful questioning' (1999: 201). Cordella suggests that 'the way in which the question is presented, therefore, can pre-determine the reply' (2004: 32). A number of researchers have looked into the different questioning techniques to determine which types are more successful in achieving the aims of the consultation, which, according to Ong et al. (1995), are to create a good interpersonal relationship, to exchange information and to make correct treatment-related decisions.

Cicourel (1999: 183) argues against the use of leading questions, stating that this type of question renders patients powerless. He proposes that patients who feel included in the decision-making believe that they have some control over the outcome of the consultation, and this in turn leads to better clinical results. This sense of inclusion is more likely to be achieved by the use of open questions. He also explains that the consultation does not consist of a rigid set of questions, but that the physician will make guesses about possible trouble-spots that will trigger other questions which may relate to the main problem. The patient's answers will also prompt further questions from the doctor, causing a change of direction in the question-and-answer sequences many times during the course of the consultation.

Harres (1998) analysed the use of tag questions in medical consultations, which fall under the category of leading questions. Harres did not dismiss this question type altogether, however. The study found that doctors used these questions not only to elicit information from patients, but also to summarise their answers and seek confirmation of their understanding of them, to express empathy and to give positive feedback. The timing of the leading or tag question may have much to do with how effective its use is.

Byrne and Long discuss the 'broad opening' technique, where doctors allow the patients to speak freely until clues are detected for the real reason for the visit:

> patients confronted with direct questions at the start of a consultation rarely give complete answers. By forcing the patient to talk, it is claimed that the process of relationship building is continued to the point where the patient feels sufficiently confident to make the real purpose of the visit apparent. (Byrne and Long, 1976: 37)

Bergmann (1992) agrees that often medical specialists use means other than direct questions, such as a simple assertion or the use of body language, to encourage patients to volunteer information.

Some have argued that the uneven distribution of questions in medical interactions can detract from building up a collaborative relationship between doctor and patient, and encourage an asymmetrical relationship. As in the courtroom, the questioner has potential control over who speaks and on what topic. One major difference between these two settings is that, in the courtroom, participants are bound by the rules of evidence, which stipulate that questions can only originate with lawyers and never with witnesses. In the medical consultation, however, patients are free to ask questions at any time. Another major difference is that questions asked in the courtroom do not seek new information. For the most part, lawyers ask questions that elicit the answers they need in order to create a story that supports their case. The information is normally already known to the questioner. In the medical setting, physicians are genuinely interested in obtaining information that will enable them to help the patient. As Ainsworth-Vaughn (1998) comments, questions in the medical setting cannot be interpreted simply as claims to power over the emerging discourse, but can in fact be the means by which power is shared. By asking a question, the doctor hands over the floor to the patient to speak. If the doctor is genuinely concerned about the patient, then much interest will be placed in the patient's answers. In 1979 Frankel conducted a quantitative and qualitative study on questions in medical interviews and found that less than 1 per cent of questions were initiated by the patient. His definition of patient-initiated questions, however, was limited to those that were first in the sequence and introduced new information. Frankel excluded what he called 'normal troubles such as requests for clarification, information, etc.' (1979: 239). Ainsworth-Vaughn (2001: 463) comments that ever since Frankel's work on 'patient-initiated' questions, there has been an overgeneralisation in the literature that stereotypes all patients as passive and powerless. Later work on the distribution of questions between physician and patient with broader definitions of the term 'question' have shown higher percentages of patient-initiated questions (Roter, 1984; Roter et al., 1988; Ainsworth-Vaughn, 2001). In a study of Chilean doctors and patients, Cordella found that 'both doctors and patients used a remarkably similar number of words in the discourse and suggests that both participants had the opportunity to take the floor during the consultation and to elaborate on their speech' (2004: 58). Cordella also found that patients could be divided into three distinct categories: compliers, apologisers and challengers, with the latter type being the most vocal.

The level of patient participation, therefore, seems to be related to a number of factors, including the patient's personality and social background, the context of the consultation, and the relationship between the physician and the patient. Nevertheless, the important finding is that a low level of patient participation leads to a sense of powerlessness, which contributes to unsuccessful communication and inappropriate medical provision. The subordinate role of patient is believed to be accentuated by doctors employing ineffective questioning techniques, by excluding the patient from the decision-making process, by talking about the patient to others in their presence, by disregarding their suggestions, by not answering their questions adequately and by using incorrect registers (Wodak, 1997). A number of studies have shown that medical outcomes are concretely improved when the patient feels empowered (see Ainsworth-Vaughn, 1998).

The register doctors use in addressing their patients has also been linked to power differentials. Shuy (1976) speaks of the need for doctors to discontinue the use of highly technical language which results in complete misunderstandings. On the other hand, Wodak comments that the doctor's use of child-like language when addressing an aged, difficult patient

> only serves to reinforce the difference in power and the patient's assumed mental inferiority. The frame conflict and the language barriers separating the two participants render cooperative face-to-face communication virtually impossible and, in the end, the patient falls silent. (Wodak, 1997: 186)

2.2.3   Patients' compliance with treatment

A number of authors have investigated the reasons behind lack of compliance and agree that a good doctor–patient relationship can help considerably in ensuring full cooperation with doctors' suggested treatments (Frey, 1998; Tebble, 1999; Adler, 2002; Ferguson and Candib, 2002; Zoppi and Epstein, 2002). Others have found that the amount of information provided to patients can help increase the level of compliance (Heath, 1992; Cordella, 2004). As discussed in the previous section, appropriate communication skills are essential in building rapport with the patient and in being able to provide the relevant information in a way that is clearly understood by the patient.

Much has been written to indicate that monolingual doctor–patient communication can be problematic and that physicians would benefit from acquiring better communication skills to achieve optimum results (Byrne and Long, 1976; Todd, 1983; Heath, 1992; Wodak, 1997; Ainsworth-Vaughn, 1998; Cicourel, 1999). When a third participant, the interpreter, is added to the interaction, a further layer of complexity is added. The crucial question to be considered is how to ensure that this extra complexity does not exacerbate the communication problems that may exist in monolingual health care provider–patient interactions. The following sections address this question with the use of authentic examples.

2.3   Treating patients through interpreters

Candlin and Candlin state that the severe lack of qualified medical interpreters is 'almost endemic in health care worldwide – such that pragmatic, ethical, clinical, and ideological issues inevitably arise' (2003: 137). The disparity that exists in the background of practising interpreters leads to a wide range of conflicting practices which create confusion among patients and medical practitioners about the role of the interpreter. While there seems to be slightly more agreement about the role of the court interpreter as a faithful and impartial renderer of others' utterances, due to the legal consequences of doing otherwise, when it comes to other non-adversarial settings, where the need for impartiality is less obvious, opinions differ. Kurz (2001) pleads for different roles for different settings. Kaufert and Putsch (1997) question whether the neutral stance necessary in the adversarial system is the best approach in the health sector. There are undeniable differences between the court and medical settings which may warrant different interpreter roles. The courtroom is a public setting, governed by strict rules of evidence, whereas the medical consultation is a private, informal setting where there is no real need for strict impartiality. The courtroom is adversarial and language is used strategically both to support and to discredit a version of facts. Medical consultations are not adversarial and the aim of the consultation is to help the patient in the best possible way. Language is also used strategically to achieve certain purposes (see section 2.2.1). The two settings, therefore, have one major factor in common: the importance of language in the interaction. Although patients are not judged by health care providers for legal purposes, the manner in which patients present their stories to a physician can have repercussions on their medical assessments. The way health care providers ask questions can also have an impact on the answers proffered. The language used by both participants will impact on the level of understanding on both sides and on the rapport that is built. The level of patient participation can determine the level of compliance to treatment. All these issues need to be considered when advocating a role for interpreters.

2.3.1 The controversy about interpreter roles in the medical setting

Concept 2.1   The direct versus the mediated approach

It is difficult to label proposed approaches to interpreting, as they often overlap in their expectations. Dichotomies such as 'visible' versus 'invisible, 'machine' versus 'human' or 'involved' versus 'uninvolved' do not adequately capture the complexity of the interpreter's tasks. It is impossible for interpreters to act as machines because they are human, and it is impossible for them to be invisible or uninvolved when they are present in a three-way interaction. Bolden (2000 391) speaks of the 'mediated interaction' and the 'directly interpreted interaction', which more adequately describe the two main approaches. In the directly interpreted interaction, the interpreter interprets every turn, and the doctor and the

Concept 2.1   (Continued)

patient address each other through the interpreter. In the mediated interaction, two interweaving conversations take place: one between the doctor and the interpreter and the other between the patient and the interpreter.

The mediated approach argues for an interpreter who does not interpret for two main participants, but who mediates between them, deciding on what to transmit and what to omit from the speakers' utterances. This has been called the 'gatekeeper' role (see Davidson, 2000). The direct approach argues for an interpreter who renders each turn accurately from one speaker to the other, leaving the decision-making to the authors of the utterances. Bolden states that the direct approach is adopted by interpreters who choose to 'embrace the role of a "translating machine"' (2000: 391), an assumption that is unwarranted. Those who argue for direct interpreting do not argue for the 'translation machine' metaphor. The only references to the interpreter acting as a machine have come mostly from the legal profession and have long since been discredited. The 'machine' metaphor argues for literal, word-for-word translations, which will for the most part lead to inaccuracy (see Hale, 1996). An accurate interpretation will attempt to render the meaning of the utterance at the discourse level, taking into account the pragmatic dimension of language, transferring the intention behind the utterance and attempting to produce a similar reaction in the listeners in response to such utterance, as the original would have (see chapter 1). An accurate rendition will also take into account the lexical, grammatical and syntactic differences across the two languages, as well as the possible cross-cultural differences. Very rarely will a literal translation produce an accurate rendition. It seems that in an attempt to continue to discredit the machine metaphor, which simplifies the complex interpreting process and undermines the high-level skills required of interpreters, many have gone to the other extreme to do away with any requirements or norms for accurate interpreting.

The direct approach does not imply that the interpreter will be 'uninvolved' or 'invisible', as in order to achieve an accurate rendition, the interpreter needs to be fully involved in the complex interpreting process. The difference lies in the focus of the involvement. Whereas under the mediated approach the interpreter is involved in deciding on the content of the utterances (i.e. what to interpret and what to omit), in the direct approach the interpreter is involved in deciding how to render most accurately what the other two participants themselves have chosen to communicate to each other.

In the arguments about the role of the medical interpreter, little is said about the consequences of each role. This is a crucial question if the best interests of patients and the goals of the health care providers are to be met.

Concept 2.2 What approach would better serve the interests of the medical profession and their patients?

Advocates of the direct approach argue that the interpreter's role is to interpret each utterance accurately to allow the doctor and the patient to communicate with each other. By so doing, doctors maintain the responsibility for directing the consultation, asking the appropriate questions, picking up on cues from seemingly irrelevant material provided by the patient, and attempting to build a rapport with the patient. Patients, on the other hand, maintain the right to decide on what to say and how to say it and to have their questions answered by a professional physician. The responsibility for effective communication still lies with the authors of the utterances. As the interaction involves three participants, the structure of the event will be different from that of a monolingual interaction. For example, the introductions at the start of the interview may involve what Tebble (1999) calls the 'contract', where the interpreter states her or his role and explains the interpreting protocol to the participants. At this stage the seating arrangement may also be discussed between the interpreter and the doctor; and during the interview the interpreter may need to ask for clarifications, or to provide insights into cross-cultural differences that may not be evident in the dialogue. Ideally, there may also be briefing and debriefing sessions between the health care provider and the interpreter (see Isaacs, 2002). Nevertheless, the bulk of the question-and-answer sequence during the history-taking phase of the interview is interpreted directly, using the first and second grammatical persons.

The proponents of the mediator-interpreter approach argue that the bilingual interaction cannot attempt to resemble a monolingual interaction and hence the direct approach of interpreting is not feasible. Interpreters become pseudo-health care providers by holding separate but related conversations with the physician and with the patient, later providing summaries of the original utterances in the other language (Bolden, 2000). Interpreters have the freedom to decide on what is and is not relevant in the utterances of each speaker and to add information that in their opinion was missed by any of the participants. They argue that such an approach helps the doctor save valuable time when the interpreter decides to omit irrelevant chunks of information from the patients' utterances, and that it provides patients with valuable information when doctors omit to provide it and interpreters decide to add it.

The majority of studies into interpreted doctor-patient interactions (Downing, 1991; Wadensjö, 1992, 1998; Kaufert and Putsch, 1997; Cambridge, 1999; Bolden, 2000: Davidson, 2000; Bot, 2003; Angelelli, 2004) have found that interpreters are for the most part completely untrained in interpreting, let alone in medical discourse or medical practice, and often have little education of any kind. Many work as volunteers, they are generally unappreciated by the system and often very few of the participants have a clear understanding of what their role is, including the interpreters themselves (Kaufert and Putsch, 1997; Cambridge, 1999; Davidson, 2000; Bot, 2003; Meyer et al., 2003; Valero Garcés, 2003b; Angelelli, 2004). Because the backgrounds of the interpreters, the working conditions and the level of understanding of role by all participants have been almost identical in most studies, the findings have also been very similar: these bilingual workers mostly take the mediator approach, and do not interpret the utterances of the interlocutors fully, but rather act as gatekeepers in deciding what information is relevant in the exchange and therefore what information to transmit from one speaker to another (Davidson, 2000). They also commonly add to the doctors' utterances when the information provided is deemed by the interpreter to be incomplete, or answer patients' questions directly rather than interpret and allow the doctor to reply. Another common trend is the consistent use of the third person rather than the first person when interpreting. Instead of interpreting an utterance in the same grammatical person it was expressed in the original, they change it to the third person by saying, for example: 'The doctor says that...' or 'She is saying that...'. Such a practice reinforces the view that two parallel conversations are taking place: one between the doctor and the interpreter, the other between the interpreter and the patient. Interestingly, the majority of these bilingual workers either think that they interpret accurately or argue that the alterations are necessary to facilitate better communication, to save the doctor's time or to provide the patients with more thorough information about their condition. However, as the examples below show, communication is often hindered rather than improved by such alterations, and both physician and patient can be excluded from the decision-making process by being denied the opportunity to hear what each has to say, but instead hearing only what the interpreter chooses to tell them.

As a result of these studies, which have shown that the majority of interpreters in the health care system in some parts of the

world do not adhere to the established codes of ethics to interpret accurately and completely and to remain neutral, many have
argued that the prescribed or 'normative' role is unrealistic and even
undesirable.

Quote 2.2   Interpreters as cultural brokers, mediators and advocates

Outcomes are most likely to improve if interpreters are assigned a role of not only
translating but also of acting as cultural brokers, mediators, and advocates.

(Meyer et al., 2003: 78)

This is a bold claim and needs to be explored and substantiated.
Firstly, the outcomes or consequences of adopting each of the different
proposed roles have not been explored empirically and need to be
researched if claims such as these are to be considered. Secondly, the
meanings and responsibilities of an 'advocate', 'cultural broker' and
'mediator' need to be clarified to decide whether such roles are feasible
or even desirable.

Roberts (1997) questions the feasibility and desirability of the confla-
tion of roles some expect of interpreters:

Quote 2.3   Is it possible or desirable for interpreters to act out many conflicting roles?

The interpreter ... is often expected to be not only a mediator between languages,
but also a helpmate and guide, cultural broker and even advocate or conciliator.
In other words, he wears many hats. But is this feasible or desirable? The feasibility
of role combination is questionable, in principle, because it is, in fact, difficult
to be a helpmate to and even an advocate of those not speaking the language
of the country and still to retain the objectivity and impartiality required to
interpret well.

(Roberts, 1997: 20-1)

Gentile et al., who advocate the direct interpreter approach, explain that
'cultural knowledge and contextual knowledge is used only to carry out
the interpreting accurately, not to assist the NES [non-English speaker]
as a cultural broker' (1996: 60–1). Cambridge (1999) argues in favour
of neutrality in the medical setting, explaining that when interpreters
identify too strongly with one side, they tend to take over the role
of 'principal' and relay their own meaning rather than the original

speaker's. As already stated, however, some argue that objectivity or impartiality is neither necessary nor desirable for medical interpreters and that it is not necessary to be faithful to the original message. Clearly, the doctor–patient situation is not adversarial and therefore the strict requirement for impartiality required of interpreters in the courtroom may not be necessary. It is assumed that in most medical situations, except in medico-legal consultations for the purpose of an insurance claim, the doctor and the interpreter are there to help the same person: the patient. However, it is difficult to understand how medical interpreters can be more helpful to the provision of health care by deviating from their role of interpreter and adopting an advocate or gatekeeper role. Any professional interpreter who has interpreted for a relative, for example, can attest to the difficulty of interpreting accurately for them (see Castillo and Taibi, 2005). The natural inclination is to speak for the patient, with whose condition one is familiar, rather than interpret for them. When such a situation arises, the patient is excluded from the interaction and becomes the subject of discussion for two people who are speaking about them in a language they do not understand, thus rendering the patient powerless. Such a situation will have negative consequences on the building of a relationship between the medical practitioner and the patient and on the patient's compliance with the treatment (see section 2.2.3).

The private, informal and relaxed nature of the medical consultation makes it more conducive for interpreters to ask for repetition or indicate when they feel there has been a misunderstanding, while still maintaining a detachment and interpreting the utterances accurately. Whereas in the courtroom cross-examiners use tactics to confuse and trip up witnesses in their questioning techniques, the aim of the physician is to be clear and to be understood by the patient, so interpreters can take advantage of the purpose of the interaction to ask for clarifications when needed. However, this does not justify unwarranted interferences from the interpreter, as a number of studies show (see Bolden, 2000; Davidson 2000; Angelelli, 2004). Bot presents us with examples of what is referred to as the 'involved' health care interpreter who aligns with one party or the other, excludes one party by talking 'about' him or her, filters information and changes the tone and force of utterances, and concludes that the examples did not prove harmful to the treatment because the therapist was aware of what was happening (2003: 34). However, it is unclear how the therapist was made aware of this situation when she had no knowledge of the language being spoken, or how the therapist understood the consequences of such interference. By using the third person and speaking about the patient to the doctor, and excluding the patient from the decision-making phase of the interview, these interpreters are reinforcing some of the factors that have been highlighted as contributing to patients' lack of compliance to treatment (see section 2.2.3). Bot does concede that 'some transgressions, such as intensive contact between interpreter and patient outside the official session, could be viewed as markedly risky' (2003: 34). Under this mediator approach, it is difficult to ascertain when it is acceptable and when it becomes 'risky' to 'transgress', and indeed how a 'transgression' is identified.

Meyer and colleagues analysed the interaction between a doctor and a patient with the use of an ad hoc interpreter and state that:

> It must therefore be permissible, and may indeed be productive to view the conduct of the ad hoc interpreter as a challenge to the professional interpreter's code(s) of practice... where the service provider is all too happy to make do... (Meyer et al., 2003: 75)

The fact that the doctor makes do with a less than adequate service constitutes no valid justification to contest the professional code of practice. Professional service providers make do with less than adequate support services for a number of different reasons, however that does not invalidate the need for improvement. The important question is not whether the doctor is happy to make do, but whether the patient is receiving adequate treatment. A number of studies have shown doctors' dissatisfaction with interpreters' services (see chapter 5). A study conducted in Madrid by Valero Garcés among 100 service providers in the health care sector found that three-quarters of those surveyed complained about the interpretation provided, attributing their dissatisfaction to lack of professionalism on the part of the interpreters. The complaints referred to interpreters conversing with the patient without interpreting, offering summary translations, lacking fluency in Spanish, lacking an awareness of different registers and medical vocabulary (Valero Garcés, 2003b: 183) – practices that would be seen as desirable in the mediator approach. In a study of untrained hospital interpreters in the United States, Davidson found that:

> The physicians generally lament the difficulties of diagnosing patients, establishing a clinical relationship, or providing adequate care to patients when using an interpreter; the interpreters tend

to focus on their role as 'linguistic ambassadors' for the patient, a stance in favor of overt 'advocacy' interpretation. Neither group, however, rests their arguments on analyses that explore exactly how, in discourse, interpreters advocate or obfuscate the conversational process. (Davidson, 2000: 384)

Vásquez and Javier (1991), two clinical psychiatrists, argue strongly for trained interpreters in psychiatric consultations to ensure an accurate rendition that will permit psychiatrists to perform their assessments adequately. They identify five basic errors commonly committed by untrained interpreters: omission, addition, condensation, substitution and role exchange. They explain these tendencies in the following way:

Omission is the process by which an interpreter completely or partially deletes a message sent by the speaker. Addition is the tendency to include information not expressed by the speaker. The tendency to simplify and explain is referred to as condensation, the tendency to replace concepts as substitution. Finally, role exchange occurs when an interpreter takes over the interaction and replaces the interviewer's questions with the interpreter's own, thus assuming the role of interviewer. (Vásquez and Javier, 1991: 164)

The characteristics outlined by Vásquez and Javier adequately describe those found in interpreters that follow the mediator approach (see next section). Vasquez and Javier further state that 'even well-intentioned untrained interpreters usually lack a sufficient appreciation of the possible consequences of an inaccurate interpretation for the patient's treatment' (1991: 164). In speaking of the South African situation, Erasmus (2000) comments that the use of untrained interpreters often creates more problems than it solves.

2.3.2 Examples of what has been described as the 'mediator', 'visible' or 'involved' interpreter

Angelelli (2004) presents a continuum of 'visibility' with regards to the performance of interpreters, with the most visible interpreters disregarding most of the established ethical obligations (such as impartiality and accuracy), and the invisible interpreters adhering strictly to them. She argues that the level of 'visibility' depends on the context, with conference interpreters being the most invisible, followed by court interpreters, and medical interpreters the most visible.

Angelelli draws from an impressive selection of data of interpreted exchanges and transcriptions of interviews with interpreters in a Californian hospital, to provide examples of what she labels the 'visible' interpreter role. She defines visibility in the following way:

> Visibility and participation are not just present in the linguistic co-construction of the conversation, they are also essential in: communicating cultural gaps as well as linguistic barriers, communicating affect nuances as well as the content of the message, establishing trust between all parties to the conversation, facilitating mutual respect, putting the parties at ease during the conversation, creating more balance (or imbalance) during the conversation by aligning with one of the parties, advocating for or establishing alliances with either party, managing the requested and given information. (Angelelli, 2004: 11)

While the interpreters in her data adhere to some of the characteristics she describes as pertaining to the 'visible' category, they do not adhere to many of the more positive ones. The examples provided show no evidence of the interpreters communicating cultural gaps, affect nuances, establishing trust between parties, facilitating mutual respect, putting the parties at ease or creating more balance in the interaction. For the most part, these interpreters create imbalance by monopolising the interaction, do not facilitate mutual respect or put the parties at ease, but instead create friction or impede the participants from building a relationship by not allowing them to communicate with each other. These well-intentioned interpreters believe they are helping by disregarding any notion of accuracy or impartiality and deliberately changing, omitting or adding to the original utterances. On the other hand, the proponents of accurate interpreting would argue that in order to be accurate, cultural gaps need to be filled and nuances and style communicated, which, according to Angelelli, are characteristics of the 'visible' interpreter. Angelelli's definition of the visible interpreter, therefore, mixes characteristics from the mediator approach and the direct interpreting approach.

Some of Angelelli's examples will be reproduced and discussed in light of the consequences that can result from interpreters' deviations from the approach of direct interpreting.

The interpreter in Example 2.1 is justifying the reason for omitting much of what patients say. His comment shows not only his belief that his role extends to being a gatekeeper, but also a dismissive attitude towards the patient:

Example 2.1 Interpreter's comment

Tú sabes más o menos cuándo el paciente está hablando tonterías, que no vienen al caso. Entonces esas ni vale la pena mencionárselas al doctor.

[You more or less know when the patient is speaking nonsense that's irrelevant. Those things are not even worth mentioning to the doctor.]

(Angelelli, 2004: 120; my translation)

A few important insights can be highlighted here. First, the interpreter presumes to know what is and what is not relevant, something he cannot possibly do for someone else, especially not in light of the dynamics of doctor–patient interaction (see section 2.2.1). What may seem irrelevant to the interpreter may not be irrelevant to the doctor, who may be able to capture indirect clues to the real problem. As Cordella explains: 'a person's condition can sometimes be understood by looking at social factors that affect health – for example, ongoing problems in the family or workplace' (2004: 121). Secondly, in being concerned with not wasting the doctor's time, the interpreter is disregarding the patient's complaint. This is consistent with the lack of neutrality proposed as a characteristic of the visible interpreter, with the interpreter advocating for the doctor in this case, not the patient. Such an attempt to help the doctor, however, may have the opposite result, as a doctor who truly cares about a patient will want to hear what the patient has to say. Finally, stating that patients usually speak nonsense assumes a superior, patronising position, where the patient is seen as ignorant and almost childlike, devoid of any right to express him- or herself freely.

Another interpreter stated that patients insist on being heard and telling their stories, but she argues that 'doctors are under time constraints, and most of the time they do not want to listen to those stories' (Angelelli, 2004: 113). Angelelli adds that 'Elda [the interpreter] has seen the disappointment in some patients' faces when they are not heard' (2004: 113). Although these interpreters claim to be helping the non-English speaker, they are in fact adding to their sense of powerlessness by not allowing them to speak. Tellechea Sánchez (2005) found very similar results in a study of 27 Spanish-speaking families in the United States. These families, who all had children with disabilities and needed constant medical attention, were interviewed about their experiences with interpreters in the medical system. Comments from the families such as *'Además los intérpretes ni siquiera traducen todo lo que tú expresas'* [Besides, interpreters don't even translate everything you say] (Tellechea Sánchez, 2005: 118), and *'El intérprete hace resúmenes... el intérprete no facilita'* [The interpreter summarises... the interpreter doesn't facilitate anything] (Tellechea Sánchez, 2005: 117) reflect their frustration with interpreters who performed the 'visible' or 'mediator' role. Tellechea Sánchez (2005) found the same behaviour in the interpreters as previously discussed: they did not interpret everything, but offered summaries and their own opinions, they had private conversations with the doctors that were not transmitted to the patients, and they decided on what should and or should not be expressed. Tellechea Sánchez argues strongly that these untrained interpreters act as a barrier to communication rather than as facilitators, increasing the level of powerlessness of the already disadvantaged patient, and advocates for adequate, compulsory training for interpreters which will ensure not only quality of interpreting in terms of accuracy, but also adherence to the role of interpreter.

Davidson (2001) found similar incidences of interpreter power in his study of untrained Spanish-speaking hospital staff interpreters in the United States and argues that:

> recently immigrated patients who did not speak English received, in very real terms, a different form of medical treatment, one mediated by a hospital employee who was not a health-care provider and who frequently, in the name of speed, cut short their more difficult-to-identify ailments... The result was a tremendous invisible power wielded by professional,[1] hospital based interpreters... (Davidson, 2001: 171)

Davidson (2001) states that physicians ask interpreters to interpret selectively what was said, although it is not clear how these instructions are transmitted to the interpreters by the physicians. In Angelelli's study, however, it was found that doctors are often not satisfied with the edited versions produced by the interpreter. Another interpreter is quoted as saying that when doctors challenge her renditions as being incomplete, she replies, 'If you like I can stop interpreting' (Angelelli, 2004: 109). An example of the type of editing that these Californian interpreters do is the following:

Example 2.2   Elda

1. Doctor: ... so it helps you or it doesn't?
2. Interpreter: (interprets accurately)
3. Patient: *No, pos, no es ... Me pega fuerte y*
4. (No ... well ... it's not ... it's a lot of pain and]
5. Interpreter: [*¿'Pero le sirve?*
6. (But, it does help you?)
7. Patient: [*Tantito estaba mejor pero esta mañana ...*
8. (Earlier I was a little better, but this morning ...)
9. Doctor: [It does help her, then?
10. Interpreter: She's not answering my question, doctor. *¿'Señora por qué no me dice si le ayuda o no el medicamento?*
11. (Listen, why don't you tell me if it helps you or not?)
12. Patient: [*Es que ... como le digo ... si no camino ...*
13. (Well ... like I say ... if I don't walk ...)
14. I: [*Señora espéreme un momentito, ieh! Vamos a hacer una cosa, cuando yo le hable, usted se queda callada y después usted habla y yo la escucho, sino no se puede y no nos entendemos.*
15. (Look, hold on a minute ... OK? Let's do something, when I talk, you keep quiet and then you talk and I listen, otherwise we can't do it and we can't understand each other)

(Angelelli, 2004: 87; my translations of the Spanish)

Example 2.2 is very illuminating of the type of mediation performed by this interpreter. She believes she is helping the doctor by not interpreting what she regards as irrelevant to the question, and in a very patronising manner attempts to force the patient to provide a yes or no answer. We can see that the doctor commences the exchange by addressing the patient in the first person, but when a number of uninterpreted exchanges take place between the patient and the interpreter, the doctor switches to the interpreter and refers to the patient in the third person (line 9). Interestingly, the interpreter makes no secret of having taken over the interview and openly states 'she's not answering **my** question' (line 10), although the patient had indirectly done so in her previous two answers (lines 3–4 and 7–8), not with a yes or a no, but with an answer that would be common of patients. Very few patients would confidently state that a medication has helped, but they would describe how they have been feeling since they have started taking it. Many examples of monolingual doctor–patient interviews demonstrate the way patients will answer questions in an indirect way (Waitzkin, 1991; Coupland et al., 1994; Cordella, 2004). In line 10, the interpreter reprimands the patient: *¿Señora por qué no me dice si le ayuda o no el medicamento?* [Listen, why don't you tell me if the medicine helps you or not?] (Note that 'señora' in Spanish is not always a politeness marker, but in many cases, such as this, an emphasis marker.) To this the patient replies in a hesitant, indirect way that she has been trying to answer the question 'Well...like I say...if I don't walk...', but she is interrupted once again by the interpreter. The interpreter proceeds to treat the patient like a child by asking her to listen and not interrupt, so that they can understand each other. The doctor is completely excluded from this exchange, hearing none of the important information offered by the patient, who was never allowed to complete her sentences. One can see no valid reason for the interpreter's interference: there were no translation difficulties, there was no pressure from the institution, there was no obstacle placed by the doctor. Had the interpreter interpreted the patient's utterances faithfully, the doctor would have been given the chance to perform his duty. The interpreter's mediator approach did not achieve anything but confusion and disempowerment for both the patient and the doctor. Angelelli agrees that the interpreter 'impacts on the participatory and responsive nature of the doctor–patient relationship', but states that it 'should not be construed as the interpreter's fault or responsibility. We may infer from this segment that Elda intervenes in response to the doctor's need to find out a yes or no answer' (2004: 88). It is not clear, however, who has given Elda the mandate to ensure that the patient answers with a yes or no. As mentioned before, doctors are accustomed to receiving indirect answers from monolingual patients, answers that can lead to probing questions that may help in ascertaining the real problems (see section 2.2.2 above). Even in cases where doctors ask interpreters to deviate from their role, a confident, professional interpreter will refuse to do so and explain her or his role, asserting that if the doctor wants a yes or no answer, the doctor will need to communicate that to the patient.

Numerous examples from this study show instances where the interpreter assumes the right to omit, change or add to the patient's or doctor's utterances, often leaving the doctor or patient out of the exchange and at times even providing the answers for the patient and the doctor. Byrne and Long suggest that 'the doctor...must also realise that many patients are likely to execute desirable medical decisions if they believe that they have been a party to the making of those decisions' (Byrne and Long 1976: 27). In instances where an interpreter takes the mediator approach, the patient would have no chance of ever being party to the decision-making. As Angelelli comments: 'If interpreters edit patients' talk and decide which information is relevant to the medical issue at hand, then it is the interpreters who are making these important decisions. And on what basis? Their own opinions and experiences? Scientific knowledge?' (2004: 137). This can be compared to Cicourel's analysis of the clerical personnel in hospitals who act as gatekeepers in deciding who is entitled to health care. He states that 'the receptionists have no training in health care delivery but nevertheless engage in brief exchanges that reveal direct and indirect information about beliefs and knowledge of health projected by the participants' (1999: 184).

Davidson concludes from his study of untrained interpreters in US hospitals that the interpreters in his sample were acting as gatekeepers rather than interpreters or even advocates. He found:

> The interpreter here evaluates the patient's response and dismisses it as irrelevant...The interpreter is acting as pre-filter for patients' utterances, screening them for relevance to the physician's questions...however, converting data by passing it through a grid of medical meanings is the central component of the process of diagnosis itself. (Davidson, 2000: 398)

Davidson also found that in interviews without an interpreter almost all of the direct questions were answered by the physician. However, those who asked questions through an interpreter received over half of those answered by the interpreter without the doctor ever hearing the question (Davidson, 2000: 390). He argues that these Hispanic patients will be seen as passive 'and also prevents the physician from following up on difficult questions or questions that display a deep misunderstanding, on the part of the patient, as to what the diagnosis or plan of treatment are' (2000: 391).

Bolden (2000) analyses the performance of one Russian interpreter during two medical interviews. She states this interpreter was highly proficient in both languages and had 'some professional interpreting training'. However, no information is given of what kind of training this was. She proposes that interpreters align to either the 'voice of medicine' or the 'voice of lifeworld' and adapt their interpreting accordingly. Mishler (1984) described two competing voices that can surface in the medical interview. The 'voice of medicine' relates to the technical medical topics that relate to pathology, pharmacology, and so on, whereas the 'voice of lifeworld' refers to everyday life events that patients bring into the consultation in order to explain their condition. He argues that doctors are normally ill-equipped to deal with the 'voice of lifeworld' and tend to spend more time on the 'voice of medicine', something that can contribute to poor communication. Below is one of Bolden's examples of this interpreter's performance. (The Russian segments are not reproduced, only the English translations in italics and the English original utterances in roman script.)

Example 2.3

Doctor: Ah, are, are you uh having a problem with uh chest pain?
Interpreter: *Do you have a chest pain?*
Patient: *Well how should I put it, who knows? It . . . sometimes it does happen.*
Interpreter (to patient): *Once a week? Once every two weeks?*
Patient: *No, this thing happens then depending on . . . on circumstances of life.*
Interpreter (to patient): *Well at this particular moment do your life circumstances cause you pain once a week or, or more often?*
Patient: *Sometimes more often, sometimes more often.*
Interpreter (to doctor): Once or twice a week maybe.

(Bolden, 2000: 396–7)

In Example 2.3 we see how crucial information is withheld from the physician. Whereas the patient makes a reference to life circumstances which affect the heart condition, the interpreter simply states that the patient has chest problems 'maybe' once or twice a week. Interestingly, after this segment, the interpreter does not wait for the doctor to ask another question and continues to conduct the consultation himself by asking the patient about a number of different possible causes for the pain. After a long exchange between the interpreter and the patient, the interpreter provides the doctor with his own diagnosis: 'Ah . . . sometimes the chest pain is stress-related sometimes it's exertion-related' (Bolden, 2000: 400–1).

Bolden argues that 'the interpreter's questions and summary translations are designed in such a way as to further the activity of the history-taking interview' (2000: 394). It is difficult to justify how an interpreter who is not a qualified physician can make such diagnostic decisions and be helping the course of the interview in any way.

Example 2.4

Doctor: And contraception, what are you using?

Patient: U::hm, on and off I've used the pill, and, uh, I've used a diaphragm also, but I don't use it that much, because, well, for one thing, I'm separated right now, uh, there isn't that much need, but when there

               [

Doctor: so

            [

Patient: is need, it's either the diaphragm or, I have taken the pill. As a matter of fact, last winter, January and February, I was very depressed, and not because of intercourse, because I find the pill calms me down, it's a very strange thing. I took the pill for a month. The pill does things. It makes my feelings even, over the month. I used to get very upset just before

              [

Doctor: Uh huh

            [

Patient: my period. Very, very upset, very nervous and very tense. I find that that helped me a bit.

(Waitzkin, 1991: 113)

Example 2.4 is an English monolingual example of a doctor–patient interaction where we can see that the doctor allows the patient to speak freely about her 'lifeworld' concerns and does not stop her when she does not produce a direct answer to the first question. In addition to telling the doctor what type of contraception she has used in the past and is using now, she provides all the reasons for her choices. She also provides information on her depression. The information that she provides, although not directly related to the doctor's question, is relevant for medical reasons. Cordella (2004) provides similar examples from her data from Chilean doctor–patient interactions. Had the patient in Example 2.4 spoken another language and used the services of any of these mediator-interpreters, only the words 'the pill' and 'the diaphragm' would have been transmitted to the doctor. By these interpreters' estimation, everything else would have been irrelevant.

Examples 2.1–2.3 demonstrate the interpreters' desire to 'help' doctors save time by editing out what they deem to be irrelevant information from the patients' answers. As discussed in section 2.2.1, none of the omissions could be considered irrelevant to a physician. Angelelli also provides examples of interpreters adding to the doctor's explanations, as explained by Joaquín, one of the interviewed interpreters:

For example, if a mother comes with a baby and asks for cough syrup, and the doctor says, 'No, tell them that we don't like giving cough syrup to babies', I take it upon myself to explain that doctors do not like to give babies cough syrup, because they think that the cough helps to clean the baby's lungs and get rid of the phlegm, and if they give the baby [this] syrup, there is a risk of sediments accumulating. So, in five seconds I have explained the patient [*sic*] the reason and the patient does not feel that the doctor doesn't want to help. (Angelelli, 2000: 115)

The argument in favour of the interpreter's action here is that the patient receives additional information to her question, which cannot possibly do any harm. However, the question it raises is this: why not allow the patient to ask the doctor the reason why cough syrup is not recommended and allow the doctor to explain through the interpreter? In this instance the interpreter may have been familiar with the reasons why, but in other more complicated cases he may not, and therefore there is no consistency as to when the interpreter should provide extra information and when the doctor should step in. Would a doctor who is accustomed to working with this type of interpreter tend to relax and expect the interpreter to take over? Or would such a doctor, as Davidson suggests, believe that the patients are not asking as many questions as English-speaking patients and therefore are less interested in their own health? These dilemmas do not arise when the interpreter interprets each turn accurately.

2.3.3   The case for the trained, faithful medical interpreter

In contrast with the studies of ad hoc medical interpreters, Englund Dimitrova (1997) analysed the work of a professional, trained medical interpreter in Sweden. The data show that the interpreter interprets every turn accurately and always uses the first person. Englund Dimitrova's points of interest in the interpreted interaction are issues of turn-taking and the use of feedback and overlapping speech, all of which are of particular relevance to Community Interpreting due to the close proximity with the interlocutors. Unlike the examples of the untrained interpreters, where the interpreters monopolise the interactions, in Englund Dimitrova's study the doctor is clearly in control and takes most of the turns, a finding that corroborates studies into doctor–patient monolingual discourse. In her words, 'doctors take the initiative and basically maintain it throughout the encounters. The fact that there is a third speaker present, the interpreter, does not change this relationship' (1997: 156). She poses the interesting question of whether the interpreter should indirectly take on the role of allocating turns to each interlocutor, by giving them face or hand signals in cases of simultaneous speech or necessary interruptions by the interpreter. When there is overlapping speech, or when the speaker is not stopping at reasonable chunks, the interpreter is forced to interrupt the speakers to have her or his turn, making turn-taking problematic. These are very important issues in triadic interpreted exchanges that need to be researched. However, it can only be done when the role of the interpreter has been decided. If the interpreter is to summarise and edit rather than interpret, there is no need for any research into turn-taking, because the interpreter is controlling that already.

Little research has been conducted which compares the outcomes of the current predominant situation of interpreters as mediators, advocates, gatekeepers and 'pseudo-physicians', with a situation where the role of neutral, accurate interpreting is adhered to. The one study that compares this situation is that carried out by Athorp and Downing (1996), where three consultations were compared: one with a bilingual nurse who acted as hospital interpreter, the second with a professional trained interpreter, and the third without an interpreter. The researchers found that the interview with the professional interpreter compared favourably to the monolingual event, with the interpreter's utterances on the whole being accurate to the doctor's and the patient's turns. On the other hand, they found that the nurse often assumed a caregiver role and reduced the number of direct interactions between the doctor and the patient. They concluded there is great benefit for the medical profession in using the services of professional, trained interpreters, as opposed to untrained bilinguals. More research into this area is crucial in order to compare the results of both roles (see chapter 8).

The proponents of a faithful rendition of the original utterances, rather than a literal or verbatim rendition, argue that this stance will not only force the medical practitioners to take responsibility for their job as health care providers, but will also empower the patients by giving them a voice through which they can express themselves in the way they wish (Downing 1991; Vasquez and Javier, 1991; Athorp and Downing 1996; Roberts, 1997; Cambridge, 1999; Tebble, 1999; Chesher et al., 2003; Tellechea Sánchez, 2005). This approach also argues that it is the only way to achieve effective communication between the doctor and the patient through the services of an interpreter, albeit the responsibility for effective communication originally lies with the main speakers. A good interpreter cannot be expected to compensate for a doctor's poor communication skills. Cambridge (1999) analysed the performance of what she calls the 'bilingual mediator' to refer to untrained 'language switchers' who act as medical interpreters. She found numerous examples of miscommunication throughout the data which are mostly attributable to the mediator's over-identification with the patient, insufficient knowledge of the specialised terminology, constant inaccuracies, offering of personal opinions and unfamiliarity with the routines and procedures of the consultation. She also states that the doctor's ignorance of the best way to speak through interpreters also contributed to the failure in the communication, as the doctor consistently used the third person, addressing the mediator rather than the patient (Cambridge, 1999: 218). As Candlin and Candlin (2003: 137) state, medical practitioners need to be trained in working with interpreters, and interpreters themselves need specialist training. Patients should also be educated on how to speak through an interpreter, on the role of the interpreter and on their right to be heard. Tellechea Sánchez (2005) found that none of the 27 families in her study had been told any of this. This situation differs somewhat in Australia, where trained interpreters are taught to explain their role to the patients when they introduce themselves. Similarly in Sweden, the *God tolksed* (Code of Good Interpreting Practice) has a section which advises interpreters to inform the interlocutors of their role (Niska, 1998).

Tebble (1998, 1999) argues for a very high standard of accuracy in medical interpreting.

Quote 2.4 Tebble's argument for accurate interpreting in medical consultations

The outcome of the consultation with all its attendant costs can depend considerably on the nature of the rapport that prevails between doctor and patient. So it is up to the medical interpreter to live up to the interpreter's code of ethics and convey what is said accurately. Conveying what is said means not just the content of the message but also the way the message is expressed. This means that the medical interpreter needs to relay the interpersonal features of each speaker's turn at talk.

(Tebble, 1999: 186)

It is worth noting that Tebble's reality of Community Interpreting in Australia is very different from that of other countries, where studies have taken place. In Australia, university training and national accreditation have been in place for over 20 years, and although there are untrained, unaccredited interpreters still working in the field, producing similar renditions to the ones quoted in this chapter, a good proportion of Australian interpreters in the major languages are trained, nationally accredited and very highly skilled, producing very accurate renditions. For these interpreters, their concern is not whether they should interpret accurately, as they have that goal already, but how best to achieve it. Communicating the manner of the speech is much more difficult than simply concentrating on the content. Maintaining a hesitant or a forceful tone, a formal or an informal register, or being aware of the significance of seemingly superfluous speech features such as discourse markers, are all aspects that add to the difficulty of achieving accuracy of interpretation. Only highly skilled interpreters can aim to achieve this higher level of accuracy.

Cordella argues that physicians and patients negotiate their meanings, express their attitudes and judgements and build up a level of solidarity through linguistic strategies, such as 'continuer markers, joint production forms, agreement markers, mirroring clarifying questions, empathic utterances and questions designed to understand the patient's health problem in a more holistic framework' (2004: 142). This is supported by much of the literature on successful consultations which emphasise the importance of dialogue in building a relationship between doctor and patient, the role of question type in eliciting the most useful information, and the need for doctors to listen for cues in patients' answers that are not directly responsive to their questions (Byrne and Long, 1976; Cicourel, 1999; Ferguson and Candib, 2002). Vásquez and Javier (1991) explain the significance of seemingly superfluous or irrelevant material produced by psychiatric patients and the importance of distorted, incoherent speech in making an accurate assessment. They comment that untrained interpreters tend to edit such information and rephrase incoherent utterances to make them coherent, hence interfering with the very important process of patient evaluation. They present telling examples of interpreters omitting information, adding clarifications of their own and assuming the role of interviewer, which led to inaccurate, at times life-threatening, assessments and treatment decisions.

2.3.4 Health care providers and interpreters working as a professional team

The argument in favour of the direct interpreting approach, as explained in Concept 2.2, does not favour the interpreter acting as a mechanical, subservient invisible participant in the interpreted interaction, but rather as an equal professional who understands the demarcation of roles, is competent in the complex skills of interpreting, is proficient in cross-cultural and cross-linguistic issues, is able to manage the interaction (e.g. stop overlapping speech, side-comments), and is aware of the discourse of the discipline and of the requirements of the setting. Professional interpreters are better able to perform a competent job when the other participants respect them as professionals, understand their role and do not expect them to act unethically. Medical practitioners and interpreters should work as a team to achieve optimal results, with each understanding the needs of the other and neither stepping into the other's role. Isaacs (2002) proposes routine pre-consultation briefing sessions with interpreters in the area of speech pathology. Ideally, such sessions should extend to all other medical interactions, although one must acknowledge the time constraints that exist in some settings, especially in public hospitals. The purpose of such briefing sessions is for the health care provider and the interpreter to have an opportunity to inform each other of their respective roles, expectations and requirements before the commencement of the interpreted interaction. Health care providers would introduce the case to the interpreter, inform her or him of the goals of the consultation, the nature of the condition, of any procedures and provide any other relevant information. The interpreter, on the other hand, would explain his or her role, the interpreting process, the basic interpreting protocols (such as direct address, introducing the interpreter to the patient and explaining his or her role, maintaining eye contact with the patient, seating arrangements, etc.), and alert the medical practitioner of obvious cultural differences, if any. Ideally, the interpreter would receive information on the case before the day of the assignment in order to prepare thoroughly, just as is the case in Conference Interpreting. If the interpreter and the health care provider have worked together before, some of the contents of the briefing session would not need to be repeated. Such an approach would greatly improve mutual understanding between the professions and in turn the service provided to patients.

2.4   Summary

This chapter has outlined the crucial need for interpreters to understand the significance of language in the medical consultation and for health care providers to understand the role and the needs of interpreters in order to provide a quality service. The chapter presented the two opposing views about the approach to interpreting in the medical setting: the direct approach and the mediated approach. A number of examples of the mediated approach are provided and their consequences discussed. It is argued that the interpreters' active interference, rather than helping redress the current problems of doctor–patient communication, accentuates them by adding a layer of control over the patient and indeed over the doctor as well.

On the other hand, the few studies that have been conducted on interpreters who take the direct approach have shown that the interpreted interactions more closely resemble monolingual doctor–patient interactions, achieving much better results. More studies should be conducted with professional, trained interpreters to analyse other issues that complicate the event. These include language-specific difficulties in finding accurate renditions, how best to transmit the manner of speech, how to manage turns, including overlapping speech, and when to interrupt to offer or to ask for clarifications when communication is not achieved, due to linguistic or cultural reasons.

One crucial question that needs to be asked is whether in the medical setting interpreters are to attempt to place the patient in the same situation as a patient who does not require the services of an interpreter (as is the case in the adversarial legal system), or whether the interpreter is to help the health care provider improve doctor–patient communication, even when a monolingual patient would not have the benefit of such help. In other words, is an interpreter able to improve on the communication skills of a physician who is a poor communicator with patients who speak his or her own language? The relaxed, private atmosphere of the medical consultation can be conducive to interpreters taking a less rigid stance than they would in the courtroom. While maintaining the goal to interpret each turn accurately, would it be appropriate for interpreters to interrupt if they feel a line of questioning is simply not working after a number of attempts, or should they adhere to interpreting every turn and let the main participants rephrase their own utterances? Would the medical interpreter be best to assume a role that fits somewhere in between the mediator or advocate role and the neutral role of the court interpreter? These are examples of ethical dilemmas that will always arise in any interpreting situation, and that will be discussed in more detail in chapter 4. Whatever role is adopted by medical interpreters, only those who are properly trained can make such choices. Untrained, ad hoc interpreters will always do what comes naturally at the time for any bilingual person, which is to offer a summary of what they remember or feel is relevant. Accuracy, even if a distant goal, can be well beyond their capabilities. Until the system changes to recognise the need for training and reward it with adequate remuneration, little will change.

Further reading

Angelelli (2004). This book reports the results of a large ethnographic study of untrained interpreters working in a Californian hospital. It contains an impressive collection of authentic data and discusses the interpreters' practices and their perceptions about their role.

Cambridge (1999).This article presents a case study which highlights the consequences of poor interpretation to the medical interview.

Tebble (1999). This article presents the results of innovative discourse based research into medical interpreted consultations. It argues strongly for the need for adequately trained and accredited interpreters.

Vásquez and Javier (1991).This article presents the perspectives from the service provider, in this case psychiatrist, on the negative consequences brought about by poor interpretation.

3
Interdisciplinarity: Community Interpreting in the Legal Context

This chapter:

- Describes the main legal settings in which interpreters work.
- Outlines the most salient issues surrounding interpreting in the legal setting.
- Presents the findings of research into legal interpreting and discusses their implication for practice.
- Discusses some of the proposed roles for each of the sub-settings.
- Highlights the strategic use of language in this setting and the need for interpreters to take this into account when deciding on how to interpret.
- Stresses the need for mutual understanding and collaboration between legal interpreters and other professionals working in the legal field to achieve optimum results.

3.1 Introduction

Quote 3.1 The role of interpreters in the legal process

...interpreters have become an indispensable part of the legal process. Unfortunately, many people who work in legal settings have little or no understanding of interpreting and its complexities. Not infrequently they treat interpreters with suspicion, distrust and a lack of respect for the skills which they bring to the job. It must also be acknowledged that the people engaged to interpret are not always skilled, experienced or fully competent.

(Colin and Morris, 1996: 15)

In chapter 2 we discussed the need for interpreters and other professionals to work collaboratively in order to perform their respective duties effectively. This need is reinforced by Colin and Morris (1996, see above), who lament the lack of understanding on the part of interpreters and lawyers about each other's work. Understanding the other's roles, expectations and needs is crucial in achieving an effective working relationship. Chapter 2 concentrated on interpreting in the medical context; in this chapter we concentrate on interpreting in the legal context. Although there is much in common to these two settings, there are also significant differences that impinge on the practice of the interpreter, as mentioned in chapter 2. This specialised branch of Community Interpreting is often referred to as Legal Interpreting, which comprises a variety of legal domains such as police interviews and interrogations, lawyer–client conferences, tribunal hearings and court hearings and trials. These different domains share the underlying legal system they serve, legal concepts and some of their discourses. However, each domain differs in terms of the relationship between interlocutors, the goal of the interaction, the privacy and the formality of the event, the roles of the participants, the role of language, and as a consequence, the implications for interpreters. Although most of the research into legal interpreting has been conducted in the context of the courtroom, the other domains present particular issues and challenges that are worth addressing.

Table 3.1 outlines the main legal domains in the English-speaking world where the services of interpreters may be required. This will not cover all the systems around the world, but may serve as a general guide to a number of common settings. Each of these settings is discussed below, drawing on the relevant literature.

3.2 Police interviews and interrogations

This initial phase of the legal process should not be underestimated. As Cotterill states when speaking of the importance of language in witness testimonies, 'the accounts presented form part of a chain of forensic narratives extending back to the original police interviews and forwards to potential future appeal proceedings' (2004: 149). Witness statements or suspects' records of interview form a very important part of the legal process. Although they are taken outside the courtroom setting, a written version of the interview, supposedly in the form of a verbatim transcript, commonly forms the basis of a case and is presented in court as crucial evidence (Coulthard, 2004). However, it is not only the content of these

Table 3.1 Main legal domains in the English-speaking world

	Police interrogations (records of interview)	Police interviews	Legal conferences	Tribunal hearings	Court hearings	Court trials
Participants	Police suspect/detainee Interpreter	Police Witness Interpreter	Lawyer Client Interpreter	Member(s) Applicant Defendant Witness(es) (Counsel) Interpreter	Magistrate Court clerk Police prosecutor Defence counsel Defendant Witness(es) Interpreter	Judge/Justice(s) Jury Prosecuting counsel Defence counsel Accused Witness(es) Interpreter
Participant relationship	Antagonistic with police (even if police attempt to maintain a friendly and cooperative interaction)	Neutral	Friendly with counsel	Neutral with members	Neutral with magistrate, antagonistic with opposing side's counsel, friendly with own counsel	Neutral with judge, antagonistic with opposing side's counsel, friendly with own counsel
Participant roles	Police as questioner Detainee as answerer	Police as questioner, witness as answerer or witness as narrator	Both questioners and answerers	Members act as questioners, applicants as answerers, without restrictions of rules of evidence	Counsel as questioners, witnesses as answerers. Rules of evidence apply	Counsel as questioners, witnesses as answerers. Rules of evidence apply
Level of formality	Informal, semi-formal	Informal, semi-formal	Informal, Semi-formal	Semi-formal	Formal	Formal
Privacy	Private	Private	Private	Semi-private	Public	Public
Goal of event	Accuse, draw a confession	Produce a statement for the prosecution case	Defend	Mediate	Choose one version	Choose one version
System	N/A	N/A	N/A	Inquisitorial	Adversarial	Adversarial

transcripts that is of importance to the court. The way in which answers are expressed, or a statement is written, may influence the assessment of its truth-value by the decision-makers. Appeals have been mounted and convictions overturned on the grounds of allegedly manufactured statements by police. The authorship of statements has been contested on the basis of forensic linguistic evidence that showed significant linguistic (i.e. grammatical and stylistic) differences between a witness's written statements as produced by the police and their oral language competence when interviewed by an independent linguist (Gibbons, 1990, 1996; Coulthard, 2004). Gibbons comments that, although some statements may have been deliberately fabricated by the police, the vast majority of the alterations were simply 'the result of a linguistically unsophisticated policeman attempting to record what he thought he heard at a single hearing' (Gibbons, 1990: 233). The imprecise transcription of police interviews was common practice prior to the introduction of mandatory recordings in most English-speaking countries. In the United Kingdom before the introduction of the PACE (Police and Criminal Evidence Act 1984) code of practice, police openly edited statements in the course of the interview and in their later compilation to make them fit the criteria for a 'good' statement (Fowler, 2003; Coulthard, 2004). A 'good' statement would present the events in chronological order, be consistent in the presentation of facts and exclude any material that may have seemed to be improbable or impossible (Ede and Shepherd, 2000, in Fowler, 2003: 200). Fowler (2003) explains that although officers believed they were writing the witness's or suspect's words, they were in fact constructing their own statement from a series of answers provided by the witness or suspect. These answers were then converted into a single, structured narrative that was chronological, relevant and coherent. Such a practice precluded any attempt to establish authorship of the text based on linguistic features, as it was collaboratively created.

> [B]y being in control of the written form in which the original interaction was to be subsequently presented to the Court, the police were able to create a misrepresentation which would significantly influence the outcome of the case and help to secure a conviction. (Coulthard, 2004: 33)

The practice was subsequently abandoned and replaced by audio- or video-recordings in most jurisdictions (cf. Laster and Taylor, 1994 for Australia; Berk-Seligson, 2000 for the US; Coulthard, 2004 for the UK).

3.2.1   The right to an interpreter in a police interview

Quote 3.2   The right to an interpreter

The right to have an interpreter present during police questioning is probably more significant than the right to an interpreter in court proceedings.

(Laster and Taylor, 1994: 136)

As it is in the police interview that suspects can forfeit their right to remain silent or to have a lawyer present which may lead to incriminating themselves, Laster and Taylor (1994) argue that the right to have an interpreter in the police interview may be even more important than the right to one in court. Despite the crucial nature of this initial phase of the legal process, the importance of using the services of competent qualified interpreters when the detainee does not speak the main language has not yet been universally recognised. Berk-Seligson (2000) highlights the stark difference that exists in the United States between court interpreting, with its established codes, standards and certification examinations, and the much less regulated area of police interpreting. She speaks of instances of poor, inaccurate and biased interpretation provided by police officers themselves, other police station staff, family members, informants, fellow inmates and even detainees. Some of these ad hoc interpreters possess less than elementary knowledge of Spanish, leading to numerous appeals against convictions on the grounds of poor interpretation in the police interview.

Nieto Garcia (2005) describes a similar situation in Spain, where the police call on untrained bilinguals to act as interpreters for Chinese speakers who are typically restaurant workers. In some jurisdictions, the caution or rights are translated into a number of languages. When these are not available in the appropriate language and there is no interpreter present, they are read in Spanish and a note is attached to the brief for the court stating that the rights were read out in Spanish but not understood by the detainee. Some jurisdictions give preference to trained interpreters; others do not. However, detainees of the same nationality or relatives of the detainee are never used as interpreters. Nieto Garcia argues for robust university training in Community Interpreting in the languages of greatest demand in Spain, such as Arabic and some Eastern European languages, to overcome this problem (Nieto Garcia, 2005: 197).

Quote 3.3   the role of the interpreter in police investigations

Perhaps it is merely naïveté on the part of law enforcement officers, or simply their lack of appreciation for the demanding nature of interpreting and translating, but the willingness of the police to entrust to non-professional interpreters the task of questioning suspects during investigative police work is playing with fire.

(Berk-Seligson, 2000: 233)

In Australia, the importance of engaging qualified interpreters during the police interview has been repeatedly recognised by law reform bodies, who recommend the legislation of the right to an interpreter during the police interview. A limited number of Commonwealth and state jurisdictions have such legislation. The Commonwealth Crimes Act 1914 stipulates that the interview cannot commence until an interpreter is present: 'the official must, before starting to question the person, arrange for the presence of an interpreter and defer the questioning or investigation until the interpreter is present' (Laster and Taylor, 1994: 137). This requirement is also present in the British PACE code of practice (Russell, 2004). Other Australian jurisdictions adhere to the guidelines contained in what is known as 'Standing Orders', which recommend a 'competent interpreter' be obtained for the interview in the event of a language barrier (AG's Department, 1991: 73–4). Although the requirement for the presence of a competent interpreter exists in either the legislation or the Standing Orders in all Australian states, there is no definition of what a 'competent interpreter' is, or what qualifications they should possess. Also, as Laster and Taylor (1994) state, police still need to make a judgement on whether the detainee requires the services of an interpreter, and at times, if they feel they can communicate through limited English, for expediency's sake, they may avoid calling an interpreter altogether. Gibbons (1995) claims that interpreter services are under-utilised by the police in Australia. However, many in the police have come to the understanding that it is in their interests to employ the services of an interpreter. As one police officer commented:

> We find that where we arrest people it's in our own interest to obtain interpreters...because the situation is that at a later time in court [*sic*] they might say they didn't understand the questions, so we obtain interpreters, and in fairness to them too, because they mightn't understand what they're in for... (Chan, 1992: 15, in Laster and Taylor, 1994: 136)

Laster and Taylor stress that providing interpreters for police interviews benefits police efficiency: 'The effort expended in obtaining evidence may be wasted if it is subsequently excluded by a court as being unreliable' (1994: 135). This seems to be accepted by Australian police in most cases, although there is anecdotal evidence which suggests that unqualified interpreters are used, especially when a bilingual police officer shares the language of the detainee.[1] Police argue that they should be able to rely on the expertise of a bilingual police officer when an interpreter is unavailable. Such a practice should not be permitted at all, on the basis that there is a major conflict of interests and that the police are not trained, qualified interpreters, as noted by the Australian Law Reform Commission (1992).

In an analysis of 49 appellate cases from California, Florida and New York, Berk-Seligson found that:

> police officers routinely are used as interpreters in the earliest investigative phases of a criminal case as well as during interviews and interrogations carried out in the police station. They also are used as interpreters of audio- or video-recorded non-English language statements of suspects/detainees, which they convert into English for police stenographers, or else translate and type themselves. (Berk-Seligson, 2000: 220)

Berk-Seligson (2000) argues strongly against the use of police as interpreters on the basis that they cannot act impartially. Through the analysis of a police interview of a Spanish speaker, where one of the constables acts as the interpreter, she shows that the 'interpreter'/officer formulated questions of his own, changed the first person singular pronoun (I) used by the interviewing officer to the first person plural pronoun (we), and in essence 'flagrantly ignored the guidelines of legal interpreting. At the same time, he became an active participant in helping the designated interrogator coerce a confession from the suspect. He in effect became an interrogator' (Berk-Seligson, 2004: 141). In other words, the police officer cannot take on the role of impartial interpreter, but instead adopts the role of open advocate for the institution. Interestingly, this is the same role that is often proposed for professional interpreters (cf. Chapter 2), except that the bias proposed is in favour of the minority language speaker.

3.2.2 Interpreting in the police context

Quote 3.4 Interpreting in a police interview

... the speech situation of the police interview or police interrogation is perhaps a more coercive one from the standpoint of asymmetrical power relationships between interlocutors, since there is no judge present to control the behaviour of the interrogators.

(Berk-Seligson, 2004: 127)

As outlined in Quote 3.4, the relationship between the police and the detainee is antagonistic, as the goal of the speech event is to accuse the suspect of an offence and to obtain a confession. This antagonistic relationship is compounded by the fact that one suspect is interviewed by two police officers and there is no lawyer present to represent the detainee (unless the detainee requests one), or a judge or magistrate to act as independent arbiter. In the English-speaking world, police are instructed to minimise the possibility for open confrontation by making the detainee feel at ease. This is achieved by the use of polite speech, colloquial language and sympathetic questioning (Laster and Taylor, 1994; Cotterill, 2004; Russell, 2004). Collaboration from the detainee is believed to be more likely when these methods are employed. This can be seen in Examples 3.1 and 3.2. The goal, however, remains accusatory: to obtain a confession through peaceful, persuasive means. Shuy states that 'even if the words of the interrogation are thought to be neutral, the event itself is enough to make questions or non-question statements seem, and be, coercive' (1997: 178). The overarching pragmatic value of the speech event constrains or even overrides the pragmatic value of utterances that occur within it .

Example 3.1

Police: And did D tell you to go in there and shag her as well?
Detainee: Yeah.
Police: So you were a bit under pressure really to go in there and – have sex with her, weren't you?
Detainee: Mm.

(Johnson, 2004: 105)

In Example 3.1 we see how the policeman uses register to establish solidarity with the detainee, reflected in the use of the slang term 'shag', and then by offering an understanding justification for the detainee's wrongful action: 'So you were a bit under pressure really...' The detainee agrees with the policeman on both counts.

Example 3.2

Police: I'm sorry for you José. A very bad thing that happened to you here. (*Pause*) You didn't want to hurt her, did you?
Detainee: *No entiendo lo que dice.* (I don't understand what he is saying)
Police 'interpreter': *¿Usted no quiso hacerle tanto daño?* (You didn't want to hurt her so much?)

(Berk-Seligson, 2004: 136-7)

In Example 3.2, we see the same trend as in Example 3.1, where the police officer expresses sympathy for the detainee by saying 'I'm sorry for you' and provides an understanding comment about the detainee's intentions not to hurt the woman as much. The use of the confirmation tag question is also important in attempting to co-construct the discourse collaboratively. Interestingly, although the interpreter is another constable, one that on other occasions showed himself to be biased in favour of the institution, in this instance he is working against the institution. By not interpreting the initial two sentences ('I'm sorry for you José' and 'A very bad thing that happened to you here'), and by changing the statement and tag into a statement with rising intonation, he is indeed interfering with the interrogating officer's attempt to build a rapport and to put the detainee at ease, instead making the exchange much more confrontational. Whether the omissions were deliberate or simply the consequence of poor interpreting skills is difficult to say, although the latter is much more likely.

Quote 3.5   Antagonism between suspects and the police

Migrants or refugees from more repressive regimes, for example, may associate the police with state terror tactics or corruption rather than seeing them as a source of help and protection. A suspect's fear of the police can create serious problems during the investigation process. It may cause minor misunderstandings to escalate into major confrontations.

(Laster and Taylor, 1994: 135)

Laster and Taylor (1994) comment that the already confrontational activity type of police interrogation can be compounded by the suspects' negative experiences with the police in their own countries.

Where an interpreter is present, the more confrontational the situation, the more problematic it can become for the interpreting task. The detainee, who may feel intimidated by the police, may cling to the interpreter for support, misunderstanding the interpreter's role as that of an advocate or even a legal representative who is there to redress the imbalance of power. Such an attitude can place extra pressure on interpreters, especially when suspects confide incriminating details in them and threaten to harm them if they disclose the information to the police.[2] Interpreters may thus find themselves in an environment where there is inherent animosity between the participants; where the detainee may distrust and even be fearful of the police based on previous experiences with police brutality in their country of origin; and where police doubt the truthfulness of the detainee's utterances, constantly trying to make them confess or to detect lies. There is also the possibility that the police will either mistrust the interpreter as someone who is biased in favour of a compatriot, or, on the other hand, expect them to act as an assistant to the police in the investigative process. On the other hand, the detainee may see the interpreter as a police offsider.

According to Russell the dynamics of the police interview change radically when an interpreter is present, 'transforming the oppositional dyad into a triadic mixture of opposition, cooperation and shifting alignments' (2004: 116). It could also be argued that the presence of an interpreter could reassure detainees that the police will respect their rights, as there is an independent witness who can testify to the contrary if asked to do so at a later stage. It is clear that the interpreter's allegiance, however, should not lie with either the police or the detainee, but rather with the communication process. They should resist pressure to take sides. A clear statement of the interpreter's obligation to remain impartial and interpret faithfully should be a routine part of the introduction to the interview (cf. chapter 4).

3.2.3 Discourse issues

An understanding of the goals of the institution and the way they are achieved through discourse strategies is necessary for interpreters to render faithful interpretations. Ironically, Example 3.2 shows an incident where a police officer who lacked adequate interpreting skills omitted essential segments of the original questions, thus interfering with his own institution's goals. It is important for interpreters to understand that the way questions are asked is of great significance. It is the English questions, not their translations, that will be taken by a court as a true record of the questions asked when they are presented as evidence. Unless there is a dispute on the basis of poor interpretation, the court will assume that the questions were accurately rendered into the other language by the interpreter. If, for instance, as in Example 3.2, the interpreter changes the tone of the question to make it more confrontational, provoking a more aggressive response from the detainee, such reaction may be misunderstood as a defensive overreaction, as it would be incongruous with the manner the question was formulated in English.

Similarly, the significance of content and manner of the suspect's answers must be understood by interpreters to maintain a faithful rendition. A parallel can be drawn between the discredited and abandoned police practice of reconstructing statements and records of interview and the current practice of many untrained interpreters who unwittingly alter the witnesses' or suspects' utterances to make them more coherent, less hesitant, more formal and more chronological, omitting what they consider to be irrelevant (Rigney, 1999; Berk-Seligson, 2000; Hale, 2004). In essence, these interpreters are doing what Coulthard (see quote 3.6) states the police used to do: they are in control of the verbal evidence, by deciding what should be and should not be included and by altering the form of the discourse.

Quote 3.6   Control of verbal evidence

In the days before tape recording police officers were very much in control of the verbal evidence. Not only did they control the topics covered in interviews, they also controlled what was recorded and what not recorded and, even more significantly, the form in which it was recorded.

(Coulthard, 2004: 20)

Krouglov (1999) argues strongly for the need to maintain the illocutionary force of stylistic features when interpreting in police interviews: 'in police interpreting, accuracy is of extreme importance and generalizations are often not helpful' (1999: 299). He found that hedges, in particular, caused major difficulties for interpreters working in the police interview. These were often omitted or their pragmatic meaning changed, a result corroborated by Hale's (1999) study of court interpreters. He also argues for the preservation of register in interpreter's renditions, stating that shifts from informal to formal 'may lead to inaccurate social or psychological evaluations of witnesses' (Krouglov, 1999: 295).

Russell (2004) argues that the apparent tolerance of obvious interpreter interventions, as presented in studies by Linell (1996) and Wadensjö (1998), cannot obtain in the context of the police investigative interview, as such a practice would have major ramifications. Recognising the complexities of interpreting, Russell poses the question of 'how much licence the interpreter should accord herself in order to facilitate comprehension between the primary participants' (2004: 117–18).

We can see, however, that even competent professional interpreters face challenges in attempting to render a faithful rendition of the interview exchanges. Russell provides examples of an interpreted police interview in the UK, where the interpreter, unlike most other interpreters quoted in other studies, for the majority of the time, interprets directly and accurately, but is faced with a challenge when there is overlapping speech. This is not a question of the interpreter's inability to interpret accurately, but a simple technical impossibility. As Roy (2000) comments, interpreters cannot interpret for two people at the same time. Roy suggests a number of alternatives the interpreter needs to choose from when confronted with overlapping speech:

1. to stop one of the speakers and allow the other to continue;
2. to momentarily ignore the overlapping speech, continue interpreting the first utterance and later interpret the overlapping utterance from memory;
3. to ignore the overlapping speech altogether; or
4. to ignore the overlapping speech momentarily, and at the end of the interpreted segment, ask the speaker whose utterance was ignored to repeat it (Roy, 2000a: 85).

These choices were evident in Hale's (2004) study of overlapping speech in the courtroom, where at times overlapping speech between the witness, the interpreter and the lawyer or police prosecutor became a struggle for power: the power to speak. Russell (2004) also found instances of these alternative strategies to overlapping speech from the interpreter in her study and comments that for the purposes of the record of interview, which is audio-recorded and later transcribed to be produced as evidence, ignoring overlapping speech altogether, or interpreting one speaker simultaneously as the other speaks, is very risky, as 'these can have serious implications for the outcome of the interview...it is self-evident that an interpreter's opinion as to what is important and what can be ignored is extremely unsafe' (Russell, 2004: 123). She suggests that the interpreter has two options: to stop the person speaking and be allowed to interpret in full, or to let the person continue, knowing that some of the speech may be lost in the interpreter's memory. Either option will influence the process (Russell, 2004: 124) and is one of those dilemmas that interpreters face through no fault of their own. Explaining the importance of strict turn-taking to each participant and using hand signals to stop people from speaking before the other is finished may be the only ways to avoid this. The strategy may not always work, but if the participants ignore the interpreter's attempts to control the flow, the outcome is no longer the interpreter's responsibility. As Russell concludes, 'interpreters must strive to achieve a fine balance between what is possible, given the nature and dynamics of the interview, and what is desirable in terms of the context of the event and the aims of the participants' (2004: 124).

Another challenge for interpreters is the use of colloquial or metaphorical language. As such utterances are almost always culturally-bound, there will always be alternative translations. Knowing the context and the background of the interlocutors can help interpreters arrive at a more accurate rendition. As quoted in chapter 1, Krouglov (1999: 296–9) provides a useful example, where the utterance of a Russian sailor *'Te tebya uroyu'* was interpreted by three interpreters as: 'I'll kill you', 'I'll get you' and 'I'll stitch you up'. When the police officer read back the record of interview, he asked in English: 'And did you say "I will kill you"?' which had been the rendition by a previous interpreter (*'Ya tebya ub'yu'*). To this the Russian speaker replied no, as he had not uttered those words. Aware of the fact that the phrase had been translated differently by three interpreters, the police officer then asked the interpreter to read the original phrase in Russian, to which the witness agreed. Krouglov states that this phrase was crucial to the investigation and therefore the police and the interpreters dedicated much time and effort in establishing its intended illocutionary meaning. Krouglov proposes that pre-session briefings with the police, where the background and the context of the case are explained to the interpreter, could help avoid situations such as this. He also argues that interpreters should explain to the parties involved the difficulties that these sorts of utterances may cause in order to avoid misinterpretations.

3.2.4 Interpreting the caution

Quote 3.7 Interpreting the police caution

It is the responsibility of the police officer to ensure that the wording and effect of the caution are understood. The implications of this caution are legally complex. Interpreting the caution accurately into another language can prove tricky. Police officers should be aware of this and be prepared to explain in plain English what the caution says and what it means.

(Colin and Morris, 1996: 31)

Much has been written about the incomprehensibility of the caution[3] (or Miranda warning[4]) to English-speaking detainees. Issues of sentence order, structural complexity, register and delivery have been cited as causing comprehension problems for detainees when the caution is read aloud to them (see Kurzon, 1996; Shuy, 1997; Cotterill 2000; Gibbons, 2003). When the caution (or Miranda warning) is read out in segments for an interpreter to interpret, the complexity is intensified.

Miranda warning

1. You have the right to remain silent.
2. Anything you say can and will be used against you in a court of law.
3. You have the right to talk to a lawyer and have him present with you while you are being questioned.
4. If you cannot afford to hire a lawyer, one will be appointed to represent you before any questioning, if you wish one.

(Shuy, 1997: 176)

The UK caution
You do not have to say anything. But it may harm your defence if you do not mention when questioned something which you later rely on in court. Anything you do say may be given in evidence.

(Russell, 2000: 5)

The Australian caution
I am going to ask you certain questions which will be recorded on a video tape recorder. You are not obliged to answer or do anything unless you wish to do so, but whatever you do say or do will be recorded and may later be used in evidence.

(Gibbons, 2003: 189)

Unless interpreters have been trained in legal interpreting and as part of their course have analysed the caution, arrived at a correct collective translation of it, practised it in class numerous times and in essence learned it by rote,[5] it would be difficult for them to interpret it adequately when confronted with it for the first time at a police station, orally. The caution is a written document, which is often read aloud verbatim, although it is also often paraphrased by police. Although the language used is not very complex, the structures (especially of the UK and Australian cautions) and the concepts can be difficult to comprehend: see Gibbons' (2003: 189) analysis. Russell (2000) found that the interpreter in her study had difficulty interpreting the caution. This interpreter, who was competent for the rest of the interview, interpreting pragmatically at the discourse level, when confronted with the caution switched to interpreting semantically at the sentence level (cf. chapter 1). Russell uses Dam's (1998) terms 'form-based' to refer to what I call semantic/sentence-level translation, and 'meaning-based' to refer to what I call pragmatic/discourse-level translation (cf. chapter 1).

The interpreter had difficulty with what seems initially to be unproblematic. Below are some examples:

Example 3.3

'You do not have to say anything'
Interpreted as:
'Vous ne devez' [You must not] in the first instance,
'Vous n'avez' [You do not have] in the second instance, and
'Vous n'êtes pas obligé' [You are not obliged to] in the third instance.

(Russell, 2000: 38)

Russell (2000) explains that in French only the final rendition is pragmatically accurate.

Another example is presented in the translation of the passive 'when questioned'. This is first interpreted as a passive, which is not pragmatically accurate in the French legal register, but later as an active, which is correct. Further examples show that the interpreter did have the ability to interpret at the highest discourse level, but needed preparation in order to do so. This is apparent in the fact that although at first he sticks closely to the text and interprets only semantically, when the same problematic phrases are presented to him a second or third time, after he has had time to think about them, he interprets them pragmatically.

Had he had access to the caution before the interview, he would have been able to prepare himself for the assignment.

Laster and Taylor (1994) and Russell (2000) recommend standard translations of the caution to overcome this problem. Russell also recommends training for interpreters: 'One could envisage the organization of contact and joint training days at local police stations, where officers and interpreters exchange views and work together to build up a partnership based on an understanding of each other's needs' (2000: 46). Such a practice is a reality in some countries where training for community interpreters is available, although such training is rarely compulsory (cf. chapter 6).

As mentioned above, very little research has been conducted into police interpreting. With the introduction of audio and video recordings, data collection has been simplified. If permission is granted to access such data, much could be gained from analysing them.

3.3   Lawyer–client interactions

As with police interviews, very little empirical research has been conducted into the discourse of lawyer–client interactions. As Bogoch states, 'Empirical studies of lawyer–client interaction outside the courtroom are scarce, and the few results available are ambiguous' (1994: 67). Again, most of the research into lawyer–client interactions has taken place in the context of the courtroom, in terms of both monolingual and bilingual interactions. The little work into lawyer–client discourse proposes a number of common themes. Rosenthal (1974) speaks of the differences between the traditional authoritarian model, which is beginning to lose currency, and the participatory model of professional-client interaction. It has been argued that under the traditional model, jargon is used as a strategy by lawyers to mystify their activity and maintain their distance and power (Bogoch, 1994). Bogoch also argues that lawyers' power is manifested in their control of the agenda for the interview: 'Another strategy derives from the professional's ability to determine what is to be included in the scope of his/her service. Thus the lawyer can determine what topics are appropriate for discussion, and can limit the client's contributions in line with this perception' (1994: 73–4). Under the participatory model clients are given more freedom to speak and lawyers speak in more accessible ways. Examples of this latter model are presented below.

Quote 3.8   The lawyer–client interview

As a lay/professional encounter, the lawyer/client interview is … inherently inter-discursive, combining two world views and two discourses. On the one hand there is the world and discourse of the law for which the lawyer is a represent-ative and spokesperson. This discourse and world are predominantly structured in terms of the sometimes strange, technical and complicated norms and categories relevant to the legal system. On the other hand there is the everyday world and discourse of the client, which is everyday only in the sense of being non-legal, non-specialized and structured in terms of twofold categories of right and wrong, justice and injustice and which is peopled with specific facts, events and situations.

(Maley et al., 1995: 54)

Based on a study of audio recordings of lawyer–client interviews in two Australian cities and two country towns, Maley et al. (1995) argue that when lawyers and their lay clients meet in a professional encounter, they bring to the encounter two separate worlds: the world of the law, with its numerous rules, requirements and constraints, and the life-world of the client, with its narratives of experience. Griffiths (1984) suggests that lawyers and clients, when discussing divorce, for example, are involved in two divorces: the lawyer with a legal divorce and the client with an emotional divorce. In order to bridge that gap, lawyers use a number of interdiscursive strategies. They constantly shift their discourse from the rules-oriented (Conley and O'Barr 1990), formal legal discourse, to the relations-oriented (Conley and O'Barr 1990), informal discourse of the client. By doing so, they are fulfilling the purposes of the law as well as creating solidarity with their clients and making the law more accessible to them. They are in essence constantly 'trans-lating' from one discourse to another: from the discourse of the law to that of their clients', and vice versa. Felstiner and Sarat speak of the lawyer–client setting as one where 'legal norms and social norms come together and shape responses to grievances, inquiries and prob-lems. In some instances these worlds may be complementary; in others there may be little fit between them' (1986: 94). This can be seen in Examples 3.4–3.6.

In Example 3.4, we can see how the lawyer paraphrases what the client says in lay terms into a legally acceptable utterance.

Examples 3.5 and 3.6 show instances where lawyers make the law access-ible to their clients by expressing themselves in very colloquial, informal

Example 3.4

Lawyer: Now what that means in simple terms is that you were effectively living as man and wife under one roof?
Client: Yeah, that's true, he had some, what you call, whatever trouble he had he call me always you know and help clean up his mess.
Lawyer: So he'd been in trouble with the police on a number of occasions, had he?

(Maley et al., 1995: 44)

Example 3.5

Lawyer: ...you've got to play the game, you've got to play the game hard, we're going to be as slippery as buggery with these people...I don't know what your instructions are...

(Maley et al., 1995: 48)

Example 3.6

Lawyer: ...and I know one judge in particular would have the cane toad on toast.

(Maley et al., 1995: 48)

language. In other words, while in Example 3.4 the lawyer is 'translating' from lay speech to legal speech, in Examples 3.5 and 3.6 the lawyer is 'translating' from legal to lay speech.

As no studies of interpreted lawyer–client interviews have been conducted (to my knowledge), one can only speculate on what takes place in such situations. It would be interesting to observe whether lawyers continue to 'translate' from one register to another, or whether they persist with the legal discourse expecting the professional interpreter to 'translate' into a more accessible register to their client, as well as to translate from one language to another. One can only hope that this is not the case, as the burden on interpreters would be considerable. Research into interpreted lawyer–client interviews is sorely needed to advance our knowledge of the practice.

3.4   Tribunal hearings

Tribunals vary in focus and scope. A number of tribunals exist to cater for different branches of administrative law. Consumer claims tribunals, Social Security Appeals tribunals, Administrative Appeals tribunals, Residential Tenancies tribunals, Migration and Refugee Review tribunals are examples. These differ across different countries. In English-speaking countries, tribunals are less formal than courts, generally do not abide by the rules of evidence, follow an inquisitorial style of investigation, are presided over by tribunal members who are not required to have any legal training, and claimants are for the most part unrepresented. Claimants/applicants and/or witnesses are given freedom to express themselves without the restrictions of the rules of evidence. O'Barr and Conley (1990) found that litigants' satisfaction levels were much higher after giving evidence in small claims courts in the US than those giving evidence in formal courts. In these fora, litigants are allowed to express themselves freely when telling their story, with all the details they believe to be important, without interruptions. This, however, O'Barr and Conley found, was a blessing in disguise for many, as they did not know how to present a case that was legally relevant. Without the guidance of a lawyer to ask the relevant questions, these unrepresented claimants often offered irrelevant or even damaging information that went against their case.

> Our study of the structure of small claims narratives indicates that many accounts of disputed events that are entirely adequate by the standards of ordinary conversation prove to be legally inadequate because of judicial assumptions about how a story must be told and how blame must be assessed. In particular, unassisted lay witnesses seldom impart to their narratives the deductive, hypothesis-testing structure with which judges are most familiar and often fail to assess responsibility for events in question in the way that the law requires. (O'Barr and Conley, 1999: 98)

Conley and O'Barr (1990) found that there were predominantly two types of witness: those who were rules-oriented and those who were relations-oriented. Rules-oriented witnesses tended to structure their narrative in a coherent, chronological way, referring only to facts that were relevant to their specific claim. Relations-oriented witnesses tended to divert from the relevant points to bring to their narrative issues of past personal relationships to explain possible motivations, hearsay evidence and other irrelevant information. Relations-oriented witnesses' narratives tended not to follow a strict chronological order, nor were they as coherent as their counterparts. (This is also true for non-English speaking claimants who present their case through interpreters.) Hale (2004) found in her study of court interpreting that Spanish-speaking witnesses also fell in either of these categories. Although interpreters tended to change the style of their speech, the orientation of the narration was for the most part translated accurately.

3.4.1   Refugee hearings

Quote 3.9   Refugee hearings

Refugee hearings are a peculiar hybrid of courtroom-style interrogation, loosely-structured story-telling, and inter-cultural discussions involving bureaucrats (who rarely exhibit an understanding of the Third World countries from which most refugees come) and claimants (who generally exhibit as little understanding of the host country as the bureaucrats do of the country of origin).

(Barsky, 1994: 65)

Here Barsky is referring to the Canadian Convention Refugee Review Tribunal and above all highlights the complex nature of these hearings as well as the cross-cultural differences that may exist between the applicants and public servants. Differences exist in the rules of procedures of these tribunals across the refugee-receiving world, although the main characteristics are shared. The Refugee and Migration Review tribunals (with their many name variations across the refugee host countries) stand out from the rest of tribunals, as their applicants are almost always from countries where a different language is spoken, and therefore the use of interpreting services is the norm rather than the exception. The Australian Refugee Review Tribunal Annual Report 2003 states that 84 per cent of hearings used the services of interpreters in over 80 languages. This situation should lead to a much improved understanding of the role of the interpreter, quality of interpretation, interpreter remuneration and, in general, better interpreting services. In Australia, the Refugee Review Tribunal and the Migration Review Tribunal, which operate under the same jurisdiction, publish an *Interpreter's Handbook* and give preference to qualified, NAATI professionally accredited interpreters. They also run workshops for their members and staff on how to work with interpreters and are sensitive to interpreting issues. However, the rate of pay remains relatively low.

The *Interpreter's Handbook*, which is accessible on the Web,[6] contains information about the tribunal, its procedures, policies and expectations of interpreters. It also provides interpreters with a useful glossary of commonly used terms and phrases, as well as with the wording of Article 1A(2) of the Refugees Convention. The Tribunal is very clear on the role it expects interpreters to play at the Tribunal. The interpreter is expected to be an independent professional whose role is clearly to interpret faithfully and impartially, as evidenced below (cf. chapter 4):

Quotes 3.10   The Refugee Review Tribunal's expectations of the interpreter's role

It is important that everything that is said is interpreted fully, not just in a précis form. It is the Tribunal Member's role to analyse the evidence given by the applicant or the witnesses. If the applicant is confused by a question or gives a confused response, the interpreter should interpret that faithfully and completely to the Tribunal Member. Interpreters must not make comments or asides to the applicant or the Tribunal Member during the Hearing (RRT, 2003a: 19).

The interpreter must not advise the applicant how to answer, or supply him or her with facts ... The interpreter is not expected to provide any cultural or other commentary. The Tribunal Member will seek clarification directly from the applicant if any cultural issues arise which may be hindering effective communication (for instance, non-verbal signs which are culturally specific).

(RRT, 2003a: 20–1)

These quotations place the responsibility for clarifications of confusing answers or of possible cultural differences on the tribunal members, who will ask the applicant or witness through the interpreter. Applicants are permitted to have an adviser, relative or friend to assist them in the presentation of their submissions in support of their case. It is such an adviser, rather than the interpreter, who has the responsibility to help the applicant prepare and present their case.

The *Interpreter's Handbook* allows for interpreters to consult reference material if needed, take notes, ask for clarifications if they misunderstand a question or answer, ask for breaks if they require them, and interrupt the speakers if they are speaking too quickly or for too long. A number of initiatives have been recommended to the Tribunal to improve the working conditions and effectiveness of interpreting services. One such recommendation, which is currently being implemented, is the availability of an interpreters' room, where interpreters can wait and prepare for the case. Another recommendation which is being considered is the provision of background material on the case in order for interpreters to prepare. Providing interpreters with background material reduces the risk of misinterpretations due to a lack of knowledge about the context and the subject matter.

Concept 3.1   What should the role of the Refugee Tribunal interpreter be? Should it differ from that of the court interpreter?

The Australian Refugee Review Tribunal is clear in their understanding of the interpreter's role. They expect interpreters working in the tribunal to abide by the same code of ethics and perform the same role as court interpreters, where accuracy and impartiality are of utmost importance. Although the system is not adversarial, and more flexibility exists in the presentation of evidence, the Tribunal argues that presentational style is important in the evaluation of credibility, just as it is in the courtroom, and therefore interpreters should provide a highly accurate rendition, not only of the facts presented by the applicants, but also of the way they are presented. In the courtroom, the argument for such a requirement is that the interpreter's role is to place the minority language speaker in the same or as similar a situation as a defendant who does not have a language barrier. In the Refugee Tribunal, the situation is somewhat different, as citizens of the host country would never present before such a tribunal, hence there is no direct comparison. The only comparison that can be made is with the other tribunals already mentioned, where witness speech styles and orientations are equally pertinent for applicants from all backgrounds.

Barsky (2000), who has written extensively on the topic of refugee hearing interpreting, argues for the opposite view. Based on his personal ideology that there should be no national borders and hence people should be allowed to move unhindered across nations, he believes strongly that interpreters in this domain should take on the role of open advocate. He proposes interpreters should improve on the claimants' narrations by changing hesitant, incoherent and even dull accounts into coherent, articulate and vibrant narratives, to maximise the claimants' chances of success. He admits that this should be the work of the lawyer, but that due to the low pay these legal aid lawyers receive and their inexperience in working with other cultures, they cannot be expected to take on the responsibility. He also suggests that the chosen interpreter needs to share the asylum seeker's political ideals to be able to help, as an interpreter who does not share the same view would prejudice the case by introducing his or her own biases. He states: 'So another function of the inter-cultural interpreter can be to, quite simply, tell a good story ... the Canadian-born interpreter who worked with me on cases involving Russian speaking claimants (from the former Soviet Union and Israel), offered claimants the advantage of bringing utterances from Russians (who are accustomed to dealing with hearing-like bureaucracies) and add the appropriate detail. As such, the story became compelling, and as a consequence,

> ## Concept 3.1   (Continued)
>
> sounded more believable...her extrapolating upon the small number of facts provided by the claimant in order to give the narrative some punch could of course backfire as a strategy if one of the flowery passages turned out to contain untrue information' (Barsky, 2000: 73).

Barsky (2000) proposes complete partiality in favour of the applicant and encourages inaccuracy from the interpreter in order to improve on the original – something that clearly goes against to the established code of ethics. Whereas he states it would be unfair to expect lawyers to take on this role due to their poor rate of pay, it is difficult to understand why it would not be equally unfair to expect interpreters to do this, as their rate of pay is even lower. There are a number of other issues to consider if interpreters are to take on the role of advocate. As Barsky admits, if interpreters add information to the account to make it more credible, apart from the fact that they would need to become very creative, they would run the risk of fabricating facts. This would have obvious adverse ramifications for the applicant. Interpreters would not be able to take an oath to interpret truly and faithfully if this role was expected of them. Similarly, if they were to polish the style, this would lead to an inconsistency between the asylum seeker's background and education and the interpreter's rendition, which can also be detrimental to the evaluation of credibility of such an applicant. Cases could in principle be determined solely from written submissions, which could be prepared by lawyers, following all the criteria of what constitutes a logical, coherent and well-expressed argument. However, this is considered to be insufficient for the applicants' assessment of credibility, hence the requirement for them to present their story orally in their own words. An interpreter changing their story to make it sound more literate would defeat this purpose. If such a system is believed to be unfair, then stakeholders should work towards changing it. Expecting interpreters to circumvent the system is not only unfair on interpreters, but also very risky.

3.4.2   Special considerations necessary when evaluating asylum seekers' claims

There are a number of issues to consider when evaluating the credibility of asylum seekers' accounts. Dirks (1977) mentions that the discourse of asylum seekers who have suffered, been displaced, tortured and experienced other traumatic experiences is rarely coherent or even chronological. Dirks further explains that:

> Camp life can drain the self-reliance of the refugee and create such a strong sense of dependence upon others to provide his primary needs that his existence is similar to that of a child. Prolonged confinement in a camp environment may in fact lead to apathy, and the loss of all emotion including hope. The regulated style of life and the lack of any personal privacy promote a loss of individual identity and an increase in feelings of aggression toward fellow residents as well as outsiders. Residents of the camps, in some instances, feel they are in a condition of social suspension as they experience no sense of progress, advancement, or achievement. (Dirks, 1977: 11–12)

It would be unrealistic for tribunal members to expect asylum seekers who have been victims of torture to express themselves in a coherent, well-structured way. The assistance of psychologists and other experts in this field should be sought to make relevant judgements. With this knowledge, an interpreter's interference with such a characteristic style would discredit the asylum seeker's claim to have been tortured.

Colin and Morris (1996) comment on this characteristic of asylum seekers' narrative style, but focus on the difficulties that this may cause for interpreters. They argue for absolute accuracy, which is much more difficult to achieve when narratives are unclear and incoherent than when they are well structured, chronological and polished.

3.4.3 Interpreters in the refugee hearing

Quote 3.11   Emotional stress in refugee hearings

When the 'case history' of an asylum seeker who has been tortured is being elicited, the interpreter may find it harrowing to have to listen to and relay details of suffering and atrocities. Non-English speakers are likely to be distressed, and consequently may express themselves incoherently or unclearly. There is always the risk that these factors will have an adverse effect on the highly accurate interpreting that is so absolutely necessary in this context.

(Colin and Morris, 1996: 62)

There is no doubt that this context presents many challenges for interpreters. The horrific stories presented by the applicants can cause overwhelming emotional stress for interpreters. The difficult, incoherent, unstructured nature of many of the narrative accounts will present serious translation challenges for interpreters who aim to achieve accuracy. The cross-cultural issues inherent in the exchange may be greater than in other legal domains, as these applicants normally would have had no connection at all with the host country, unlike migrants who are permanent residents. As explained in chapter 1, many cross-cultural issues can be bridged in an accurate pragmatic rendition. In order to achieve this, however, interpreters need to be competent and highly skilled, as Kalin confirms:

> Because of the close links between language and culture, however, even excellent translators fulfil this task only when they attempt to communicate in their translations the cultural context of words and concepts. Interpreters used in the asylum procedure often not only lack this sophistication; sometimes they are also not qualified or they make mistakes because of fatigue resulting from a lengthy hearing. All this may distort the communication between asylum-seeker and refugee tribunal. (Kalin, 1986: 233)

Competent interpreters always consider the cultural context in their renditions. There is no such thing as a 'basic translation task', as Barsky (2000) puts it when he compares what tribunals expect interpreters to do and what he would like them to do. If a translation does not consider the cultural implications of the message, it cannot be classified as 'professional translation'. A major problem arises when incompetent interpreters are employed for such sensitive matters, impacting on the outcome of the case. Barsky quotes the following from the experience of an immigration lawyer:

> I had one [interpreter] who translated 'socialist party' as 'social group' ... I've seen cases where a claimant with two university degrees is made to sound completely garbled [by incompetent interpreters]. That can cause contradictions where there are none ... These contradictions are grounds for rejecting claimants; incompetent interpreters, therefore, like other links in this system, can undermine a potentially valid claim. (Barsky, 1994: 43)

There are cultural differences that may require the interpreter's clarifications. Although the Australian Refugee Review Tribunal expects members to ask for clarification from the applicant regarding cross-cultural differences, this can only occur when the member is aware that such differences may exist. Barsky (1994) provides the example of the word 'brother' which means 'fellow member of the tribe' in some Ghanaian groups. Such subtleties need to be clarified by the interpreter, if there is any risk of ambiguity. As Barsky (1994) rightly comments, the Ghanaian speaker will have no reason to suspect that the word does not carry the same meaning in the host country, and neither will the tribunal member. Detailed research into the extent to which it is necessary for interpreters to interrupt to provide crucial cross-cultural information that could not have been transmitted in an accurate pragmatic rendition or clarified by the applicant and member themselves needs to be carried out (cf. chapter 8).

Linguistic difficulties faced by interpreters at the Refugee hearing

Example 3.7

By counsel (to the interpreter):
Q. You're not making an exact translation. I am sorry, I hate to trouble you. I know that this is hard. He said well-founded. You have to translate the whole sentence and you have to try and be precise

(Barsky, 1994: 45)

Terminological precision in this tribunal is crucial. Terms such as 'well-founded fear', 'persecution' and 'nationality', for example, all relate to the definition of 'refugee' under the UN Convention. Such terms, however, may be very difficult to translate into other languages, especially if the interpreter is untrained and unprepared. The convoluted structure of the definition, with its long sentences containing a number of embedded clauses, coupled with the difficult concepts they represent, makes it difficult not only for the interpreter to understand, retain and translate, but also for the applicant. As with the police caution, unless the interpreter has been trained and has carefully studied the text before hand, it would be virtually impossible to translate accurately. For some languages, this text would need to be completely restructured to be translated. Such reorganisation cannot be done orally when the interpreter is interpreting the text piecemeal. The text would have to be known to the interpreter or presented in writing for a sight translation. The tribunal member will not be able to judge adequately where to make the breaks for the interpreter to interpret. Once the definition is read out, the member normally explains the definition in simpler terms to the applicant, which the interpreter needs also to interpret. A written simplification of the text, using bullet points for each embedded clause, and having it translated and published in the most popular languages, would improve its comprehension.

Quote 3.12   Definition of the term 'refugee'

The term 'refugee' is defined in Chapter 1, Article 1 of the Convention. In particular, Article 1A(2), as amended by the Protocol, defines a refugee as a person who:
   'owing to well-founded fear of being persecuted for reasons of race, religion, nationality, membership of a particular social group or political opinion, is outside the country of his nationality and is unable or, owing to such fear, is unwilling to avail himself of the protection of that country; or who, not having a nationality and being outside the country of his former habitual residence, is unable or, owing to such fear, is unwilling to return to it'.
   In the case of a person who has more than one nationality, the term 'the country of his nationality' shall mean each of the countries of which he is a national, and a person shall not be deemed to be lacking protection of the country of his nationality if, without any valid reason based on well-founded fear, he has not availed himself of the protection of one of the countries of which he is a national.

(RRT Report, 2003b: 13)

3.5   Courtroom hearings and trials

Most of the research conducted into oral legal language in the English-speaking world, and into legal interpreting, has concentrated on the courtroom setting. One practical reason for this bias may be the availability of recorded data from a forum that is open to the public. Another reason may be the perception that the courtroom setting, with its many rules, traditional, ritualistic procedures and protocols, and fixed participant roles, is a much more interesting and even important setting to study. As a public forum, it inevitably attracts more attention than private encounters. The studies into the language of the courtroom have been influential in the research into court interpreting, as their findings directly affect the work of the court interpreter. Having an understanding of the strategic purposes for which language is used in the courtroom is essential for interpreters to perform adequately.

3.5.1   The language of the courtroom

The bulk of the research into spoken courtroom language has been in relation to the adversarial system, as orality in this system is essential. Cases are presented to a magistrate or a jury in the form of oral evidence. Evidence is adduced via questions and answers. A number of researchers have compared the adversarial hearing or trial to a battle, with language as its main weapon (Du Cann, 1986; Maley and Fahey, 1991). As such, language is used strategically by lawyers to achieve specific ends. Both sides, the adversaries, have the opportunity to present their version of the story (their case) through examination of their own witnesses. This is called examination-in-chief or direct examination.[7] They also have the opportunity to challenge the other side's story by cross-examining their witnesses. The purpose of examination-in-chief is to elicit a story that will convince the decision-makers of its veracity and merits. This is done by the careful use of strategic questions, used to elicit relevant information that is pertinent to their own case. The purpose of cross-examination is to discredit the evidence presented by the other side, so strengthening their own case. Both purposes are achieved by the tactical use of language in the form of question types, repetition, modality, intonation and the careful choice of words with specific connotations (Danet and Bogoch, 1980; Harris, 1984; Drew, 1992; Stygall, 1994; Moeketsi, 1999).

On the other hand, the language of witness testimonies is crucial to the outcome of a case, in both adversarial and inquisitorial settings. Although witnesses may not realise the effect of the language they use, research has repeatedly found that the content, coherence, delivery, manner, register and style of a witness testimony all impact on the impressions formed by the decision-makers. These impressions relate to the credibility, competence, intelligence and trustworthiness of the witnesses, which in turn impinge on how convincing the whole case is and hence its success (O'Barr, 1982; Giles and Sasoon, 1983; Conley and O'Barr, 1990; Gibbons et al.,1991; Moeketsi, 1998; Berk-Seligson, 2000; Hale, 2004). The whole process is further complicated by the constraints imposed by rules of evidence, which determine what can be said, in what form and by whom.

3.5.2 Interpreters in the courtroom

The literature on court interpreting can be divided into a number of themes. These include:

- the availability and provision of professional interpreters;
- the performance and challenges of practising interpreters;
- the training of interpreters;
- the ethical obligations and role of the interpreter.

It is generally agreed, that there are deficiencies in all of these areas.

The availability and provision of professional court interpreters

Kelly states that although unqualified interpreters continue to be used in US courtrooms, it is now rare and 'court personnel recognize the need for trained interpreters' (2000: 132). This is corroborated by Berk-Seligson (2000), who states that US courts are becoming increasingly aware of the consequences of poor interpreting which has led to a number of appeals.

The meaning of 'qualified' is difficult to ascertain when the term is used in relation to court interpreting. 'Qualified' can refer to interpreters adequately and formally trained through degree programmes, but also to interpreters who have been certified or accredited by examination alone. As compulsory pre-service training is still not a reality anywhere in the world, it can be safely assumed that the pool of competent, highly skilled and trained court interpreters continues to be low. Some languages are better equipped than others, a fact determined by the demand and the availability of training courses. Spanish, for example, is the language of highest demand in the United States, and therefore it is likely that there will be more trained, competent Spanish interpreters available than interpreters of other languages of lesser demand. The same can be said for other countries, referring to the languages relevant to each.

Whereas in some instances the poor provision of qualified interpreters is inevitably related to the limited availability of such interpreters (Dobinson and Chiu, 2005), in other instances, the low level of interpreter service use may relate to issues of misunderstandings about the need for qualified interpreters and to misconceptions about the impact of their use. Carroll argues that 'professional interpreting services are not always provided, and that the Court does not fully recognize the dangers inherent in using non-professional interpreters' (1995: 67). He argues that there are four main possible reasons for such underutilisation:

1. judges believe that it is more difficult to assess the credibility of witnesses when they speak through an interpreter, preferring to hear someone speaking in limited broken English;
2. there is suspicion that those who speak through interpreters are devious and evasive and use the interpreter as a tactic;
3. that interpreters do not give a literal translation of the answers and therefore cannot be trusted;

4. that judges are capable of ascertaining the language skills of a defendant or accused and hence can determine when they need an interpreter.

He suggests that these misconceptions are shared by lawyers, who often advise their clients to avoid the use of interpreting services if they can make themselves understood with their limited knowledge of the language.

These objections and excuses, which are common across countries (cf. Morris, 1999), can be understood and justified in some instances, especially when courts have experienced the services of incompetent interpreters. It is true that it becomes more difficult to evaluate the credibility of a witness when speaking through an interpreter. However, if the interpreter is trained to maintain important supra-segmental features, stylistic features and register in their rendition, this problem will be reduced to an insignificant level. The problem arises when untrained interpreters – who continue to be the majority – ignore features that are crucial to the assessment of credibility to the judicial officer, because in their view they are either irrelevant or superfluous, or because they simply do not possess the interpreting skills necessary to provide a fully accurate rendition. In any case, listening to someone speaking in a language for which they are less than competent will also make the evaluation of credibility very difficult. With regards to the second objection, the reasons for speaking through an interpreter are almost always genuine. It is difficult to imagine why anyone with a good command of a language would relinquish their opportunity to express themselves. Nevertheless, if the interpreter renders a faithful interpretation and abides by the code of ethics, the court should have nothing to fear. The misconception of literal translation equating to faithfulness is one that has been discussed in chapter 1 and will not be discussed further, suffice it to say that attempts are being made to distil this myth. The final reason for the underutilisation of professional interpreter services is the erroneous belief that a judge can determine better than the person in question how competent they are in the language, based solely on a series of simple questions. This is a practice that is becoming less common, especially in Australian courts. Since 1995, a number of initiatives has been implemented to educate the legal profession and the judiciary on the work of interpreters, on the interpreting process, the meaning of accuracy and on how best to work together. For example, in 1996, the Law Society published the *Guide to Best Practice: Lawyers, Interpreters, Translators* (Sydney: The Law Foundation of New South Wales), to which interpreters and interpreter educators contributed. Since then, the Bar Association, the Department of Public Prosecutions and the National Judicial Commission have all held seminars for their members on working with interpreters. Robinson and Chiu (2005) state that although there is no absolute right to an interpreter, with the common law principle of the judge's discretion still in force, judges and magistrates now tend to err on the side of caution.

The situation in other countries may not be as positive, possibly because they are relatively new to Community Interpreting. In Austria, for example, Kadric (2000) states that courts accept only selective interpreting, where the interpreter is permitted to interpret only parts of the proceedings, thus making the provision of interpreting services totally inadequate. Kadric found that judges become impatient at hearing long segments in another language and interrupt the witnesses, not allowing them to resume, or at times interrupt the interpreter, not allowing them to complete their interpretations. In the Civil Code system, defendants have the right of reply to the other side's testimony. However, in bilingual cases, the interpreter is not permitted to interpret the plaintiff's testimony simultaneously to the defendant, which denies the defendant's right to hear and to respond. Kadric comments:

> Overall, the non-German-speaking party is not given a full chance to interact and communicate with the court...If the rights of the non-German-speaking party are further curtailed by a lack of interpretation, due process is clearly violated...Courtroom proceedings must ensure equal opportunity of interaction for all parties. In the case of non-German-speaking parties, this is only possible with interpretation at all stages of the proceedings. (Kadric, 2000: 162)

Many more examples of inadequate provision of interpreting services as well as of poor working conditions could be provided. However, the scope of this chapter does not allow for further detail on this topic.

Interpreters' performance

Much of the data-based linguistic analytical research into court interpreting has focused on the performance of practising interpreters and on their interaction with the other participants. Through detailed micro-linguistic analysis, following the traditions of conversational analysis, discourse analysis and pragmatics, these studies have looked at the different aspects of interpreting that make it a highly complex practice. Although most of these studies are descriptive, they suggest strong practical applications for training and practice. The two major and most comprehensive studies into court interpreting are Berk-Seligson's (1990/2002) and Hale's (2004). Both studies deal with multiple interpreters, hundreds of hours of data and present not only qualitative appraisals of isolated examples, but also quantitative analyses of complete cases which provide clear trends. Both studies also use experimental, discourse analytical and ethnographic methods.

Berk-Seligson's (1990/2002) major study found, through an analysis of the interaction between all the participants in the bilingual courtroom, that in some way they all misconstrued the interpreter's role: for example, interpreters took it upon themselves to rephrase questions or to instruct lawyers on how to ask them, or to reprimand witnesses for not answering relevantly; lawyers and judges often shifted to the interpreter their responsibility to speak directly to the witnesses and expected interpreters to 'fix' situations that they themselves could not. Berk-Seligson also found that interpreters' changes to the original questions and answers were not inconsequential, altering their pragmatic effect, which in turn affected mock jurors' evaluations of the witnesses' trustworthiness, convincingness, intelligence and competence. She found that the interpreters in her sample tended to insert many of the features considered to belong to the 'powerless testimony' style, which, according to O'Barr (1982), has a negative impact on how witnesses are rated by jurors. Berk-Seligson uses the results of her study to argue for adequate training for court interpreters.

Hale (2004) analysed the discourse practices of the lawyers, the witnesses and the interpreters, first by analysing the questions, then the answers, and then both in combination. In her study of courtroom questions she found that the lawyers' practices corroborated what had already been found with regard to the use of courtroom questions. A majority of interpreters demonstrated a lack of understanding of the specific purposes of certain question types, including the use of tags and other questioning strategies, such as discourse markers, repetition and modality. The majority of interpreters arbitrarily altered or omitted these features in their rendition of the questions, changing their pragmatic intention and force. Some of the changes related to inherent cross-linguistic differences, but some to individual choice. With regard to the answers, witnesses fell into distinct categories (as identified by O'Barr 1982; Conley and O'Barr, 1990). The sample of interpreters in this study showed a tendency to alter the witnesses' style, thus impinging on their potential evaluation by the magistrates. However, their changes were not consistent. Some interpreters improved on the witnesses' styles, making powerless narratives into powerful ones; others did the opposite. Experimental studies showed that when the renditions were fully accurate, that is, maintained not only the propositional content but also reproduced the style and register, the results on the evaluation of credibility, intelligence and competence were almost identical to the results achieved when the originals were evaluated by Spanish speakers. However, the inaccurate renditions, which changed the style, achieved very significant differences as compared to the evaluations of the originals. This result strongly suggests that it is possible to place the minority speaker in a very similar situation to that of a mainstream speaker when the interpreting is accurate in terms of content and style. The analysis of the whole interaction demonstrated a power struggle between all participants, resulting in instances of overlapping speech, reprimands and switches to the use of the third person, making the work of the interpreter more difficult. Samples from the data were extracted and presented to practising interpreters, who had the advantage of seeing the utterances in front of them. The results showed that even when features such as discourse markers, tag questions and hesitations were visible, many of these interpreters still omitted them, following the same trend as the interpreters in the sample. The ones who kept these features were mostly those who had been trained and had been made aware of their significance. When questioned about issues relating to the legal system, the language of the courtroom and role, divergent responses were produced. Hale concludes that adequate training is necessary for interpreters to understand the reasons behind certain linguistic features and the significance of language style in the courtroom. Education of the lawyers and the witnesses about the role of the interpreter, the meaning of accuracy and the complexity of the interpreting process is also necessary to improve the overall service.

A number of smaller studies found similar results in relation to pragmatic alterations of the originals (Rigney, 1997, 1999; Rios, 1997; Berk-Seligson, 1999; Fraser and Freedgood, 1999; Mason and Stewart, 2001). Other studies have looked at the interpreters' treatment of register (Berk-Seligson, 1989a; Dueñas Gonzalez et al., 1991; Hale, 1997a; Brennan, 1999), finding that interpreters tend to raise the register or level of formality when interpreting into English, copying the style of the lawyers, and lower it when interpreting into the other language, copying the style of the witnesses. Instead of allowing the participants to carry on the process of accommodation between them, thus giving them the opportunity to assess their speech level, many interpreters act as a filter and remove this process from the interaction by taking care of the accommodation themselves. In such situations, no one except the interpreter is aware that this is happening, and the main interlocutors are under the mistaken belief that each is speaking in the same register.

Studies of politeness in court interpreting have produced different results. Berk-Seligson (1989b) found that interpreters tend to add politeness markers and therefore increase the level of politeness. Hale (1997b), in a small-scale study of four court cases, found that the interpreters interpreted politeness adequately, taking into account the pragmatic differences across the two languages and making the necessary lexical and syntactic adjustment to produce accurate renditions. Mason and Stewart (2001), in a case study, found that the interpreter altered the face-threatening components of the original utterances by failing to interpret pragmatically.

All of the studies discussed highlight the immense difficulties encountered by court interpreters. Not only do they need to attempt to render an accurate version of what they heard with very little time to think and often with no opportunity to prepare for the assignment, they must do so within the constraints of the courtroom and amidst the conflicting expectations of those who speak through them, who often misunderstand or simply are not aware of all the challenges. These challenges are discussed in chapter 5, drawing not only on what has been already written on the subject, but also on the voices of practising interpreters.

Further reading

Berk-Seligson (1990/2002). This book reports the first and one of the largest data-based studies into court interpreting. Set in the United States, it researches the performance of a number of Spanish-English interpreters and their impact on the legal process.

Cook, Eades and Hale (1999). This special issue of *Forensic Linguistics* provides a compilation of research papers on different aspects of the discipline. The articles cover a wide range of topics from different perspectives.

Hale (2004).This book reports the results of one of the largest data-based studies into court interpreting. The data are drawn from 17 cases in Australia which were interpreted by Spanish-English interpreters. The book studies the discourse practices of the interpreters, lawyers and witnesses in fine detail.

Laster and Taylor (1994). This book was written by two academic lawyers and
    provides a very useful overview of the state of the profession and of the main
    issues surrounding legal interpreting in Australia.
Mikkelson (2000). This manual is a useful introduction to court interpreting for
    those wanting to know more about the discipline or wanting to become court
    interpreters.

Part II

Practical Applications

4
Analysing the Interpreter's Code of Ethics

This chapter:

- Explores the purpose and applicability of the interpreter's code of ethics.
- Compares and discusses a number of different codes of ethics from around the world and highlights their commonalities.
- Analyses the description and intention of the main concepts of the interpreter's code of ethics.
- Presents the views in favour and against the interpreter's code of ethics, including the voices of interpreting practitioners.

4.1 Introduction: practising interpreters' views about the code of ethics

> **Quote 4.1**
>
> I set it as the bible of my daily life practice.
>
> (Respondent 7)[1]

> **Quote 4.2**
>
> Codes of behaviour are pretty much a matter of common sense. However, a uniform code of ethics aims at maintaining the desired level of professional conduct for all practitioners, and hopefully promotes a certain degree of awareness in the service provider.
>
> (Respondent 6)[2]

> ### Quote 4.3
>
> The code of ethics is a mess and quite ridiculous.
>
> (Respondent 3)[3]

These three quotations reflect the main attitudes expressed by practising interpreters in response to a survey about the code of ethics conducted by the author. These are, respectively, the very positive attitude from those who pledged a blind adherence to it; the measured attitude, mostly from interpreters with training who view the code as a guide requiring professional common sense; and the very negative, stating that the code is of no use at all (the minority of responses). What can cause such disparate reactions? Why is it that some interpreters find the code so useful, others are indifferent to it and yet others find it useless? In this chapter these questions will be explored by analysing a number of codes of ethics from around the world, reflecting on the intention of each of the common points and drawing on the voices of practitioners.

The practitioners' voices were gathered by way of a survey of Australian practising AUSIT[4] members and/or NAATI[5]-accredited interpreters, conducted by the author between April and July 2005. The questionnaire was sent to 500 interpreters with only 21 returned – a very poor response rate of 4.2 per cent. This response may be indicative of the indifference towards research from the majority of practitioners. Trained interpreters are well represented among the respondents (see Table 4.1). They consistently participate in professional development opportunities and research projects, something that may have skewed the overall responses to the survey.

Table 4.1 Respondent profiles

Language spread	33.3 per cent European, 28.57 per cent Semitic, 23.8 per cent Asian, 9.52 per cent Auslan, 4.76 per cent Scandinavian.
NAATI accreditation	80.95 per cent professional, 14.3 para-professional, 4.76 per cent nil
Interpreting training	61.9 per cent trained (7.7 per cent at TAFE[6] level, 46 per cent at BA (university) level and 46 per cent at postgraduate (university) level), 38.1 per cent untrained.
Experience	47.6 per cent 10–20 years, 28.6 per cent 5–10 years, 14.8 per cent < 5 years, 9.52 per cent > 20 years.

4.2   The aims of a code of ethics and controversies surrounding it

A professional code of ethics provides guidelines for practitioners on how to conduct themselves ethically for the benefit of the clients they serve, the profession they represent and themselves as practitioners. Neumann Solow states that a 'code of ethics protects the interpreter and lessens the arbitrariness of his or her decisions by providing guidelines and standards to follow' (1981: 39). In most professions, a code of ethics complements and reinforces what was learned in a professional course of study. In the absence of widespread compulsory pre-service training for community interpreters, the code of ethics has become the only consistent standard for most countries around the world through which general rules of conduct and practice are set. These codes have been generally upheld by professional associations, employing agencies, institutions requiring the services of interpreters and by practising inter-preters themselves as the standard to which interpreters should aspire. The positive aims and objectives of a code of ethics are adequately reflected in this comment from a practising interpreter:

> The code of ethics reminds me that I have a standard to uphold and also gives me the means to do that. It also reminds me that I am a professional and as I use it, others also know this. I find it both encouraging and supportive in and as I do my work. When a situation occurs, I am able to 'access' my code of ethics, which I use as a guide to then make the best or most appropriate (or professional) decision at the time. It also helps me to justify why I make a certain decision while using it in my work. (Respondent 8)[7]

Respondent 8 regards the code as a constant reminder to self and to others of the professional nature of the work; as a means of support and encouragement in what is a very lonely profession, devoid of much institutional or other external support; and as guidance and direction in making and justifying difficult decisions in the course of the work. This interpreter's comment further illustrates that the code is received with different degrees of acceptance by practitioners. Neither its rejec-tion nor its endorsement is universal. The interpreters' profiles shed some light on the possible reasons for this discrepancy (see Table 4.1). It appears that interpreter training and accreditation can make a difference to their perception. If we look at the profiles of the four interpreters quoted above, we find that the interpreter who completely rejected the code (Respondent 3) is the only one with no NAATI accreditation or interpreting training. The one who regards the code as a 'bible' (Respondent 7) has NAATI professional accreditation but no interpreting training. The other two, who offer positive but measured responses, both have interpreting training. Respondent 6 has NAATI professional accreditation and a BA in Interpreting and Translation, and Respondent 8 has NAATI para-professional accreditation and a Certificate in Interpreting. This trend is consistent among the other interpreters in the survey. However, since the sample is small, it cannot be considered to be fully representative and further research is needed to confirm this hypothesis (cf. chapter 9). It can be safely stated that the code of ethics would constitute a topic of discussion in any course of study. Graduates would have been trained to reflect on the meaning of the code, its applicability, its shortfalls and limitations and to evaluate their practice against this backdrop. Such an academic background would lead to the types of responses provided by the trained interpreters in the sample.

Concept 4.1   The need for a uniform code of ethics

There are a number of reasons to support a uniform code of ethics. It provides interpreters with guidelines to help them make appropriate decisions in their work. Such guidelines, as Neumann Solow (1981) comments, can help to protect the interpreter from making arbitrary choices which could have negative consequences. If all interpreters abide by the same code, all participants in the interpreted exchange will have the same clear expectations of the interpreter's role, reducing the possibility of conflict. It has been argued that a well-defined role, as outlined in a uniform code, is crucial to professionalise Community Interpreting (Gentile et al., 1996; Roberts, 1997). A code should not only protect the interpreter and elevate the status of the profession, but also protect the interests of those who speak through interpreters (cf. chapter 1). Tseng (1992) comments that a code of ethics is crucial for the interpreting profession, both to earn public trust and to act as an internal control mechanism.

Public trust earned solely from reliance on a code of ethics, however, may be problematic and risky. As Wallmach (2002: 12) comments, the existence of a code of ethics does not guarantee that interpreters will adhere to it. This can be due to a number of reasons: ad hoc, untrained interpreters may simply not be aware of the code; they may not fully appreciate its applicability to their practice; or they may not be capable of abiding by its principles due to lack of competence. Others may not agree with the code's prescriptions and may see no reason for following them. As one of the interpreters in the sample commented: 'Some interpreters have no idea of ethics, or if they do, they ignore it and "do their own thing", which does not throw a very pretty light on the profession' (Respondent 6). This respondent is highlighting the fact that when an interpreter acts unethically, this not only affects that particular interpreter, it also has repercussions on all the participants involved, as well as on the profession as a whole, diminishing the public trust that is so crucial.

Wadensjö comments that in order to 'achieve more than interpreters' paying lip service to official Codes of Conduct, a thorough understanding of professional rules and recommendations is needed; of what they imply in theory and in actual interpreter-mediated interaction' (1998: 286). Such an understanding can only be achieved through careful study and debate on what each principle means in practice, the reasons for upholding each of the guidelines and the consequences of not doing so. However, an academic debate of the issues must be accompanied by practical training to acquire the necessary knowledge and skills. Much more than the mere existence of a code of ethics is needed in order to ensure quality of interpreting services. There is large contradiction between the high standards expected of interpreters, as outlined in the code of ethics on the one hand, and the total absence of any compulsory pre-service training, low institutional support and poor working conditions to allow interpreters to meet those standards on the other. In view of this, some have questioned whether it is realistic to expect community interpreters to adhere to a code.

Concept 4.2   Challenging the interpreter's code of ethics

In recent years some have questioned the validity, usefulness and applicability of the code of ethics, in particular with regards to the requirements for accuracy and impartiality. The general argument has been that the code prescribes an impossible ideal which does not reflect the performance of real-life practitioners, and that it expects interpreters to interpret literally, act robotically without professional judgement and to be completely invisible (Wadensjö, 1992; Barsky, 1996; Kaufert and Putsch, 1997; Jacobsen, 2002; Angelelli, 2004). These criticisms raise a number of questions that this chapter will attempt to answer.

First, does the code prescribe literal translations under their accuracy requirement and a mechanical performance that dismisses any personal or professional judgement from interpreters?

Second, does the existence of a code of ethics assume that all practising interpreters, at all times, will be willing and/or able to abide by it simply because it is there or because they have read it?

Concept 4.2   (Continued)

Third, is the code of ethics of any use to practising interpreters? Does its usefulness depend on the individual's interpretation of it, on their level of education
and training, or on the situation?
   Fourth, should the code be changed to match the practice of those who do
not abide by its principles or should their practice change to meet the code?

In describing the work of court interpreters, some have alluded to
the interpreters' 'injunction to translate literally' (Mason and Stewart,
2001: 59) or to 'the requirement for verbatim versions of source texts'
(Jacobsen, 2002: 62). These claims have been reinforced by often quoted
but misconstrued ideas of the meaning of accuracy or of the interpreting
process held by some judicial officers, as evidenced in statements such
as these:

> Vocabulary typically used in courtrooms must be capable of literal
> translation...
> > (Minder, 1998: 12. From a US trial court judge, quoted in
> > Mikkelson, nd: 1)

> An interpreter really only acts as a transmission belt or telephone.
> > (US judge, quoted in Berk-Seligson, 1990/2002: 210)

> The interpreter should look upon himself rather as an electric trans-
> former, whatever is fed into him is to be fed out again, duly trans-
> formed.
> > (Wells, 1991: 329. Australian judge, quoted in Hale, 2004: 8)

Although such metaphors reflect very little understanding of the
complex nature of interpreting (cf. chapter 1), making it seem like a
simple process able to be performed by any bilingual, regardless of
their level of bilingualism and interpreting skills, for the most part they
represent a lay person's way of expressing that faithfulness is crucial.
Non-linguists cannot be blamed for not understanding such a specialised
practice. The judiciary appear to be using the mechanical metaphor to
express their frustration with the performance of some interpreters who
do not abide by the ethical requirements, as evidenced in the following
quotation from a Malaysian magistrate who complains that interpreters:

...will converse with the witness for a long time, we don't know what's happening, suddenly he says 'his answer is no'. So I ask 'Why are you talking to him all this while?' He says, 'No, I was explaining the question to him'. That's not the role of my interpreter. If the witness does not understand the question, he just has to say 'I don't understand the question'. It's not up to the interpreter to explain the question to him. (Ibrahim, 2004: 256)

This magistrate is not proposing that the interpreter should act like a machine, but should interpret accurately. The complexity of achieving such a task may not be known to those who speak through interpreters, and it is up to the interpreting profession to educate them about its meaning.[8] However (as explained in chapter 1), some argue that accuracy of interpretation is unachievable or even undesirable, and they have expressed this in language that can only perpetuate the misconceived belief that the act of translation is a simple task. Alexieva (1997) refers to interpreters being required to act '*simply* as an interlingual mediator' (1997: 170). Anderson (2002: 212) asks: 'Should the interpreter be a *mere* echo, or should he be an advisor and ally?' Barsky refers to the interpreter's role being '*downplayed* and *restricted* to the performance of *basic* translation tasks' (1996: 45). Kaufert and Putsch argue that the role of the interpreter is 'not *simply* to interpret ethical issues in an *objective* and *linguistically accurate* manner' (1997: 74). The use of these derogatory terms to describe what is one of the most difficult tasks to achieve – an accurate rendition – can only be counterproductive. These statements can be misconstrued as undermining the interpreting task. There is nothing *basic, mere* or *simple* about the task of accurate, objective interpreting (see chapter 1 for a full discussion on accuracy).

Does the code of ethics support the idea of accuracy equating to literalness, or the interpreting process to a simple mechanical process? Section 4.3 analyses a number of codes of ethics from around the world to answer these questions.

4.3   Comparison of codes of ethics from around the world

Sixteen codes of ethics from nine countries (Australia, Austria, Canada, Colombia, Indonesia, Ireland, United Kingdom, Spain and United States) were selected at random. The International Criminal Tribunal for the

Former Yugoslavia is also included. The codes can be divided into three broad areas:

1. interpreters' responsibility to the authors of the utterances, which includes accuracy, impartiality and confidentiality;
2. interpreters' responsibility to the profession, which includes professional conduct issues such as dress, punctuality, and solidarity; and
3. interpreters' responsibility to self as a professional, including the need for professional development, role definition, adequate working conditions and pay rates.

Not all codes share all of the above mentioned aspects. Only the clauses shared by most of the codes were therefore analysed, and are presented in Table 4.2.

The distribution shows that not all codes speak of the three most quoted tenets which fall under my first category of responsibility to the authors of the utterances: accuracy, impartiality and confidentiality. Of these three, the most prominent is confidentiality, with 81.25 per cent of the codes including it, followed by accuracy with 75 per cent and impartiality with 68.75 per cent. This seems to indicate that it is believed that the interpreter's commitment to professional secrecy is paramount if they are to be accorded the trust needed to discuss private matters in the presence of a third party. Interestingly, accuracy is not mentioned by every code, which may indicate that some codes take this for granted. Similarly, impartiality is omitted by 31.25 per cent of the codes. Whether this means it is also taken for granted or it is not considered necessary is difficult to say. The entries for accuracy, impartiality and role, which are

Table 4.2   Frequency of main aspects included in the codes of ethics

Aspect included in the codes of ethics	Frequency and percentage of the 16 codes
Confidentiality	13/16 (81.25 %)
Accuracy	12/16 (75 %)
Impartiality/conflict of interest	11/16 (68.75 %)
Professional development	8/16 (50 %)
Accountability/responsibility for own performance	7/16 (43.75 %)
Role definition	6/16 (37.5 %)
Professional solidarity	5/16 (31.25 %)
Working conditions	4/16 (25 %)

the three controversial concepts that have been discussed by a number of researchers, will now be analysed.

4.3.1 Accuracy

Does the code of ethics prescribe literal renditions?

The entries on accuracy from the sample of codes presented in Table 4.3 do not seem to support the claim that codes of ethics prescribe literal renditions or a machine-like, unthinking performance. All the entries under accuracy speak of the interpreter's or translator's obligation to be faithful to the original. However, none mentions the need to produce a literal, word-for-word (verbatim) rendition of the original. Some of the codes attempt to explain the meaning of accuracy by explicitly speaking against a literal rendition. Others are less explicit about its meaning.

Table 4.3 Entries on accuracy

Code	Accuracy
Australia (AUSIT) 1999	(#5) Interpreters and translators shall take all reasonable care to be accurate
	i) In order to ensure the same access to all that is said by all parties involved in a meeting, the interpreter shall relay accurately and completely everything that is said.
	ii) Interpreters shall convey the whole message, including derogatory or vulgar remarks, as well as non-verbal clues.
	iii) If patent untruths are uttered or written, interpreters and translators shall convey these accurately as presented.
	iv) Interpreters and translators shall not alter, make additions to, or omit anything from their assigned work.
	v) Interpreters shall encourage speakers to address each other directly.
Canada The Association of Visual Language interpreters of Canada (AVLIC)	Every interpretation shall be faithful to and render exactly the message of the source text. A faithful interpretation should not be confused with a literal interpretation. The fidelity of an interpretation includes an adaptation to make the form, the tone, and the deeper meaning of the source text felt in the target language and culture.

Table 4.3 (Continued)

Colombia Asociación Colombiana de Traductores e Intérpretes (ACTI)	The translator is under the obligation to...guarantee that the translation be faithful to the original. Fidelity does not exclude necessary adaptations to give the text the intended form, atmosphere and meaning.
Indonesia Indonesian Translation Service Code of Ethics	The...Service will provide translation and interpreting which is faithful to the original text. The...Service and its translators and interpreters will make every effort to provide the user with the same impression from the translation that he or she would obtain if able to use the original. ...We undertake to provide fair and true translations or original texts in the light of information provided by you concerning intended language register and style, intended target audience and the purpose for which the work is to be used or relied on.
Ireland Irish Translators' and Interpreters' Association	4.1 Members of the Association should endeavour to the utmost of their ability to provide a guaranteed faithful rendering of the original text which must be entirely free of their own personal interpretation, opinion or influence. 4.3 Where an interpreter or translator is working in any matter relating to the law, the client's statements must be interpreted or translated by the idea communicated without cultural bias in the presentation, by avoidance of literal translation in the target language or by giving of advice in the source language.
Spain Grupo Trinor (private agency)	An interpreter should ensure the best possible communication between the persons who are using our services. To this end, the interpreter will endeavour to do the assignment with accuracy and speed and will take all the necessary steps to ensure that all interlocutors understand the content of the dialogue in question. Naturally, the quality of the service provided will always depend on the extent to which the customer co-operates and the quality of the original (whether it be speech or text).

USA National Association of Judicial Interpreters and Translators (NAJIT)	Source language speech should be faithfully rendered into the target language by conserving all the elements of the original message while accommodating the syntactic and semantic patterns of the target language. The rendition should sound natural in the target language, and there should be no distortion of the original message through addition or omission, explanation or paraphrasing. All hedges, false starts and repetitions should be conveyed; also English words mixed into other languages should be retained, as should culturally bound terms which have no direct equivalent in English, or which may have more than one meaning. The register, style and tone of the source language should be conserved.
California Rules of Court – Rule 984.4 Professional conduct for interpreters	An interpreter shall use his or her best skills and judgment to interpret accurately without embellishing, omitting or editing.
Cross-Cultural Health Care Program (CCHCP)	Interpreters must transmit the message in a thorough and faithful manner, giving consideration to linguistic variations in both languages and conveying the tone and spirit of the original message. A word-for-word interpretation may not convey the intended idea. The interpreter must determine the relevant concept and say it in language that is readily understandable and culturally appropriate to the listener. In addition, the interpreter will make every effort to assure that the client has understood questions, instructions and other information transmitted by the service provider. Interpreters must interpret everything that is said by all people in the interaction, without omitting, adding, condensing or changing anything. If the content to be interpreted might be insensitive or otherwise harmful to the dignity and well-being of the patient, the interpreter should advise the health professional of this before interpreting.
State of Washington Department of Social and Health Services (DSHS)	Interpreters/translators shall always thoroughly and faithfully render the source language message, omitting or adding nothing, giving consideration to linguistic variations in both source and target languages, conserving the tone and spirit of the source language message.

Table 4.3   (Continued)

International Criminal Tribunal for the former Yugoslavia	Article 10 – Accuracy
	(a) Interpreters and translators shall convey with the greatest fidelity and accuracy, and with complete neutrality, the wording used by the persons they interpret or translate.
	(b) Interpreters shall convey the whole message, including vulgar or derogatory remarks, insults and any non-verbal clues as the tone of voice and emotions of the speaker, which might facilitate the understanding of their listeners.
	(c) Interpreters and translators shall not embellish, omit or edit anything from their assigned work.
	(d) If patent mistakes or untruths are spoken or written, interpreters and translators shall convey these as accurately as presented.

The Association of Visual Language Interpreters of Canada's (AVLIC) code states that 'a faithful interpretation should not be confused with a literal interpretation. The fidelity of an interpretation includes an adaptation to make the form, the tone, and the deeper meaning of the source text felt in the target language and culture.' The Irish code is also specific about the need to avoid literal translations. The Colombian code mentions necessary adaptations in order to achieve the intended 'atmosphere and meaning'. The Cross-Cultural Health Care Program (CCHCP) code states that 'Interpreters must transmit the message in a thorough manner, giving consideration to linguistic variations in both languages and conveying the tone and the spirit of the original message. A word-for-word interpretation may not convey the intended meaning.' The only code that mentions what may possibly be misconstrued as a literal translation is the International Criminal Tribunal code: 'Interpreters and translators shall convey with the greatest fidelity and accuracy, and with complete neutrality, the *wording* used by the persons they interpret or translate' (emphasis added). The other possible source of confusion could be the statement that there must be no omissions or additions 'from their assigned work', which is found in the Australian Institute of Interpreters and Translators' (AUSIT) code. In an attempt to clarify this point, I have argued (Hale, 1996, 1997b) that often additions or omissions are needed in order to achieve accuracy. In fairness to the drafters of these codes, however, one can assume that what was meant are additions or omissions from the core message, rather than from the number of words in an utterance.

The sample entries on accuracy do not support a prescription for literalness. The statement that the whole message, including vulgar terms, obvious untruths, hedges, repetitions, register and style, needs to be interpreted, especially in the legal interpreting codes, does not imply a literal rendition. It simply emphasises the importance of such seemingly unimportant or superfluous features of discourse (see Mikkelson, 1998; Berk-Seligson, 1990/2002; Hale, 2004).

In explaining the meaning of accuracy, Mikkelson quotes Obenaus, who points out that 'the fact that legal texts require precision and impose restrictions on the translator is all too often misconstrued to mean that they have to be translated literally, leading to unsatisfactory and awkward results' (Obenaus, 1994: 248, in Mikkelson, 1998: 23).

Jacobsen, commenting on the code of ethics, states:

> Not surprisingly, therefore, the principle of *Accuracy and Completeness* disregards issues such as linguistic differences, cultural differences, or problems of ambiguity or non-explicitness, and it is seemingly based on the rather naïve assumption that all interpreters perform equally well at all times. (Jacobsen, 2002: 64)

Kaufert and Putsch concur and add that:

> Ethical guidelines that are based on neutrality, completeness, and accuracy often fail to take into account issues such as class, power, disparate beliefs, lack of linguistic equivalence, or the disparate use of language. (Kaufert and Putsch, 1997: 72)

The entries in the codes do not mention any of the difficulties faced by interpreters when attempting to achieve accuracy, such as those mentioned by Jacobsen (2002) or Kaufert and Putsch (1997), and numerous other difficulties not mentioned here. Nor do they concede that accuracy of interpretation is a lofty objective that may not always be achieved for a number of reasons, some beyond the interpreter's control (cf. chapter 5). The code only speaks of the highest ethical standards interpreters should strive to achieve. On the other hand, they do not state that difficulties in achieving full accuracy may not exist. A code of ethics by itself cannot provide interpreters with a thorough understanding of their role, the interpreting process, the difficulties of achieving accuracy and the many other complex issues surrounding their work. Codes of ethics for other professions do not attempt to outline how to perform each of their required tasks. Expecting a code of ethics to do so would naively assume that it is capable of doing so. It would also be oversimplifying what is in fact an extremely complex matter. The elaboration of the code needs to take place in the training of interpreters. The question is whether the codes should make a qualification to this effect, to avoid unrealistic expectations. The New South Wales' interpreters' oath – 'I will truly and faithfully interpret all the evidence and other matters touching the matter now before the court to the best of my skills and ability' – goes a step further towards acknowledging that there are limitations in the process. Over-reliance on a code of ethics to solve all issues relating to the profession is a real risk. Some may assume that the existence of a code of ethics is all that is needed for interpreters to perform their work competently and professionally. Such a belief dismisses the need for pre-service formal training, for in-service professional development, for adequate working conditions and for the need for those who speak through interpreters to help facilitate the process – issues that would be accepted without question in any other profession.

Does the code of ethics prescribe an unthinking performance from interpreters?

There seems to be no evidence to support the codes' prescription of a robotic or mechanical role for interpreters. The California Rules of Court state that 'an interpreter shall use his or her best skills and judgment to interpret accurately'; and the code of the National Association of Judicial Interpreters and Translators (NAJIT), in its preamble, states:

> While many ethical decisions are straightforward, no code of ethics can foresee every conceivable scenario, court interpreters cannot mechanically apply abstract ethical principles to every situation that may arise. This Code is therefore intended not only to set forth fundamental ethical precepts for court interpreters to follow, but also to encourage them to develop their own, well-informed ethical judgment.

These codes mention the need for professional interpreters to exercise their judgement when applying the code's guidelines to their practice, something a machine cannot do. Such an injunction is supported by the practising interpreter quoted above (Respondent 6) and the interpreter quoted below (Respondent 4).[9] Dueñas González and colleagues concur, commenting that novice interpreters tend to follow rules of conduct strictly but as they gain confidence they:

> learn how to apply these rules in accordance with common sense and their intelligent assessment of the situation. One characteristic that distinguishes professionals from mere employees is that they are able to apply independent judgment and the benefit of experience to resolve difficult conflicts. (Dueñas González et al., 1991: 474)

The AUSIT code asks interpreters to encourage speakers to address each other. The CCHCP, after stating the need for complete fidelity in the health setting, states that 'if the content to be interpreted might be insensitive or otherwise harmful to the dignity and well-being of the patient, the interpreter should advise the health professional of this before interpreting'. Both instructions force the interpreter to step out of the strict interpreting mode to enter into a clarification mode where the interpreter speaks for her- or himself. If the interpreter was acting as a machine, such judgement and discretion would not be possible.

Interpreters' understanding of the accuracy requirement

It is apparent, however, that some interpreters may still misunderstand the spirit of the codes, as the following quotation from a Swedish interpreter seems to indicate:

> According to the ethical rules I should stick absolutely to the letter. (Wadensjö, 1998: 251)

This interpreter's understanding goes counter to Dueñas González and colleagues' advice: 'Interpreters must uphold the spirit of the canon of ethics, and must not become entangled in following the letter of the rules' (Dueñas González et al., 1991: 474). As speculated above, the interpretation and application of the code may be dependent on the formal training, preparation and experience of the interpreter, as one Australian interpreter commented, when asked 'How does the interpreters' code of ethics guide you in your practice?'

Quote 4.4

I find that it is my knowledge, my experience, and what I learnt during my degree that guides me. In other words, professional common sense is my best guide. Naturally, you ought to have a degree in Interpreting and Linguistics to acquire the professional bit in 'professional' common sense. If I did not have an academic background, I do not think the code of ethics would be a clear guide to follow when confronted with a complex situation.

(Respondent 4)

This interpreter is supporting the argument that a code of ethics by itself, without any academic background, cannot be a useful guide for any complex situation, simply because it cannot cover every possible situation. Interpreters need to use their professional judgement. However, if they have not been trained as professionals, that judgement may be lacking.

The interpreters surveyed were asked about their understanding of accuracy and provided with three possible answers that represented the three main approaches to translation: translation at the lexical level; translation at the sentence level; and translation at the discourse level (cf. chapter 1). Only one respondent (4.76 per cent of the sample) answered that accuracy meant 'a literal, word-for-word translation'. This was Respondent 19, a Portuguese interpreter with para-professional NAATI accreditation, no interpreting training and only primary-level general education. None of the respondents chose answer b: 'A translation of each separate sentence which will remain the same regardless of context'. The rest (95.23 per cent) chose the following as their understanding of accuracy: 'A translation which takes into account the whole discourse and reproduces the intention and the impact of the original'. This result clearly indicates that at least these interpreters do not understand the ethical requirement for accuracy to mean a literal translation. Whether they are consistently able to achieve accuracy according to their understanding of it is a different matter. The interpreter's performance will depend on a number of factors – bilingual competence, interpreting skills, physical factors such as fatigue, working conditions, background knowledge, clarity of source utterance, to name just a few. Having a clear understanding of the goal to be achieved is only the first step towards achieving it. In hindsight, interpreters will often think of better renditions they could have opted for. Using such situations as learning experiences, interpreters can build up their mental repertoire. This is particularly true in settings where the discourse is formulaic and repetitive.

The sample was also asked if they considered the meaning of accuracy to differ according to context; for example, is the level of accuracy needed in the legal context different from that in the medical context? The majority (80.95 per cent) answered no. Four (19.01 per cent) answered yes, but only two offered explanations for their answer:

> Accuracy is interpreted differently in the contexts of conference interpreting and court interpreting, and so is impartiality. This is because the interpreter's role in these two settings is different. The purposes, the parties involved are different. (Respondent 4)

> There might be situations where someone is expressing that his/her condition is good. Within the legal context, it may imply getting away without being discovered and/or punished, but may also mean that he/she did not have anything wrong. In a medical context it may mean that he/she is healthy... (Respondent 5)[10]

These answers do not refer to the same differences. Respondent 4 is arguing that accuracy implies different things in different contexts, such as conference and court interpreting. Whereas in conference interpreting the interpreter is expected at times to summarise, improve on the style of the speaker, omit hesitations and repetitions (cf. chapter 1), in the courtroom that would not constitute complete accuracy (cf. chapter 3). This respondent argues that this is because of the different roles and purposes in each of the contexts, and suggests that codes of ethics should reflect these differences. As this respondent has a postgraduate degree in Interpreting and Translation, it can be assumed that this is a topic that was discussed in the course of study.

Respondent 5, on the other hand, is attempting to explain the concept that a term can have different meanings according to context, and therefore the same word will be translated differently into the target language, but still be considered accurate. This is not explained in the code of ethics. As this respondent does not have interpreting qualifications, it can be assumed that this is a concept that was devised from their extensive experience.

4.3.2 Impartiality

Table 4.4 lists the entries under impartiality or conflict of interest in the different codes of ethics. The interpreter's and/or translator's obligation to observe strict objectivity to ensure that personal feelings,

Table 4.4 Entries on impartiality

Code	Impartiality Conflict of interests
Australia (AUSIT) 1999	(#4) Interpreters and translators shall observe impartiality in all professional contracts Objectivity i) A professional detachment is required for I/T assignments in all situations. ii) If objectivity is threatened, interpreters and translators shall withdraw from the assignment. Responsibilities related to impartiality i) Interpreters and translators are not responsible for what clients say or write. ii) Interpreters and translators shall not voice or write an opinion, solicited or unsolicited, on any matter or person in relation to an assignment.
Austria Austrian Association of Certified Court Interpreters	(#1) Unbiased and impartial
Canada Society of Translators and Interpreters of British Columbia	Indirectly, 'members shall not use their professional role to perform functions that lie beyond the scope of a language professional, such as advocacy, counselling or improper disclosure of information'.
The Association of Visual Language interpreters of Canada (AVLIC)	Members shall remain neutral, impartial, and objective. They will refrain from altering a message for political, religious, moral, or philosophical reasons, or any other biased or subjective considerations.
Indonesia Indonesian Translation Service Code of Ethics	The ... Service and its translators and interpreters will remain even-handed, dispassionate, independent and objective in all professional matters and especially in the exercise of all professional discretion and judgements concerning translation and interpreting issues.

United Kingdom Institute of Translation and Interpreting	Members shall interpret impartially between the various parties in the languages for which they are registered with the Institute and, with due regard to the circumstances prevailing at the time, take all reasonable steps to ensure complete and effective communication between the parties, including intervention to prevent misunderstanding and incorrect cultural inference.
USA National Association of Judicial Interpreters and Translators? (NAJIT)	Court interpreters and translators are to remain impartial and neutral in proceedings where they serve, and must maintain the appearance of impartiality and neutrality, avoiding unnecessary contact with the parties. Court interpreters and translators shall abstain from comment on cases in which they serve.
California Rules of Court – Rule 984.4 Professional conduct for interpreters	An interpreter shall be impartial and unbiased and shall refrain from conduct that may give an appearance of bias...An interpreter shall not make statements about the merits of the case until the litigation has concluded.
Cross-Cultural Health Care Program (CCHCP)	An interpreter's function is to facilitate communication. Interpreters are not responsible for what is said by anyone for whom they are interpreting. Even if the interpreter disagrees with what is said, thinks it is wrong, a lie or even immoral, the interpreter must suspend judgment, make no comment, and interpret everything accurately.
State of Washington Department of Social and Health Services (DSHS)	Interpreters/translators shall disclose any real or perceived conflict of interest which would affect their objectivity in the delivery of service. Providing interpreting or translation services for family members or friends may violate the individual's right to confidentiality, or constitute a conflict of interest.
International Criminal Tribunal for the former Yugoslavia	Article 8 – Impartiality 1. Interpreters and translators are bound to the strictest impartiality in the discharge of their duties. 2. Interpreters and translators shall not give legal advice to any person, whether solicited or not, nor refer suspects or accused to specific defence counsel.

opinions, beliefs or interests do not interfere with the main aim of producing accurate renditions is very strongly reflected. The injunction to disqualify oneself as an interpreter if there is any suspicion of an insurmountable conflict of interest that will interfere with accuracy is explicitly stated in the codes. However, a definition or explanation of impartiality is not offered by any of the codes. Most offer a set of 'don'ts' under this heading, which include refraining from giving advice or altering the original to suit their own ideologies, beliefs or interests. Some of the codes remind interpreters and/or translators that they are not responsible for what is being said or written, and therefore they should not feel personally involved or inclined to change the content if it is offensive or a patent untruth, for example. The legal codes, such as the NAJIT code and the California Rules, state that interpreters should not only remain impartial but should also avoid the appearance of bias. This is consistent with the adversarial common law system. Judicial officers also must be neutral and be seen to be neutral, hence their avoidance of any contact with any party in the proceedings. The avoidance of unnecessary contact with those for whom interpreters will interpret is a logical continuation of this principle. One of the codes speaks directly against interpreting for friends and relatives, as this constitutes an obvious conflict of interests.

What is impartiality and can it be fully achieved?

Quote 4.5　Serle on objectivity

I do strive for objectivity in the full knowledge that it is a vain task, but the struggle is everything.

(Serle, 1973: 59)

The requirement for 'absolute' accuracy or objectivity, as expressed in the codes, can only refer to the interpreter's aim, rather than to consistent performance. In dealing with human interpreters and human communication, exactness is not an achievable goal. As some have argued (e.g. Rudvin, 2002; Wallmach, 2002), the interpreter cannot be expected to be devoid of subjectivity. They 'cannot be wholly "neutral" any more than [they] can be wholly invisible' (Rudvin, 2002: 223). Interpreters will inevitably form their own opinions about the people for whom they are interpreting, about the fairness of the process, about the likely truthfulness of the utterances, about the quality of the professional services, and so on. This is unavoidable and the codes of ethics acknowledge it:

> Even if the interpreter disagrees with what is said, thinks it is wrong, a lie or even immoral, the interpreter must suspend judgment, make no comment, and interpret everything accurately.
>
> (CCHCP)

> Members shall remain neutral, impartial, and objective. They will refrain from altering a message for political, religious, moral, or philosophical reasons, or any other biased or subjective considerations.
>
> (AVLIC)

> Interpreters and translators are not responsible for what clients say or write.
>
> (AUSIT)

These statements acknowledge that interpreters will often disagree with what the speakers say for political, religious, philosophical or other reasons, or may even consider that the speakers are lying or are immoral. These are all subjective judgements that interpreters will form when they participate in any interaction. What the codes of ethics expect of interpreters, however, is for them to be aware of and to control their subjectivity so that they do not interfere with their ability to render the utterance faithfully. If they believe their subjectivity constitutes a conflict of interest, making it impossible for them to render an accurate interpretation, then disqualification from the job is advised. In other words, ethical behaviour on the part of the interpreter implies that even if the interpreter disagrees with a statement uttered by one of the parties, the interpreter will not alter it to suit their beliefs. The 'linguistic actor' metaphor (Laster and Taylor, 1994) can be used here to reflect the principle of impartiality. The actor who takes on the role of a criminal will not be expected to be one in their personal life. Similarly, the interpreter who speaks for someone else is not expected to be, think or act like that person in their personal life.

As some have stated, it can be very difficult for interpreters to remain impartial under conditions of extreme emotion (Barsky, 1996; Mason, 1999; Wallmach, 2002). Community interpreters are made privy to the most intimate information affecting others, which may include such distressing accounts as domestic violence or child abuse. The truthfulness of those accounts is unknown to the interpreter. Making a conscious effort to remain impartial can help avoid emotional involvement and possible burn-out. As Smirnov comments: 'Community interpreters must therefore have a proper understanding of their role and professional ethics, as they will have to function in situations of unbalanced power relationships and high emotional tension' (1997: 215). Garber also mentions that the imbalance of power in community settings has led many to prescribe the advocate role for community interpreters. He states that in Ontario this belief has mostly been abandoned as interpreters 'recognize that the power of the client is enhanced through his ability to speak as directly as possible to the service provider with the confidence that he understands and is understood' (Garber, 2000: 19).

Interpreters, however, are not alone in this. Other service professions share these dilemmas.

One of the interpreters in the sample presented the issue of impartiality as an ethical dilemma, although he still claims to abide by the code's requirements:

Quote 4.6

I am a committed Muslim and sometimes an issue would be raised that contradicts my beliefs and I find myself, in the process of interpreting, emphasizing it against my own beliefs.

(Respondent 5)

Another interpreter, in speaking of the guidelines found in the code states:

Quote 4.7

So far, I have never come upon a situation that I have needed to call on them and they have not been able to give me an 'answer' as to what to do or how to behave. I may not always 'like' it – but it is there. It's then up to me whether I do the 'right' thing or not.

(Respondent 8)

These interpreters admit that at times it is difficult to apply the code to their practice, mostly due to pressure from their own beliefs or opinions, but they nevertheless do it. In contrast, Respondent 3, who opposes the code, deliberately goes against it 'on a daily basis, if not hourly'. This interpreter has made a conscious decision to disregard the code, as it is of no value at all to their practice.

In speaking about the role of legal mediators, Greatbatch and Dingwall comment that:

> Like other professionals, such as television interviewers, mediators may be accused of bias even though they have avoided the direct expression of opinion. Nonetheless, the maintenance of a neutralistic stance provides a first line of defence against such charges. (Greatbatch and Dingwall, 1999: 274)

No one can deny that total impartiality is impossible. However, a conscious 'neutralistic' stance can go a long way in assuring as much impartiality as is possible to allow for an ethical performance. For Miguélez (2003) impartiality is crucial in achieving an accurate interpretation in community interpreting, supporting the ethical requirements stated in the codes of ethics. The logic behind this argument is that interpreters with a personal interest in an outcome may change the utterances to facilitate that outcome, although the result of such interference may be different from the one expected, as much of the research has shown (cf. Hale, 2004). According to Rudvin, 'One of the underlying assumptions among interpreters and service providers alike is that 'being neutral' equals translational equivalence' (2002: 231), an assumption with which she disagrees. This is not explicit in the codes of ethics. Being neutral cannot equate to being faithful, as faithfulness requires much more than neutrality. Neutrality, however, can facilitate faithfulness of interpretation. A conscious attempt to remain neutral is simply one of the many aspects that can help an interpreter render a faithful interpretation.

Concept 4.3   Does forming an opinion constitute unethical behaviour?

Acknowledging the difficulties and paradoxes inherent in the situation and the negative feelings that often ensue, might help alleviate the burden or feelings of guilt that many interpreters have . . . in respect to professional neutrality requirements.

Indeed . . . interpreters could be trained to use their negative feelings as paralinguistic cues, and use those cues to enhance their interpreting skills, thus improving performance, rather than suffering the burden of not feeling 'professional' because one has, simply by harbouring negative emotions, broken an ethical requirement to be neutral. (Rudvin, 2002: 224)

As Rudvin states, the difficulties associated with the need to remain impartial must be acknowledged. Disagreeing or agreeing with what the parties state does not constitute unethical behaviour and it would be ludicrous for interpreters to feel guilty about forming judgements about any situation. What constitutes unethical behaviour, according to the code, is the deliberate alteration of an utterance to reflect the interpreter's own beliefs, goals and purposes. As one of the interpreters stated: 'My thoughts and feelings sometimes make my job difficult – but the code of ethics helps sort that out' (Respondent 8).

4.3.3   Role

Table 4.5 outlines the entries which refer to the interpreter's role. Only the NAJIT code explicitly states what the role of the interpreter is:

> The function of court interpreters and translators is to remove the language barrier to the extent possible, so that such persons' access to justice is the same as that of similarly situated English speakers for whom no such barrier exists.

The AUSIT code advises interpreters to explain their role to those who are unaccustomed to working with interpreters, but it does not define it. The AVLIC code mentions that it may be appropriate for interpreters to comment on the effectiveness of communication, the interpreting process and suggest appropriate resources and referrals. All other codes state what the role of the interpreter is not. As with the entries on impartiality, the codes seem to be attempting to rectify the practice of many practitioners who are mostly ad hoc and untrained. As discussed in chapter 2, research has found that a high percentage of practising interpreters, in certain sectors and in certain countries, show an open lack of impartiality and provide lay advice, give their own opinions on what the speakers should say and indiscriminately edit the utterances. These practices are explicitly opposed by the codes of ethics. However, one of the Australian interpreters who responded to the survey expressed resentment to this:

> The code was whipped up by some people who could see something through a keyhole and who believed they saw the whole world. What they saw was a bunch of unruly ethnics, recently anointed by NAATI, working in the Community domain in Australia in the 1980s with little idea of impartiality, confidentiality or punctuality, and the Code was a response to that highly specific problem. It displays almost no realistic grasp of the contemporary translation and interpreting industry. (Respondent 3)

Table 4.5 Entries on role

Code	Role
Australia (AUSIT) 1999	Under #1, professional conduct: 'Interpreters and translators shall explain their role to those unaccustomed to working with them' (p. 12). The role is not explicitly presented in the code. It is implicit in the entries for accuracy and impartiality
Canada Society of Translators and Interpreters of British Columbia	Members shall not use their professional role to perform functions that lie beyond the scope of a language professional, such as advocacy, counselling or improper disclosure of information.
The Association of Visual Language interpreters of Canada (AVLIC)	Members will refrain from using their professional role to perform other functions that lie beyond the scope of an interpreting assignment and the parameters of their professional duties. They will not counsel, advise, or interject personal opinions.
Association of Translators and Interpreters of Alberta (ATIA)	...it may be appropriate for members to comment on the overall effectiveness of communication, the interpreting process and to suggest appropriate resources and referrals.
USA National Association of Judicial Interpreters and Translators? (NAJIT)	The function of court interpreters and translators is to remove the language barrier to the extent possible, so that such persons' access to justice is the same as that of similarly situated English speakers for whom no such barrier exists.
Cross-Cultural Health Care Program (CCHCP)	An interpreter's function is to facilitate communication. Interpreters are not responsible for what is said by anyone for whom they are interpreting. Even if the interpreter disagrees with what is said, thinks it is wrong, a lie or even immoral, the interpreter must suspend judgement, make no comment, and interpret everything accurately.
State of Washington Department of Social and Health Services (DSHS)	Interpreters/translators are not to counsel, refer, give advice, or express personal opinions, to individuals for whom they are interpreting/translating, or engage in any other activities which may be construed to constitute a service other than interpreting/translating. Interpreters/translators are prohibited to have unsupervised access to clients, including but not limited to phoning clients directly.

Amidst the vast range of levels of education, experience, competence and background, it would be unrealistic to expect the code of ethics to cater for every practitioner's specific needs. It may very well be that it is most useful to those entering the profession. It may be that novice professionals tend to follow guidelines strictly. More experienced professionals are able to rely more on their professional judgement, which is based on the core principles of the code.

The role agreed by the codes, therefore, is for the interpreter to be the means by which communication between two people who speak different languages can be achieved. The codes speak against the interpreter acting as an advocate, a counsellor, a gatekeeper or anything other than an interpreter. This, of course, does not exclude occasions when the interpreter needs to intervene to ask for clarifications or to explain an obvious cross-cultural misunderstanding, nor does it preclude the interpreter from sight translating routine documents, forms or non-complex materials, as these are all functions of an interpreter.

Concept 4.4   The role of the interpreter as prescribed by the code of ethics is challenged

The role prescribed by the code of ethics is one that has been challenged by a number of scholars (see chapters 2 and 3). The early literature on the role of the interpreter and on what interpreters were expected to do was largely based on personal opinions rather than on any empirical research. In an attempt to fill the gap, descriptive discourse analytical studies began to show the actual performance of real-life community interpreters. These studies demonstrated that many interpreters performed very differently from the prescriptions in the codes of ethics. These studies however, as a general rule, described the work and performance of ad hoc, untrained and for the most part incompetent interpreters. A number of researchers seem to indicate that since descriptive research has demonstrated that interpreters do not interpret accurately, such a norm is impossible, and in turn prescribe a different norm – that interpreters should be free to choose what to interpret and what not to interpret, and define their own role accordingly. They also argue for extra roles for the interpreter, such as 'advocate, counsellor, mediator, culture brokers, medical assistants and case managers' (Kaufert and Putsch, 1997: 75) – roles that constitute different professions which require their own adequate formal training. This alternative position is very ambivalent, especially for new trainee interpreters, who need guidance and direction. It is difficult to gauge the contents of an alternative code of ethics which would omit any requirement for accuracy and impartiality and impose these extra roles for which interpreters have no expertise. 'A good deal of descriptive work has been carried out on the ethnography of the courtroom and on courtroom discourse which has led to substantial agreement on the answer to the first question . . . [what the interpreter actually does] . . . in contrast, there is far from consensus on the answer to the second question [what the interpreter ought to do]' (Ibrahim, 2004: 248). More research is needed on what the role(s) of the interpreter ought to be, on whether such a role changes according to situation, participants and context and on the reasons behind the prescribed roles.

Practising interpreters' descriptions of their role

Table 4.6 lists the descriptions of role provided by eight of the practising interpreters in the sample (the other respondents did not provide an answer to this question).

All the interpreters offer a definition of their role that refers to facilitating communication between people who speak different languages. Some definitions are more specific than others. Respondent 1, for example, states that although their responsibility is to ensure that communication has occurred, the speakers do not relinquish the responsibility for ensuring that the information provided was understood. Respondent 5 simply states his role is to act as a conduit as well as possible. Although it is unclear what acting as a 'conduit' means, one can assume it refers to becoming the means by which communication can be achieved. This metaphor has been discredited as being equal to the machine metaphor. However, one can argue that the two metaphors refer to very different things. The machine metaphor assumes that interpreters act robotically, without thinking, because all they need to do is match words. The conduit metaphor implies that the interpreter is a link, the means by which two people who do not speak the same language can connect. Such a metaphor is valid for interpreters, as it does not explain how that connection is achieved, but that it is the interpreter's aim. Respondent 3 speaks of restoring access to the interlocutor, reader or text by removing the language impediment. Similarly, Respondent 7 states his role as being 'an agent of social justice'. It is unclear what this means in concrete terms, but one can assume that it relates to issues of access and equity, where language becomes the barrier in being awarded access to social services. This interpreter clearly views himself exclusively as a public service interpreter. Respondent 4 reproduces the three main tenets of the code of ethics: accuracy, impartiality and confidentiality as constituting the interpreter's role. Only two interpreters mention the need to facilitate cultural understanding or acting as a cultural bridge if this becomes an issue during the interaction

Table 4.6 Descriptions of role

Respondent	Answers to: What do you consider to be your role as a professional interpreter?
1	To ensure that communication has occurred, but not necessarily to ensure that the information has been understood. That is the responsibility of the parts involved.
2	My role as a professional interpreter is to facilitate communication between people, who otherwise would not be able to do so.
3	Person responsible for doing all that is possible, given the best available understanding of all the relevant technical, theoretical and ethical problems and their solutions, to restore to the client, direct linguistic access to interlocutor, reader or text.
4	1. To interpret into the other language everything said by the parties to a bilingual exchange and to produce a pragmatically accurate interpretation. 2. To remain impartial at all times. 3. To observe confidentiality in accordance with the code of ethics.
5	To act as a conduit between two parties as best as I can.
6	To assist two or more people who do not speak a common language to communicate with one another. To educate on cultural differences *if* they become an issue at the interview.
7	An agent in the delivery of social justice.
8	I consider my role to be a facilitator of communication and at times, a cultural bridge. That is: because I have a knowledge of both languages and cultures – when I am working with a deaf and hearing client (who don't have these abilities or knowledge), it's my role (to the best of my ability) to make communication occur (intent, meaning, etc.), and for both parties to understand each other and where they are coming from (cultural background, etc.).

which can impinge on accuracy. The fact that the others do not mention this cannot be understood to mean that they do not see a need for such clarifications when needed. The definitions provided by these interpreters are short and do not offer examples of how such a role is achieved, but none openly contradicts the role stipulated by the code of ethics.

In answer to whether the role of the interpreter differs according to setting, most agreed that the practical application of the role differed due to the limitations or demands of the setting. For this reason, some suggested that there should be different codes of ethics for the different types of interpreting.

Quote 4.8

It seems clear to me that the current code of ethics is outdated. I understand the circumstances, purposes, and practitioners for which the code was originally written. But it is about time a more thorough code was published. In my opinion, it would be more useful if the code of ethics had perhaps a general section and then some specialised sections relating to legal, medical and business interpreting in particular, for example.

(Respondent 4)

4.4 Ethical dilemmas

Quote 4.9

There are times when I don't 'like' it but I choose *not* to break my code of ethics. In one situation, I *really* struggled – but followed my code of ethics and at the end of it all I knew it was the best/right thing to do and I even felt more 'professional' for doing it. So I appreciated the code of ethics more that day than I think I ever have before. And it made me proud to be a professional Auslan[11] interpreter. I also knew (as I was making my decision) that my organisation, the clients and my peers are affected by my decisions – so following the code of ethics was the thing to do.

(Respondent 8)

Ethical dilemmas may arise due to a number of reasons: conflicts of interests; lack of competence in the assigned area of work; competing demands and expectations from the participants in the interaction; conflicting or unrealistic demands from a higher authority; poor working conditions that impinge on the interpreter's ability to perform; overlapping speech; sensitive cross-cultural issues; sensitive personal issues that make impartiality very difficult. Such situations become ethical dilemmas because the solution offered by the code is difficult to apply (often requiring great courage and confidence from the interpreter to enforce the professional stance known to be the right one) or because the code does not explicitly offer a solution. It is in those situations that interpreters need to use their professional judgement to discern whether they can apply the principles of the code, whether they need to disqualify themselves if their personal subjectivities or lack of competence are the reasons for their inability to comply, whether they need to make a stand to enforce the code amidst the pressures from the other parties, or whether they need to flout the code for a higher good.

Respondent 8 speaks of a time when they were presented with an ethical dilemma. The respondent knew what the code prescribed and struggled to abide by it, as it clashed with their personal feelings. After making the professional decision that adhering to the code was the right choice, this respondent felt very good about it, proud not to have succumbed to self-generated pressure, akin to having passed a trial. Interpreters are constantly 'tempted' to breach the code. Resisting such temptations demonstrates professional integrity and should ultimately strengthen interpreters and the profession and achieve a better result for the interlocutors.

However, there are times when, for reasons of higher importance, the code cannot be applied in full. Interpreters often wonder how to apply the confidentiality clause in dangerous or life-threatening situations. Such situations are very rare and a study to quantify their frequency would be very useful (cf. chapter 8). The typical questions posed at workshops on ethics are:

- What do I do if the patient tells me before the consultation that he is going to commit suicide but does not tell the doctor?
- What should I do if a suspected criminal tells me he will kill me if I tell the police what he just told me?

One of the respondents, a medical interpreter, disagrees with the confidentiality clause in specific cases: 'I believe the life of a human being should be above any confidentiality concerns/clauses' (Respondent 4). These are the situations when interpreters need to make a professional decision to flout that aspect of the code for a greater good. The code should act as a guide to be applied judiciously, not blindly. Respondent 8 expressed this in the following way: 'I see it as my guide not a rod for my back'.

There are a number of ways such ethical dilemmas can be dealt with. However, avoiding them in the first place by not being left alone with the patient or the suspect is the preferred alternative. In any case, the code applies to the interpreted encounter, and not to any interactions before or after the professional encounter. During those interactions, the interpreter is not acting as interpreter but as a private citizen and is therefore not bound by any professional code of ethics. According to the code, it is the information obtained during the interpreted interview that must not be disclosed.

Pressures from the participants during the interpreted interaction can be another source of ethical dilemmas for the interpreter:

> Sometimes although rarely, there are people who see the interpreter as their ally or advocate, and expect the interpreter to take their side. (Respondent 2)

> Both parties want me to be on their side, as it were. (Respondent 4)

> Both parties do feel that they can relate to you since you are the one who can speak their language during that particular conversation, so they tend to converse with you rather than through you. (Respondent 7)

If the speakers see the interpreter as their ally, they will assume that asides to the interpreter that may be offensive to the other party, or statements that may be detrimental to their case, will not be interpreted. On the other hand, they may assume that the interpreter will add information the party has forgotten to state. Such expectations contradict the code of ethics' accuracy and impartiality clauses and hence interpreters who want to act ethically will not yield to the pressure to breach the code. This creates a dilemma if the other participants are not aware of the code and of the role of the interpreter. Tebble (1998) suggests that explaining the role (which she calls the 'contract') at the outset can avoid these ethical dilemmas. Respondent 8 stated that participants often have incorrect assumptions regarding their knowledge of the other participants' background, beliefs or intentions or about the role of the interpreter. In those situations, this respondent explains the role and what is involved in the interpreting process and 'hopefully the job goes smoother for all concerned' (Respondent 8).

Another source of ethical dilemma is the service providers' reliance on the interpreter to act as a cultural broker or as an adviser or to perform duties that are within the service provider's realm. Interpreters often complain that they are pressured by service providers to give them information they are not qualified to provide, such as commenting on the state of mind of a patient, on the credibility of the person's answers, on the cultural characteristics of people who speak that language, or even being asked to comfort the person or take them to lunch. Some service providers may feel that the interpreter will know everything there is to know about cultural differences and will rely on them to solve all cross-cultural issues. This pressure from the service provider is confirmed by Kaufert and Putsch, two Canadian medical practitioners, who argue that interpreters should serve as 'mediators, advocates, culture brokers, medical assistants, and in some cases, case managers' (1997: 75). Some interpreters will succumb to this pressure and provide personal, lay opinion, which for the most part will be as good as or at best slightly better than the service provider's guess, but not as reliable as any answer supplied by the speaker him- or herself. Others will tell the service provider that they are not qualified to provide such information and that they can ask the client if they wish.

Offering cultural information can be risky. The majority of cross-cultural differences that are reflected in the language, such as politeness, indirectness or other pragmatic considerations, should be bridged in an accurate pragmatic rendition of the original, without the need to interrupt the flow. Interpreters need to be fully aware of such cross-cultural pragmatic differences. There may be other cultural issues that can arise during the course of an interview which will cause miscommunication where an interpreter may feel the need to interrupt to clarify – for example, the convention to kiss or shake hands when being introduced in some cultures, or the avoidance of eye contact in others. However, it is only the very broad cultural conventions that an interpreter can safely highlight. Other differences are mostly individual and relate to such varied factors as education, class, religion, upbringing and personality, to name just a few. As Isaacs qualifies: 'each individual from a given culture will assume the beliefs, values, attitudes, and behaviours of the broader cultural context to varying degrees. It would be impossible to provide a checklist of "do" and "don't" rules' (2002: 26). Generalising will inevitably lead to stereotyping. Examples such as the following cannot be very helpful in advancing cross-cultural understanding.

Example 4.1

Richard Nixon fell into this pitfall when visiting Latin America. On arriving, Nixon gave the OK sign. However this gesture has a very different meaning in Latin America...Richard Nixon was very embarrassed and the Latin Americans were very offended.

(Singelis, 1994: 280)

In attempting to promote cultural sensitivity, the above statement is ironically very culturally insensitive, as it groups all the different North, Central and South American Spanish and Portuguese-speaking countries as one, with one unified culture, and one single port of entry. Not only do all the separate countries have their cultural differences, different regions within each country have their own characteristics as well. Suffice it to say that the sign described above does not constitute a rude gesture in all the Latin American countries.

Example 4.2

Another [Hong Kong Chinese] mother of a child with a cleft palate and other congenital facial anomalies assumed that these were due to her having seen horror films and pictures of evil gods during the initial stages of her pregnancy.

(Chan, 1992: 225)

Interpreters cannot be expected to suggest to medical practitioners that all Chinese mothers have the belief described above. Such an assumption would be offensive to the Chinese. Medical practitioners would be better advised to ask the patient why she believed this to be the case and then offer accurate medical advice.

Kaufert and Putsch mention that communities from the Horn of Africa, Italy, Greece, China, Korea and Mexican-Americans believe that 'telling the truth to the affected individual is disrespectful, may be dangerous, and/or may shorten his or her life' (1997: 74). Such generalisations are extremely risky. It is very unlikely that all people from those countries hold these beliefs and therefore impossible for the interpreter to confidently state it. If an interpreter were to tell a physician that such were the case, even to say that only some communities may feel this way, one is left wondering what the physician would do. Tell the patient a lie? Would the patient's right to know about their condition be denied based solely on the lay opinion of an interpreter? Would the patient die without knowing their condition? How would the patient be able to give informed consent for treatment? A whole list of ethical dilemmas arise as a consequence of the interpreter providing a stereotypical view of the patient's cultural background which does not take into account that person's agency or individual idiosyncrasies, circumstances or life experiences. Garber (2000) presents an example of a Central American man who spoke reasonable English and visited a medical practitioner in Canada. At the end of the consultation he was given a prescription. Garber states that the patient saw this as a piece of paper with illegible writing on it but did not know what it was or what it was for, as in his country of origin, doctors administer the medications themselves. Garber argues that if an interpreter had been present, if he had not spoken English, this misunderstanding would not have taken place. However, as an experienced Spanish interpreter myself, I would not have known that this patient did not understand what the purpose of the prescription was unless he said so, as in most Spanish-speaking countries prescriptions are issued by doctors in the same way as in Canada. It is very unrealistic and unfair to expect the interpreter to hazard a guess when misunderstandings are caused by cultural differences that are not obvious to anyone present.

The above argument does not suggest that cross-cultural differences do not exist or that they may not be a source of misunderstanding. Nor does it suggest that service providers should be insensitive to potential cultural differences. What it does suggest is that cultural differences can be varied and complex and that interpreters need to be confident that the cause of the misunderstanding is a cross-cultural issue before deciding to offer an explanation. To my knowledge there has been no thorough research conducted into the frequency with which interpreters need to interrupt an encounter to provide a cultural explanation; or whether different interpreters of the same language would agree on the cultural explanations provided by each other. Such a study is sorely needed (cf. chapter 8) to ascertain the extent to which cultural brokerage in interpreting is needed.

4.5   Summary

The comparison and analysis of 16 codes of ethics from nine countries demonstrated that claims that the codes prescribe literal renditions under the accuracy requirement and a robotic, mechanical performance from interpreters is not evident and therefore unjustifiable. A code of ethics, in its many versions, does not provide any detailed descriptions or in-depth discussion of the meaning of accuracy and of the many difficulties interpreters may encounter in striving to achieve it. Nor does it offer any explanation or discussion of the complex nature of the interpreting process, the controversies surrounding the notion of absolute impartiality or of the possible need to flout the confidentiality clause under certain circumstances. A number of the codes indeed advise that professional judgement is required to apply the general guidelines of the code. Expecting a code of ethics to cover all the many different aspects of such a complex profession in detail is unrealistic and inconsistent with other professions. Such thorough training and debate should take place in pre-service formal training and in-service professional development opportunities.

The mere existence of a code can neither guarantee that interpreters will be capable of abiding by its high standards nor that all interpreters will be willing to adhere to the code even when capable of doing so. The current situation shows inconsistency between the high standards set by the code and the lack of a compulsory pre-service training requirement, compounded by a lack of institutional support. The high standards of accuracy in particular should constitute a goal to which interpreters must strive, acknowledging that a consistent, 'perfect' performance is impossible and that, due to a number of factors, including those that are beyond the interpreter's control, such a goal will not always be achieved. Interestingly, the majority of the interpreters surveyed relied most strongly on the code when confronted by ethical dilemmas and were grateful to be guided by it. All the interpreters, except one, indicated that the code was considered to be useful for their profession, although the trained interpreters stressed that it was their academic training that allowed them to make sense and appropriate use of the code.

The final question that remains to be answered is whether the code should be amended to match the practice of those who do not abide by it or whether their practice should change to match the principles outlined in the code. The code needs to be interpreted correctly as a general guide to practitioners to help them make their best professional judgements. The theory and skills of the interpreting practice must be learned and debated in formal training. A code of ethics cannot fulfil that role. Refining and improving the code as a working document, informed by professional practitioners, is a desirable move. However, adjusting the code to limit the standards to meet the lowest possible denominator can only be detrimental to the profession and, most importantly, to the people it serves.

Further reading

Chesher et al. (2003). This article presents the response of a worldwide survey on community interpreters' views about their role and ethical obligations.

Dueñas González, Vásquez and Mikkelson (1991). A thorough manual on the most salient issues of court interpreting. Although its focus is on court interpreting, it is a useful reference for community interpreters in general.

Kaufert and Putsch (1997). This article debates a number of different ethical dilemmas encountered by interpreters in the health care sector and presents different views on ways to deal with them.

Roberts et al. (2000). This is the second book of proceedings of the Critical Link conference series. It is a compilation of papers from the Critical Link 2 conference held in Vancouver, where the theme concentrated on professional issues.

5

The Practitioners' Voices: Views, Perceptions and Expectations from Legal, Medical and Interpreting Practitioners

This chapter:

- Outlines some of the main issues and challenges faced by community interpreters.
- Presents the views of medical and legal practitioners about their expectations and perceptions of interpreters.
- Presents the views of practising interpreters about current issues relating to their practice.
- Discusses how the results of research can be applied in the practice to help meet interpreters' issues and challenges.

5.1 Introduction

Community interpreters face a number of challenges which are rarely recognised by those involved in the interaction. This chapter outlines some of the main challenges and discusses the possible applications of research to the practice to help overcome them. In this chapter, the views, perceptions and expectations of medical and legal practitioners and practising interpreters are presented and analysed. The chapter argues that the responsibility for quality interpreting services does not lie solely with interpreters, but with all the participants involved in the interaction, as well as with the system that trains, accredits and employs them. The disparate expectations, perceptions and opinions held by the different stakeholders as well as the lack of institutional support are highlighted as a main reason for many of the challenges interpreters face.

5.2   Sources of challenges faced by interpreters

The main sources of challenges faced by community interpreters can be divided into four main areas: interpreting-related issues; context-related issues, participant-related issues and system-related issues (see Figure 5.1).

5.2.1   Interpreting-related issues

Linguistic difficulties, skills-related difficulties and time constraints

The linguistic difficulties related to the interpreting process have been discussed in chapter 1 and will not be repeated here. Although some

---

Interpreting-related issues
  Linguistic
    Lexical gaps
    Grammatical differences
    Semantic differences
    Pragmatic differences
  Skills-related
    Complex and multiple skills required
  Time
    Time constraints on the interpreting task
  Cultural
    Cross-cultural differences that can lead to miscommunication
Context-related issues
  Working conditions
  Lack of background information
  Constraints of the activity type
Participant-related issues
  Negative attitudes from users of interpreting services
  Participants' misunderstanding of the interpreting process
  Participants' misunderstanding of the interpreter's role
  Participants' lack of awareness of the interpreter's professional needs
System-related issues
  Insufficient pre-service formal training opportunities
  Lack of compulsory requirement of pre-service formal training
  Lack of institutional support
  Poor remuneration

Figure 5.1   Challenges faced by the community interpreter

research has been conducted into cross-linguistic issues, in Translation Studies and in Interpreting Studies (Whitney, 1986; Hatim and Mason, 1990; Baker, 1992; Hervey et al., 1995; Hale, 1999, 2001), much more research is needed, in particular in relation to spoken language and in a variety of language combinations. How much of that research has been read and applied by practising community interpreters is difficult to ascertain, but it can be assumed that those who have completed a formal interpreting course that covered theory are more likely to know about the results of research and to apply them to their practice than those who have learned on the job. A former student of the author, now a practising interpreter, wrote after a difficult court job, where she felt she performed to her satisfaction:

Quote 5.1   The value of research

Nunca me podría haber desempeñado de la manera en que lo hice si no hubiese hecho las materias de interpretación con vos o leído tus trabajos ... Cuanto más trabajo en los tribunales, más me doy cuenta del valor práctico de tus investigaciones para los intérpretes.

[I would never have been able to perform in the way I did if I hadn't done the Interpreting subjects with you or read your work ... the more I work in court, the more I realise the practical value of your research for interpreters.]

(Alejandra Hayes, 30 November 2005, email communication with Sandra Hale)

In Quote 5.2, Cambridge proposes three of the most common challenges often quoted by interpreters: dealing with constant register shifts; interpreting coarse language; and coping with vicarious trauma. Although only the first two are of a linguistic nature, the last one is also worth mentioning.

Quote 5.2   Three challenges interpreters face

Public Service interpreters regularly work with clients of non-English-speaking background (NESB). In linguistic terms one of the major challenges for PS interpreters is the constant shift in register between client and Public Service Provider (PSP), and the use of dialect words and idiosyncratic language by an NESB client group of vulnerable, frightened and often not well-educated people. If a PS interpreter is going to fulfil his/her duty as 'alter ego' to each speaker, they must be adept at these register shifts and able to relay the curses and the 'rude bits'. For interpreters from some cultural backgrounds, this can present particular

> **Quote 5.2   (Continued)**
>
> challenges, especially for the women, in assignments such as rape or child abuse... The training implications of this type of challenge must not be overlooked. Vicarious trauma and the need for confidential support are also real issues.
>
> (Cambridge, 2004: 50)

With regards to Cambridge's first challenge, in Community Interpreting the registers can shift according to setting and participants. There may be participants of varying social backgrounds who come together in an encounter, speaking in different speech styles, social dialects and registers. In a monolingual situation, the speakers would enter into a process of accommodation, where they would adjust their speech to arrive at a middle ground. Those who argue for accuracy in interpreting (Berk-Seligson, 1990/2002; Dueñas González et al., 1991; Cambridge, 2004; Hale, 2004) propose that the same should apply in an interpreted interaction. Interpreters need to attempt to maintain the register of the original speaker to allow the speakers to accommodate, if that is indeed their wish. It may very well be, as in the case of cross-examination, that a register differential is deliberate on the part of the prosecutor. Results of research (Berk-Seligson, 1990/2002; Hale, 1997) have shown that there seems to be a tendency on the part of interpreters to take over the accommodation phase, producing utterances that are in the same register as those of the hearer rather than the speaker. This is the natural inclination, and therefore the easier option. Being conscious of the different registers and maintaining them in the interpretation is a difficult task and a challenge for interpreters. But such a skill can be acquired through training and practice, as Cambridge suggests.

The second challenge identified by Cambridge refers to expletives or coarse language. These can present challenges for a number of reasons. Interpreters may not be prepared to quickly produce a rendition that carries the same illocutionary force and achieves the equivalent perlocutionary act as the original, unless they have covered such possibilities in training. It may be against the beliefs of some interpreters to swear and so they may refuse to interpret accurately, resorting to omitting the utterance or to reporting that the person has sworn. Such options would change the reaction in the listener, not provide the listener with an opportunity to reply and deny the speaker their choice to swear. Interpreters who feel this way do not think of themselves as interpreters,

speaking on behalf of someone else, but rather as authors of the utterances, responsible for their content and style.

The third challenge presented by Cambridge, vicarious trauma, can
be a real issue for interpreters working with victims of torture, rape,
domestic violence and any other type of violence. Not unlike the police
or social workers who have to deal with these issues, interpreters need
debriefing and support after difficult assignments, something that very
rarely, if ever, happens.

As for the other two challenges mentioned under the category of
interpreting-related issues, interpreting skills relate to the different
modes of interpreting required, as explained in chapter 1. The acquisition of these skills through training and practice is the interpreter's
responsibility.

Cross-cultural differences

As mentioned in chapter 4, cross-cultural differences may pose challenges for interpreters. Many cross-cultural differences are reflected in
the way people express themselves in language. For example, the way
politeness is expressed in different languages is culturally bound, but
the conventions used through language can be reflected in an accurate
pragmatic rendition. If, for instance, the target language uses indirectness to express politeness and the source language does not, an accurate
rendition would change a direct statement into an indirect one, to
match the original polite intention. There are, however, cultural differences that may require some intervention in order to avoid misunderstandings, as it may not be possible to reflect such differences through
language. Obvious examples are the use of hand gestures and general
body language. Other, more subtle differences, however, may not be
easy to pinpoint, and it is often difficult to judge whether they are a
result of a general cross-cultural difference, a social difference that is
shared by any language group or a personal preference.

In a practitioners' forum, an interpreter provided the example
presented as Scenario 1 as one where the interpreter's intervention to
explain a cultural difference was warranted.

Scenario 1

An Arabic-speaking man is discussing with his lawyer his fight for the custody of
his children in a divorce case. The lawyer explains that the Family Court expects all
parents who are seeking custody to complete a parenting course. The client says
he will not do that, as such a course is for women, not men. The lawyer says that if

---

Scenario 1 (Continued)

that is his response, they cannot negotiate; they must go to court and let the judge decide the case. The interpreter interrupts to explain that in the Arabic culture the man's reaction is acceptable. The lawyer ignores the interpreter's intervention and leaves.

Most of the other interpreters in the room disagreed with this interpreter's decision to interrupt. One Anglo-Australian interpreter commented that the attitude of the Arabic-speaking client could be found in Anglo-Australian men too. Others said that the lawyer would be aware of the generally male-dominated Arabic-speaking culture, but that generalisations are inappropriate, as not all Arabic-speaking men would have this attitude. Others said it was up to the lawyer to explain the Family Court's culture to his client, one that this man should accept if he wants custody of his children. In any case, the interpreter's intervention achieved very little in concrete terms.

Scenario 2

A Spanish-speaking Central American man is giving evidence, in the course of which he discusses his and his wife's indecision about how to spend a substantial amount of money they won on the lottery. The couple could not decide whether to use the money towards paying off their mortgage or to pay for their daughter's fifteenth birthday party celebration. The interpreter interprets faithfully, but does not intervene to offer any cultural explanation. The lawyer does not ask any questions relating to this issue, which is peripheral and irrelevant to the case.

To someone unfamiliar with the witness's culture, spending thousands of dollars on a girl's fifteenth birthday would seem unreasonable. To those familiar with his culture, it would not be surprising at all. Fifteenth birthday parties are still a major event for some families in Spanish-speaking countries, a type of debutante or coming-out event. It is not unusual to spend as much on this celebration as on a wedding reception. The dilemma for the interpreter is to decide whether to intervene or not. If the interpreter does not intervene, even if the utterance is accurately rendered, it is not faithful to the original, as it cannot possibly portray the same intention and produce a similar reaction in the listener. If the interpreter interrupts to explain this cultural difference, since in this case it is irrelevant, she or he may be told that such information is not required.

Scenario 3

An Australian aboriginal person is suspected of committing a crime and is being questioned by police. The police ask if he committed the particular crime. The suspect states unequivocally that he did and agrees with all accusations presented in question form by the police. Such a record of interview will most likely incriminate the suspect. The interpreter does not intervene to offer any cultural clarification.

In Scenario 3, the interpreter knows that in Aboriginal culture, the principle of gratuitous concurrence is common (see Eades, 1994), where, when confronted with direct questions, Aboriginal people will agree simply to please the questioner. The interpreter does not know if this particular suspect is abiding by this cultural trait or is admitting to the truth. Once again, the interpreter is faced with a dilemma: should the interpreter have changed the form of the question to make it less direct and more akin to the conventions of Aboriginal culture? Should the interpreter have intervened to explain the cultural differences to the police and ask that the explanation appear in the record of interview? Or should the interpreter have remained silent and hope that the cultural difference will be highlighted in court?

The wider the gap between the two cultures that come into contact, the more challenging this issue becomes. It is, however, unclear what interpreters should do, except use their professional judgement to decide whether an intervention is warranted. As mentioned in previous chapters, this is an important area that has not attracted much attention and requires research to inform the practice.

Kelly (2000) conducted a survey of 100 questionnaires distributed to judges, interpreters, interpreter trainers and administrators, prosecutors, defence lawyers and legislators in Massachusetts. The results obtained from the question 'Should interpreters interpret (convey) cultural differences in the courtroom?' were mixed: 53 per cent of judges said no, while negative responses from the others ranged from 47 per cent from prosecutors to 29 per cent from interpreters and defence lawyers. The mixed perceptions may be related to a lack of understanding of what constitutes cultural differences, of how expert the interpreter is at identifying it, and of how to convey such differences. Many questioned the interpreter's expertise; others commented that if the interpreter had the expertise, then their role would change to that of an expert witness and another interpreter should be hired for the rest of the case. Some considered that cultural differences should be conveyed to the defence team outside of the courtroom. Some replied that such interventions were warranted 'only when language does not convey such differences' (Kelly, 2000: 139). Kelly highlights the difficulties encountered when a single language is spoken in a number of countries, where what may be a cultural issue for one group, may not be for another (see discussion in chapter 4). She explains that it is those obvious cultural differences that clearly apply to a whole society that must be transmitted rather than personal idiosyncratic differences. Kelly concludes that:

> The interpreter's cultural intervention should not derive from sympathy with the defendant or a belief in his guilt or innocence. Such action should occur due to the existence of identifiable differences between the host and defendant's cultures. One should not advocate for either culture, only the factual presentation of concrete differences which may have a bearing on the outcome of the case. (Kelly, 2000: 145)

In a survey of interpreters and service providers conducted in Austria, Pöchhacker (2000) found that interpreters were much more comfortable with the idea of explaining cultural differences than were the service providers, who did not consider it to be necessary.

These surveys constitute a good starting point for further research in this area which looks at specific instances of cross-cultural differences that present challenges to interpreters and on how they can be overcome (cf. chapter 8).

5.2.2   Context-related issues

Issues relating to context have been discussed in detail in chapters 2 and 3 in connection with the medical and legal domains. In these two chapters, the constraints of the different activity types, especially the courtroom, are highlighted. Working conditions in any setting, however, need to be adequate for interpreters to perform well. It is not unusual to see interpreters working for long hours by themselves, with no breaks, no seat to sit on, no table to lean on to take notes, and nothing to drink. It is very likely that if interpreters requested any of these basic requirements, they would be granted unconditionally, although according to some this is not the case: 'I work in [the] State/County Court... and the Administrative Office of the Court here just turns a blind eye and deaf ear to our complaints and suggestions for better working conditions in order to meet our ethical obligations of accurate interpretation' (interpreter writing to an e-bulletin, in Morris,

2000: 250). However, even if simple requests were heeded, many interpreters would not be confident enough to demand anything that is not readily provided to them.

Working in pairs for long assignments is common in Conference Interpreting but not in Community Interpreting. Working as a team with another interpreter would not only satisfy issues of occupational health and safety by avoiding unnecessary fatigue, it would also serve as a quality assurance mechanism. Such a move would, of course, have budget implications, hence the resistance to implement the practice.

Another challenge for interpreters is interpreting without any prior knowledge of the subject matter or acquaintance with the participants. If interpreters are not provided with any information or material in advance, they are not given the opportunity to prepare adequately. The prevailing mistrust of interpreters has led to reluctance to provide any briefing information, with the excuse that the issues are confidential and cannot be divulged. This argument does not hold, since interpreters are bound by a code of ethics which prescribes confidentiality, and the same issues will be discussed in the presence of the interpreter once the assignment commences. The misconception that interpreting is 'just saying what someone said in one language in another' has been often stated by service providers as the reason for not needing to give interpreters any prior information or materials. Many misinterpretations (as discussed in previous chapters) would have been avoided if interpreters had been given adequate materials and time to prepare.

5.2.3   Participant-related issues

As community interpreters work in a participatory framework, the behaviours of all participants influence the interaction and the effectiveness of the interpreting activity. At the micro level, matters such as seating arrangements, eye contact, turn-taking and overlapping speech are important considerations in the interpreted interaction. At the macro level, the attitudes towards interpreters from the other participants and their understanding and expectations of their work and their role impinge on the performance of the interpreter (cf. Hale, 2004, 2005). Interpreters often find themselves caught in a struggle between a number of competing demands and expectations from those around them. The rest of this chapter will present the results of a small survey conducted in Sydney, Australia among lawyers, medical practitioners and interpreters, about their different perceptions and expectations of interpreters' work.

The service providers' responses

Twenty medical practitioners and 21 legal practitioners responded to the questionnaire. It must be noted from the outset that the response rate was only 20 per cent for each group, with 100 questionnaires being sent out or personally delivered to each group of professionals. This poor response rate may indicate a general lack of interest on Interpreting issues from these service providers.

Three-quarters (75 per cent) of doctors and two-thirds (67 per cent) of lawyers reported working with an interpreter at least monthly. The most commonly spoken languages of their patients and clients were Chinese, Vietnamese, Russian, Arabic and French. All of the medical practitioners and the majority of legal practitioners called on government or private agencies to provide interpreters. Only two lawyers sometimes contracted interpreters directly. This indicated that they had very little control over which interpreters they were allocated.

Perceptions of interpreter professionalism   A number of questions aimed to discover whether these service providers regarded interpreters as professionals or not. These related to issues of qualifications, trust, assessment of competence, remuneration and interpreters' rights and responsibilities.

When asked about the qualifications they required interpreters to have, the lawyers' responses demonstrated a better understanding of interpreters' requirements. None of the lawyers answered 'nil', compared to 46 per cent of doctors; none of the lawyers expected interpreters simply to know two languages, compared to 23 per cent of doctors. The majority (62 per cent) of lawyers required interpreters to have NAATI professional accreditation, compared to only 23 per cent of doctors, and 14 per cent required formal qualifications in addition to NAATI professional accreditation, compared to only 4.8 per cent of doctors. A third (33 per cent) of lawyers give preference to the best qualified interpreters, compared to a little over a quarter (26.7 per cent) of doctors. This, however, is understandable in light of the fact that most do not contract their interpreters directly. In response to the question on whether interpreters should be university trained, 52 per cent of lawyers said yes, compared to only 30 per cent of doctors. Although lawyers seem more aware of accreditation requirements and training needs for interpreters and slightly more give preference to trained interpreters, neither group seems to value formal tertiary qualifications, which gives interpreters no real incentive to train. Such a low perception of the need for formal education may be due to the fact that, since trained interpreters are in the minority, many of these medical and legal practitioners may not have had the opportunity to experience working with trained interpreters and have not experienced the difference between those who are trained and those who are not. Such a perception reinforces the misconception that Interpreting is not a skilled profession that requires training. Ironically, a majority of service providers (80 per cent of doctors and 100 per cent of lawyers) considered interpreters to be professionals, yet most did not consider it essential for them to undergo the same rigorous training required of other professionals. Even though 45 per cent of doctors and 48 per cent of lawyers claimed to have noticed a difference between trained and untrained interpreters, some noted they do not always know if interpreters are trained or not. However, very few gave preference to the best qualified interpreters, with some observing that they would if they were booking the interpreter directly. In other words, they do not demand any qualifications from the booking agency, but are content to be assigned any interpreter. This may indicate that even if they see a difference between competent and incompetent interpreters, they do not consider it important enough to contact the booking agency to provide them with feedback on the interpreter's performance or to demand trained interpreters. It does not seem to be universally recognised that an incompetent interpreter will affect the service providers' ability to perform their professional duty. It is important to highlight that if the interpreter is not performing adequately, then the service provider cannot either.

When asked about how they assess an interpreter's competence, both professional groups provided similar responses: 0.05 per cent of doctors and 4.76 per cent of lawyers assessed them on their accent, 10 per cent of doctors and 19 per cent of lawyers on their body language, 20 per cent of doctors and 33.3 per cent of lawyers on their general appearance, 30 per cent of doctors and 23.8 per cent of lawyers on the coherence of the utterances in English, and 60 per cent of doctors and 79.2 per cent of lawyers on how smooth the exchange was. As can be seen, some respondents chose more than one answer, indicating that their assessment is formed with reference to a number of factors. Lawyers assigned more importance to body language, accent, general appearance and general smoothness than doctors did, but less to the client's incoherence, as ways of assessing interpreter competence. The most popular way of assessing competence for both groups, however, was the smoothness of the exchange. This related to interpreting everything directly and accurately.

Other answers that were shared by both groups were feedback from their clients or patients and their families, and their own knowledge of a second language.

There were a number of answers that were given exclusively by medical practitioners:

- the interpreter's understanding of mental health issues, demonstrating an awareness that background knowledge is important for interpreting;
- their level of involvement/detachment, where the most detached are seen as the most competent, with one stating that those 'too eager to help' do not show professionalism; and
- the relevance of the patients' answers and questions.

Answers that were unique to lawyers included:

- interpreters' renditions being either much shorter or much longer than the original;
- interpreters talking over the witness; and
- interpreters explaining to lawyers that the client did not understand instead of interpreting the client's utterance and letting the client say they did not understand.

These responses are very illuminating as they reveal these practitioners' evaluations of the interpreter's work, without their having any expertise in the matter. Only 15 per cent of the medical practitioners and 33.3 per cent of the lawyers had read any material on Interpreting or attended an Interpreting-related course. Nevertheless, some of their answers are valid whereas others may be unjustified. Although feedback from the patients/clients or their relatives can be useful, they cannot be taken as expert advice, as they are not qualified to assess the work of the interpreter. Similarly, doctors and lawyers who have some knowledge of another language cannot presume to be Interpreting experts. Blaming the interpreter for the incoherence or irrelevance of the patients' or clients' utterances is also unjustified, as the interpreter may be rendering an accurate interpretation of the original. Interestingly, no one stated that the interpreters' qualifications would be a good indication of competence.

Remuneration is closely linked to whether an occupation is considered to be skilled or unskilled. Lawyers were slightly more generous in their opinion about rate of pay for interpreters. Two-thirds (66.6 per cent) of lawyers deemed an hourly rate of Aus\$35–75 (£15–32) to be appropriate, whereas three-quarters (76 per cent) of medical practitioners believed a rate of Aus\$15–55 (£6–23) to be adequate remuneration for interpreters. These fees do not reflect a professional's rate of pay. They are, however, consistent with these service providers' previous responses on qualifications required. If interpreters are not required to have any qualifications, they cannot expect to be paid a high hourly rate. Regardless of the fact that most respondents considered interpreters to be professionals, these two questions about qualifications and remuneration reveal the truth about this issue. Many still think of Interpreting as an unskilled occupation, requiring no training and hence not meriting professional remuneration. Such a situation perpetuates mediocrity. If interpreters have no financial incentive to train and improve, the quality will remain static or deteriorate. A study of a small group of physiotherapists in New South Wales (Lee, Lansbury and Sullivan, 2005) revealed that physiotherapists' attitudes towards interpreters were so negative that they considered them a waste of money, preferring family, friends and bilingual staff, with professional interpreters seen as the last resort. One of the physiotherapists even suggested that the Health Care Interpreter Service should be voluntary. Such negative attitudes among health care practitioners need to change if interpreted exchanges are to be effective.

Trusting interpreters to do the right thing is a good indicator of the service provider's confidence in their competence and professionalism. Interestingly, the vast majority (90 per cent) of doctors claimed to trust interpreters, with fewer (81 per cent) of lawyers stating the same. It may be that lawyers expect more of interpreters than doctors do, considering the strategic importance of language in the legal domain. The ones who responded to the contrary had the explanations shown in Table 5.1.

The responses from both groups for the most part indicate a mistrust of interpreters when they openly take on the 'mediator' or 'gatekeeper' role (cf. chapters 2 and 5), lose their impartiality and edit the utterances. Medical practitioners and lawyers alike agree that interpreters should interpret directly, accurately and impartially. This replicates Mesa's (2000) survey results, which found that doctors and patients valued accuracy and impartiality very highly.

With regards to interpreters' rights, lawyers had much more to say than medical practitioners, with only 33 per cent of lawyers not replying to this question, as compared to 60 per cent of doctors who said they did not know. A number of respondents from both groups mentioned issues relating to occupational health and safety, such as working under

Table 5.1   Question: Do you trust interpreters?

Respondent	Answer
10 (medic)	Generally. However, I speak seven languages and have often experienced unethical behaviour, coaching, putting interpretations after what was said.
17 (medic)	No. Some interpreters appear to carry on side-conversations separate to the direct purpose for which they are engaged.
18 (medic)	Some interpreters, yes. Some interpreters, no, usually obvious when they are making their own conversation/interpretation.
10 (lawyer)	Not entirely! Sometimes I have difficult legal concepts to explain and I am not sure the ideas are communicated.
16 (lawyer)	Yes, generally. Experience leads me to be aware that some interpreters are not entirely trustworthy. Sometimes it is blatantly apparent that an individual interpreter is not interpreting accurately, assisting beyond interpreting and/or imposing his/her own prejudices/values.
17 (lawyer)	Not always. There are some who 'add value', that is, purport to provide their own version of advice, rather than simply interpreting.
19 (lawyer)	No, not always. A lot of the time they seem to carry on an independent line of conversation. As a lawyer, there are important things I need to explain and I am not always confident my words are being directly translated.
21 (lawyer)	Generally yes, but sometimes interpreters may become partisan.

safe conditions. A number of others stated interpreters should simply have standard employees' rights. Although this may seem like a basic right, as most interpreters work on contract, most do not enjoy any of the entitlements of full-time permanent employees, such as holiday and sick leave. Many of the respondents stated interpreters had the right to be treated as professionals, with impartiality, civility, courtesy, respect and fairness, with one medical practitioner stating interpreters should be treated as professional peers and members of the team. This included valuing their professional judgement. A number of lawyers referred to interpreters' professional needs, such as having the right to ask for a break, to slow down or to have questions phrased in a clearer way. A number of lawyers also made reference to their own responsibility for clarity of language, which they saw as an interpreter's right: 'To have words or expressions that can be communicated, i.e. not use convoluted language' (Respondent 10). Lawyers and doctors both mentioned the interpreter's right to refuse work that is beyond their competence, to receive enough notice for the job, not to be placed in a compromising position and to be able to communicate their needs in order to perform their work effectively. Although not every respondent replied to this question, their answers were all valid and, if applied consistently, would help improve interpreters' conditions. The fact that 60 per cent of doctors and 33.3 per cent of lawyers could not think of anything to say on this indicates that most doctors, at least, are unaware of interpreters' professional needs.

With regards to the interpreter's responsibilities, only two lawyers and three medical practitioners did not reply. By far the most popular answer was to interpret accurately (76 per cent lawyers; 50 per cent doctors), with others adding impartiality, integrity and professionalism to the interpreter's responsibilities. Under this category, two medical practitioners made the following extra comments:

> To interpret accurately and not become 'emotionally' or 'culturally' involved with the family.
>
> (Respondent 14)

> Act professionally and *not* distort what you say or worse, the situation. Some interpreters become emotionally attached to patients and start advocating for them. This is inappropriate.
>
> (Respondent 17)

These answers argue strongly for interpreters to remain impartial and interpret accurately, supporting their obligations under the code of ethics. They show the doctors' frustration with past experiences of interpreters who act against the principles set out in the code. Yet, these doctors seem to do little to ensure that unethical interpreters are not given further work. They see the deficiencies of poor interpreting, but take no responsibility for improving it.

A number of lawyers qualified their requirement for accuracy by stating 'to the best of their ability' or 'as much as possible', showing awareness that full accuracy may not always be possible. A number stated that interpreters need to alert lawyers when interpreting problems arise, when miscommunication is perceived or when inconsistencies due to the interpreting process are possible. A number stressed that interpreters should not contribute their own advice or opinion.

After the obligation to be accurate, the responses related to being ethical and arriving on time, keeping the information confidential, being non-judgemental and patient. One medical practitioner expected interpreters to notify them of any cultural differences. Two of the responses demonstrated a lack of understanding of the interpreter's role by saying that the interpreter was responsible for ensuring that the patient understood the consultation, assigning the interpreter what is the doctor's responsibility.

Understanding of the meaning of accuracy The majority of medical practitioners expected interpreters to be accurate. This was supported by their answers on the meaning of accuracy, which reflected a correct understanding of it. Three-quarters (75 per cent) of respondents chose 'A translation which takes into account the whole discourse and reproduces the intention and the impact of the original' as signifying accuracy. Only 10 per cent believed accuracy meant interpreting each sentence, the meaning of which will remain the same regardless of context; 15 per cent believed accuracy to mean a word-for-word, literal translation. Interestingly, one of the respondents who chose this last answer claimed to be multilingual himself. This answer may be due to a misunderstanding of what 'literal' means. One of the respondents who chose this answer explained: 'I am a psychiatrist. The interpretation of muddled talk is part of the assessment' (Respondent 10). This statement supports what was argued in chapter 2, that the manner of speech is just as important as the content of the speech, in both the legal and medical contexts, and should be included in an accurate rendition. However, it does not support the concept of a verbatim, literal translation. It argues for interpreters to maintain the incoherence of the original in their rendition, rather than attempt to reconstruct the speech into a coherent, well-expressed statement. One doctor stated: 'Sometimes words don't translate, e.g. "depression" may not have a single word and must be described. I need to know this' (Respondent 11).

Lawyers' responses were slightly less consistent. A bare majority (57.14 per cent) of respondents chose 'A translation which takes into account the whole discourse and reproduces the intention and the impact of the original' as signifying accuracy. A considerable minority (28.6 per cent) believed accuracy meant interpreting literally, at the word level, and 19 per cent believed accuracy to mean interpreting at the sentence level. These results show that despite the fact that lawyers seem to be more aware of interpreters, of their qualification requirements and their rights and responsibilities, they do not have as good an understanding of the meaning of accuracy as doctors appear to have, according to this small sample. The insistence on a literal, verbatim translation said to be prevalent in the legal profession, is shared by only 28.6 per cent of the respondents in this sample.

The question on accuracy was related to two others (questions 13 and 14) which elaborated on specific examples of accuracy:

Q.13:   *If the interpreted version of your patient's/client's answer is incoherent and hesitant, do you think*:

a. It is your patient/client who speaks in that manner and the interpreter is accurately rendering the same manner?
b. It is the interpreter who is having trouble interpreting?

Q.14:   *If you ask a long, difficult and potentially confusing question, do you expect the interpreter to*:

a. Clarify, simplify and shorten your question?
b. Render your question in the other language accurately by maintaining the level of difficulty and potential confusion?
c. Tell you that s/he thinks your patient/client will not understand that question, to please rephrase it?
d. Tell your patient/client without your knowledge that they should ask you if they don't understand?

In response to question 13, a large majority (85.71 per cent) of lawyers and a smaller majority (70 per cent) of medical practitioners chose option a, being consistent with the high percentage who claimed to trust interpreters to interpret accurately and competently. However, some ticked both options, indicating that sometimes they may suspect the interpreter of being inaccurate. The way they form judgements on the issue of accuracy is not explained, but it may have to do with the previous answers on assessing competence. The interpreter's general appearance and conduct and the overall smoothness of the exchange may determine whether service providers suspect the interpreter of being inaccurate. This result is encouraging for interpreters. It may be of course that the interpreter is sometimes the culprit of the confusion and the incoherence. However, it is reassuring to see that the majority of respondents would trust interpreters to interpret faithfully.

In response to question 14, the answers were not as clear cut. What is clear from the answers is that most do not approve of interpreters holding private conversations with their patients or clients which exclude them from the exchange, evident in the fact that only one medical practitioner and no lawyer chose answer d: 'Tell your patient/client without your knowledge that they should ask you if they don't understand'. Interestingly, however, almost two-thirds (65 per cent) of doctors chose answer c: 'Tell you that s/he thinks your patient/client will not understand that question, to please rephrase it', with almost half (47.62 per cent) of lawyers choosing this answer. These service providers would like interpreters to tell them when they think the patient or client does not understand a question, rather than interpret the question accurately and wait for the patient or client to say if they do not understand. These results match Mesa's (2000), who found that medical practitioners expected interpreters to alert them to potential miscommunication. Consistent with this choice, only 20 per cent of doctors chose answer b: 'Render your question in the other language accurately by maintaining the level of difficulty and potential confusion'. However, a higher percentage (38.1 per cent) of lawyers chose this. It is the answer that falls under the ethical requirement of accuracy. A surprising 30 per cent of doctors chose answer a: 'Clarify, simplify and shorten your question', which goes against the concept of accuracy. Only 14.29 per cent of lawyers chose this. These answers contradict the responses elicited under question 13 and the previous ones which stated that the groups expected interpreters to interpret accurately. Under this question, considerably more doctors than lawyers showed a willingness to relinquish to the interpreter their responsibility for clarity and for ensuring that their patients understand them. Such inconsistency reveals confusion about their understanding of the role of the interpreter, confusion which presents a challenge for interpreters in attempting to please those for whom they interpret, while meeting their ethical obligations.

Understanding of the interpreter's role   When asked about what they considered to be the role of the interpreter, 87.71 per cent of lawyers and 60 per cent of doctors chose: 'To ensure all utterances are interpreted accurately from and into English, leaving the responsibility for clarity to you and your patient/client'. This seems to contradict what most answered for the question discussed above. Once again, a significant difference is found between lawyers' and doctors' understanding of the role. However, 33.3 per cent of lawyers and 40 per cent of doctors chose: 'To ensure that your patient/client clearly understands what you are trying to say by simplifying your words and expressions'. This indicates that some lawyers ticked both answers, being unsure of which was correct. Although a majority overall opted for the role as prescribed by the code of ethics, a significant minority chose the opposite, relinquishing their responsibility for effective communication and passing it to the interpreter. This confusion was also reflected in the way they addressed their patient or client: 30 per cent of doctors and 42.86 per cent of lawyers stated addressing their patient/client directly, in the first and second persons. The majority either used a mixture of forms or the third person alone. Consistent with this lack of a uniform understanding of the interpreter's role, 45 per cent of doctors and 38 per cent of lawyers claim to explain the interpreter's role at the outset to their patient or client. Some of the ways they explain their role are given in Table 5.2.

Table 5.2 Explanations of the interpreter's role provided by service providers

Respondent	Explanation of role
2 (medic)	To say exactly what I ask and reply with exactly what you say.
10 (medic)	I ask for direct interpretation. I often ask advice re cultural issues.
11 (medic)	This is an interpreter from the Health Care Interpreter Service who will assist with my assessment. The interview is confidential.
14 (medic)	The interpreter will translate information for us.
17 (medic)	I need to discuss complicated medical and health issues and I have requested an interpreter to ensure the content of our discussion is not impeded by a language barrier. The interpreter is there to translate directly what I am saying plus the response of the patient.
20 (medic)	The interpreter will repeat exactly what I say and exactly what you say. Please talk to the interpreter as if you were talking to me. The interpreter will keep all the information confidential, and will not disclose it to anybody except myself.
4 (lawyer)	To interpret what they say into English.
12 (lawyer)	That they are there to interpret, not to assist the client by making your story.
13 (lawyer)	That the interpreter is present to assist in the communication process.
16 (lawyer)	Exact translation of all said.
20 (lawyer)	Required for clarity of instructions and for their understanding of court.

All these responses show a basic understanding of the interpreter's role. However, when specific questions are put to these service providers about what an interpreter should or should not do, confusion and misunderstandings emerge. It would be unfair to expect service providers to have a sophisticated understanding of interpreting issues, as that is not their profession. It is not surprising, however, that such confusion exists among them, as there is parallel confusion also among practising interpreters, many of whom are neither accredited nor trained. If there was consistency among interpreters, more consistency could also be expected among the professionals they serve.

The practising interpreters' response

Five hundred questionnaires were sent to the home addresses of NAATI-accredited interpreters, or via the AUSIT e-bulletin, and 23 interpreters with a wide variety of language combinations responded. This, once again, was a very low response rate – 4.6 per cent – and much lower than that of the service providers. It indicates a lack of interest from the majority of practising interpreters in participating in research, and hence the sample may be positively biased as only those most interested responded. Cambridge's assessment may be an adequate explanation for this problem.

Quote 5.3   Interpreters' interest in research

The academic community seems to have a bit of a blind spot about the meaning of the word 'freelance'. It means a person without the support of an institution of any kind – no 'auspices', no library facilities and nobody paying for one's time let alone costs, when doing anything other than interpreting. These factors will necessarily depress any trend towards practitioners taking part in research or attending conferences.

(Cambridge, 2004: 50)

The high number (66.6 per cent) of trained interpreters in the sample is consistent with previous surveys. Trained interpreters tend to demonstrate greater interest in participating in research. The majority of inter-preters (83.3 per cent) held NAATI professional accreditation. Most of their responses were reported in chapters 4 and 5 when discussing perceptions of role and the code of ethics. The responses that will be reported and evaluated in this section relate to professional rights and responsibilities, usefulness of research to their practice and self-evaluation.

Interpreters' opinions on what constitute their rights and responsibilities
When asked about what they considered to be their rights, most interpreters provided more than one answer. The most popular answer (provided by 15 interpreters, or 65 per cent) related to being treated as a professional, as a peer and member of the team, with due respect and consideration. This was followed by adequate working conditions, which included appropriate breaks, drinking water and a separate waiting room (26 per cent). The next two most popular answers (17.4 per cent) indicated as a right being trusted by those around them and not questioned on their competence, and being briefed before the assignment in order to be adequately prepared. These were followed by appropriate remuneration and an understanding from the other participants of the interpreter's role and code of ethics (13 per cent). Other answers included having the right to refuse an assignment, having institutional support and being allowed to interpret what was said, which assumed other speakers' responsibility to speak clearly.

Interestingly, many of the rights expressed by interpreters were the same as those considered to be their rights by the service providers. These were: to be treated as professionals, with respect and consideration, to be provided with adequate working conditions, to be able to refuse an assignment and for speakers to speak clearly. The rights that were not recognised by service providers were: adequate remuneration, to be fully briefed and to have institutional support. When asked whether they believed these rights were met, their responses were mixed: 17.39 per cent answered 'no', 17.39 per cent answered 'yes', 30.43 per cent answered 'mostly yes', 13 per cent answered 'mostly no', 8.69 per cent answered 'yes and no', with the remaining 13.1 per cent not replying.

The interpreters who answered 'no' related their answers to low pay, lack of institutional support, poor working conditions, misunderstanding of their role, participants expecting them to perform tasks beyond their duty, not perceived as a professional and as a peer with needs, but more as a 'helper', and not considered a participant in the exchange.

Of those who answered 'yes', only two gave their reasons. One was a full-time employee of a government interpreter agency who enjoys the rights inherent in a permanent full-time position. The other interpreter provided a very interesting response:

> ## Quote 5.4
>
> Yes. I consider that the respect given to me is because of my own respect for myself in the first place, followed by my respect to my profession and last but by no means least, the respect by my clientele to me is a reciprocation of my respect for them.
>
> (Respondent 15)

The other answers provided instances when their rights were not observed. These included participants not understanding the interpreting process or the interpreter's role, with one interpreter commenting that such violations of rights are not deliberate. A number of interpreters said that they are generally respected by the other professionals but not by the non-English-speaking client/patient, by the 'lower-rung' service providers and by the booking clerks.

In general, most responses were positive regarding the treatment they received from other professionals. These results match the perceptions expressed by the service providers in the sample. This indicates that, for a good proportion, service providers treat interpreters adequately. The professionalism of the interpreter, as expressed in Quote 6.4, may have a strong influence on how interpreters are treated by the other participants in the exchange. Confident, competent interpreters inspire respect. It was interesting to read that it is often the non-English speaker and the lower-rung public servants that do not respect interpreters as professionals. Previous research (see Hale and Luzardo, 1997) found that non-English speakers often misunderstand or are unaware of the interpreter's role, causing a dilemma for interpreters who wish to abide by their code of ethics.

It is also apparent that the underlying issues include poor working conditions, low remuneration and the absence of compulsory pre-service training. These are factors over which the participants of the exchange have little control.

In answer to what the interpreter's responsibilities are, all the responses mentioned performing professionally by abiding by the code of ethics, with special mention of the need to maintain accuracy, impartiality and confidentiality, to interpret to the best of their ability and to update their knowledge and skills. In relation to this last answer, some mentioned professional development courses, others glossaries, and one mentioned updating their knowledge and skills 'through reading the results of research and other publications in the field, attending conferences and other PD events ... ' (Respondent 4).

Interpreters' perceptions of the usefulness of research When asked whether the results of research could help them to improve their practice, an overwhelming 94.12 per cent said 'yes'. They were then asked what questions they considered should be addressed by research, to which they provided the impressive list outlined in Table 5.3.

Interestingly, the proposed research questions fall under the categories of interpreter challenges as explained in Figure 5.1: Interpreting-related issues, context-related issues and participant-related issues. A number

Table 5.3 Questions interpreters consider should be addressed by research

Respondent	Research questions
1	Expectations and intentions of parties to liaison interpreting. Understanding on behalf of professionals on working with interpreters. Variations in practice around the world in different settings.
2	Outcomes of minority language speaker experiences with and without interpreters. Practical issues: access to interpreters, competencies of interpreters in various settings.
3	Countless. Empirical definition and examination of the notion of 'complexity' for example. Division of that into different types of attributes of speech (ellipsis, anaphora, length of utterance, lexical density, frequency of conditional clauses, etc.). Articulation of the causes of prominent relationships between certain attributes and the problems they cause, elimination of other causes such as those arising out of setting, attitudes of others present, etc. Developing practical and specific types of training to counteract these things.
4	How to optimise *chuchotage* during court hearings and other legal conferences so that the NES [non-English speaker] is in the same position as if she or he spoke English.
5	On the problem of changing dialects within one language, as in the case of standard Arabic and its many dialects.
6	Compliance with the code of ethics and uniformity by all practitioners. Take account of complaints and suggestions from service providers and non-English speakers about interpreting performance.
7	Perceptions and expectations of service users. How to improve the two-way communication.

Table 5.3   (Continued)

Respondent	Research questions
8	I think this questionnaire is a good start. If nothing else, it's made me really think again about what is involved in my work and just how supportive and even comforting the code of ethics is to me.
9	You know better than I!
10	How can interpreters achieve pragmatic equivalence in interpreting.
11	How to elevate awareness of the true role of the interpreter.
12	A comparison of the performance of trained and untrained interpreters.
13	Cognitive studies on the process of interpreting. Interpreter training, including note-taking and memory training.
16	In the legal and medical contexts in particular – exploration of the possibility and then effect of training for professionals working with interpreters. Expectations of clients. Understanding of the impact and implications of a 'third person'.
17	How to improve the whole image of this interpreter business/industry.
21	How can an interpreter interpret for a professional who does not speak English (because she or he has not learnt English well in the first place) and a 'client' who has been in Australia for 40 years and forgot how to speak Portuguese.

of the questions have been addressed in this book, others are suggested for further research in chapter 8. The suggestions from interpreters are very valid, practical suggestions, and demonstrate a desire to learn and improve. Respondent 8 comments on the usefulness of the questionnaire as a means to reflect on performance.

Interpreters' means of self-evaluation   An overwhelming number (90.5 per cent) of respondents stated they regularly perform self-evaluation of their performance. The majority said they did this by going over their assignments in their minds after completion to see if there is anything that caused them problems for which they need to be better prepared next time, or need to seek advice from colleagues or from their employer. Some mentioned discussing difficult situations with their peers, always maintaining confidentiality. One respondent stated talking to student observers or peer observers to provide feedback. Respondent 6 reflected on 'the smooth flow of the conversation' as a form of evaluation, which matches the most common method of evaluating competence used by lawyers and medical practitioners.

The survey asked interpreters if they based their practice on any theory of Interpreting and whether they would be able to substantiate their choices if asked to do so. Not many replied to this question, which reflects a lack of awareness of the theories or of their relevance to the practice. The ones who did respond indicated that they relied on the theories of Interpreting and linguistics learned in class, especially mentioning Pragmatics and the main Interpreting studies authors. Others claimed to rely on the code of ethics. Their responses on substantiating their choices were very similar, referring to the same theories and the code of ethics, with some adding references such as dictionaries and other publications as useful resources.

5.2.4 System-related issues

Many of the issues faced by community interpreters arise from problems within the system, which are mostly interconnected. Poor remuneration, which is a major complaint from practising interpreters, is linked to a lack of recognition of Community Interpreting as a highly skilled profession, which in turn is reflected in the non-compulsory nature of pre-service formal university training. As training is not compulsory, the demand for such courses is low, leading to a shortage of supply. The absence of any formal requirements for interpreters to practise means many jobs that should be performed by professional interpreters are performed by family members or other volunteers, reinforcing poor institutional support. If services can be acquired at no cost to the institution, there is no incentive to provide any support. The issue of quality of services does not seem to be considered by the system as a strong enough reason to promote change. As Morris says, the system's attitude needs to change.

Quote 5.5 System-related issues

As long as the system's *attitude* to the employment of interpreters remains unchanged, the consequences of ignorance about the interpreting process will similarly remain with us – and those who should benefit from quality interpreting will instead suffer from the substandard product they are offered, whether for lack of competent interpreters or because of the unsatisfactory conditions in which

---

Quote 5.5 (Continued)

interpreting is provided. If judges can only 'call attention' to a parlous state of affairs, who will take steps to correct it?

(Morris, 2000: 246)

The question of whose responsibility it is to remedy the situation remains unanswered. Arguably, it is the responsibility of all those involved: the interpreters themselves, the service providers and the service recipients to put pressure on policy-makers to instigate the necessary changes. Interpreters alone cannot be expected to take on the full burden. If quality is to be ensured, compulsory formal training needs to be prescribed, commensurate remuneration guaranteed and adequate working conditions provided. Research can do much to describe and highlight the issues, demonstrate the needs for training, provide useful information for the improvement of interpreters' performance; but it needs to be read and considered seriously by the interested parties in order to have any effect.

5.3 Conclusion

This chapter has outlined the main issues and challenges faced by community interpreters. These were divided into four categories: Interpreting-related issues, context-related issues, participant-related issues and system-related issues. The chapter concentrated on presenting the real voices of two of the participants – the service providers and the interpreters – in the interaction to highlight their views, perceptions and general ideas about the work of the interpreter, through the analysis of a survey. The other participant – the service recipient – is noticeably missing. Very little research has been done to access their voices, with few exceptions (Hale and Luzardo, 1997; Tellechea Sánchez, 2005). More research is needed to fill this gap. It was finally noted that in order for real changes to occur, all participants need to take responsibility for the system to implement improvements. Such improvements relate to compulsory training and accreditation, commensurate professional remuneration and adequate working conditions.

6
Community Interpreting Training

This chapter:

- Discusses the main issues surrounding Community Interpreting education and training.
- Briefly outlines the different types of courses.
- Reports on the voices of a group of Community Interpreting educators.
- Outlines the most widely shared curriculum contents and teaching methodologies.
- Argues for a discourse-based approach to training.
- Proposes an integrated training framework.

6.1 Introduction

Training[1] is probably one of the most complicated and problematic aspects of Community Interpreting. The many issues surrounding training can be divided into four broad areas:

1. lack of recognition for the need for training;
2. absence of a compulsory pre-service training requirement for practising interpreters;
3. shortage of adequate training programmes; and
4. quality and effectiveness of the training.

All four broad areas are inextricably connected. If the need for training is not recognised, compulsory training will never be enforced. If training is not compulsory, the demand for courses will be limited, hence reducing their availability. If courses are few in number and short in duration, their contents will be compromised, impinging on their quality. This in turn affects their effectiveness in improving practice, thus reinforcing the fallacy that training is not essential.

6.2   Lack of recognition for the need for training

Quote 6.1   Lack of understanding of the complexity of interpreting

The lack of understanding of the nature of bilingualism and the variation in linguistic forms leads to non-appreciation of the skills involved in interpreting. Consequently, there is a lack of recognition of the need for training in these skills which, in turn, leads to unreal expectations of lay bilingual people as interpreters.

(Barnett, 1989: 97)

The lack of understanding highlighted by Barnett can be found in all parties involved in interpreted encounters: service providers, their clients and untrained, ad hoc interpreters. Service providers who do not understand the complexity of interpreting will rely on volunteer bilinguals to interpret for them and expect accurate renditions. As Valero Garcés states: 'if someone speaks two languages, it is still widely believed that he/she must be able to translate and interpret... this misconception is further perpetuated by the overriding need to assist people immediately, making qualifications a secondary consideration...' (2003b: 182).

Bilingual volunteers who 'help' as ad hoc interpreters often do not realise that there is more to interpreting than simply offering to each party a summary of what they understand. This attitude is anecdotally confirmed by students on Interpreting courses who had previously acted as 'natural interpreters', to borrow Harris's (1977) term. They often comment that they were ignorant of the complexity of the task before commencing the course, assuming that all they needed to acquire from a course was specialised terminology (see Schweda Nicholson, 1994; Ko, 1995). It is not until students are made aware of the many issues surrounding accurate interpreting and are trained in how to interpret accurately that their practices change from those inspired by intuition and natural inclination to those based on informed choices and trained skills. It is also common to find negative attitudes towards training among experienced practising interpreters who are accredited but untrained. NAATI's proposal to introduce compulsory professional development for practising interpreters to maintain their accreditation has revealed a strong division among those who are vehemently opposed to training and those who are strongly in favour of it.[2] Those practising interpreters who oppose training either feel that there is nothing further for them to learn or that the poor remuneration and working conditions do not warrant the investment of money, time and effort on their part to train to improve their skills, knowledge and performance.

Those who are the recipients of the services do not appreciate the difficulties associated with interpreting, evidenced in the fact that they will often ask a child or a friend to act as their interpreter. In a survey of non-English-speaking users of interpreting services, Hale and Luzardo (1997) discovered that although more than three-quarters (78 per cent) of the respondents believed interpreters should be university trained, 18 per cent thought they did not need any training at all, and when asked about whose services they normally used, 69.9 per cent stated calling a professional. Of the 27.7 per cent who said they would take a friend or a relative, the reasons they gave included being there when you need them, knowing you and your background, providing advice and support, or simply the fact that they had always used a relative or friend. The admissibility of these ad hoc volunteers attests to the perception that they can adequately perform the duties assigned to them, even if most believe a professional would do a better job.

Another obstacle is lack of financial support. Institutions' frequent need to cut costs often means that funds will not be allocated for the provision of professionally trained interpreters, as they are not perceived to be necessary.

Quote 6.2 Poor institutional monetary support for interpreting services

With public-sector institutions often unable, or unwilling, to pay for professional interpreting services, there are few incentives for engaging or investing in higher-level training. Indeed, little training for interpreters working in community settings is offered at an academic level. This lag in the academization of the profession is one of the crucial differences between conference and community interpreting, and has profound implications for the development of research.

(Pöchhacker, 2004a: 30)

Pöchhacker (2004a) attributes many of the problems associated with training to lack of financial support. Low pay cannot give aspiring practitioners the incentive to commit to long, formal, specialist education. The low demand for such courses in turn cannot support the running of formal degrees by universities. Although shorter, informal courses are an alternative, the unavailability of academic degrees impacts on the development of research in Community Interpreting, which in turn impacts on the quality of training and eventually the practice. It is against this generally apathetic attitude towards training that those who believe in its essential role must battle.

6.3   The need for compulsory pre-service training

Compulsory pre-service training in Community Interpreting is far from being a reality anywhere in the world (see Niska, 2005). The main reasons, as stated in section 6.2, are a lack of recognition for the need for training and a lack of financial support and incentives. This situation has led to a lack of uniformity in interpreters' backgrounds and consequent deficiencies in their practice. As Laster and Taylor (1994) comment, it would be unfair to blame interpreters for their shortcomings, when it is the system itself that allows them to practise without any formal training or uniform testing.

Quote 6.3   Lack of uniformity in the entry to the profession

Many of the deficiencies blamed on individual interpreters, now and in the past, are the result of systemic problems, such as the lack of uniform education and testing to promote high levels of technical competence.

(Laster and Taylor, 1994: 14)

There are a number of reasons behind the need for compulsory training. The most important is that of equipping community interpreters to provide quality services, in order to avoid the potential negative consequences associated with incompetent interpreting (highlighted in chapters 2 and 3). Bowen and Kaufert (2003) argue that the fundamental reason for providing trained interpreters is to ensure the basic right to equitable services to those who do not speak the language of the host country. Gile also comments that when community interpreters are forced to learn on the job, mistakes are inevitable, and the price to pay for the parties involved, and in particular for individuals in crisis who need them, can be very high, perhaps too high. It seems obvious that some sort of training is highly desirable in most settings and indispensable in others, in particular in court settings. (Gile, forthcoming)

Erasmus goes as far as to suggest that the use of untrained, unprofessional, ad hoc interpreters 'often creates more problems than it solves' (2000: 199).

Training also has a social function. As Gentile and colleagues comment, 'a major catalyst of professional socialization is a course of training which qualifies graduates for entry into the profession' (Gentile et al., 1996: 69). Gile (1995) agrees. It will be difficult for the status of Community Interpreting to advance in the absence of compulsory formal training. Other professionals who work with interpreters, who have been required to acquire professional qualifications in order to practise, understandably tend not to treat interpreters as equals. Corsellis agrees that 'linguists working in the public services should become regulated professionals, like their colleagues in other public service disciplines such as doctors, lawyers or nurses and for the same reasons' (2005: 154). As Pöchhacker comments, 'the high status enjoyed by conference interpreters since the 1950s is largely due to a strong market (with financially potent institutional clients) and university-level training' (2004a: 30). The low status of Community Interpreting as a profession leads to a poor sense of professional identity. When interpreters are insecure about their professional status and competence they tend to undermine their work as interpreters and attempt to take on roles they consider to be more important, such as acting as pseudo-welfare workers, health workers or para-legals (see Hale, 2005 for a full discussion on the interpreter's identity crisis). Moeketsi and Wallmach, in an article which describes the BA in Court Interpreting offered by the University of South Africa, state that 'when conceptualising the type of training program needed for court interpreters, one of the primary motivators was the need for personal development and empowerment, and not only for training in interpreting skills' (2005: 80).

6.4 Community Interpreting courses

As pre-service training is not compulsory, courses in Community Interpreting vary significantly in terms of scope, duration and focus. Some are generalist courses, some include translation, others specialise in legal or medical interpreting, others combine as many specialisations as the course time will permit. Some courses receive funding for a one-off delivery to train a group of interpreters quickly to cater for a specific need, but for which there is no continuity or consistency (see Straker and Watts, 2003; Foley, 2006). Others are permanent, offered by tertiary institutions as part of their syllabus of regular courses.[3]

Community Interpreting courses range from the very short orientation courses (approximately 20 hours) run by employers such as hospitals; to longer, more structured courses offered by colleges (approximately 60 hours); to single elective subjects which can be undertaken at universities as non-award courses (approximately 60 hours); to full degree courses at both undergraduate and postgraduate levels (1–4 years' duration) (cf. Niska, 2005; and see list of courses in chapter 9). The shortest courses tend to be non-language-specific, covering only issues relating to ethics and role. Longer courses include language-specific practical classes where students are exposed to simulated situations. University courses include theory and practice.[4]

Sandrelli (2001) distinguishes between professional and basic training, arguing that professional training courses are normally run by non-academic institutions, with the participation of other professionals who work with interpreters in the field, local authorities and practising interpreters. On the other hand, she describes basic training in Community Interpreting as the type offered by academic institutions as an elective subject in another course or as a preparatory subject for the perceived more complex skills required for Conference Interpreting. Although most Community Interpreting courses in Europe seem to fall under either of these two categories, this may not always be the case, especially in other parts of the world. Some formal university degree courses combine the practical with the theoretical and graduate professional community interpreters, some with external accreditation or certification (see Niska, 2005, and the list of courses in chapter 9).[5]

Unfortunately, the majority of Community Interpreting courses are of short duration and superficial. When writing about the situation of Community Interpreting training in Spain, Taibi and Martin lament that 'the training time is not enough for theoretical issues ... and practical skills ... to be dealt with adequately. This, in turn, reflects the lack of awareness in Spain regarding the need for Public Service Translation and Interpreting and, indeed, its very existence as a specialized professional activity' (2006: 94). Benmaman, in speaking of court interpreting training in the United States, agrees that short, informal courses are only 'stop-gap measures', and that 'more permanent and comprehensive solutions' are needed to address the educational needs of interpreters (Benmaman, 1999: 112). Short, superficial courses may even be counterproductive, creating a sense of complacency in governments and policy-makers who may be led to believe that such courses are sufficient to ensure quality in interpreting services.

6.5   Challenges faced by course designers and educators

The main challenges faced by course organisers relate to three key areas: recruiting suitably qualified teaching staff; attracting students with adequate bilingual and bicultural competence; and deciding on the most relevant course content and most efficient teaching methodologies (Valero Garcés, 2003b; Niska, 2005; Taibi and Martin, 2006). Until the discipline becomes established, it is difficult to find staff with the relevant academic and research background, and even when such a pool of highly qualified teachers exists, the ever-changing nature of migration trends makes it difficult to find staff with competence in the new language(s) of need.

Ensuring that the students have the bilingual and bicultural competence needed to become community interpreters can also be a challenge. On the one hand, those with adequate bilingual skills in the well-established languages may not be attracted to the profession, given the poor remuneration, limited work opportunities and unfavourable working conditions. On the other, those who speak the rarer languages, which may be in higher demand, may not be fully competent in the language of the host community.

These two obstacles impinge on the content and effectiveness of the courses. Time constraints and limited resources lead to compromises in the curricula. No course can claim to cover all the areas necessary to train students adequately for the complex task of Community Interpreting. The duration of the course will determine how much it can cover. Therefore, course designers are always forced to prioritise when choosing what to include. Prioritising, however, is difficult in the absence of any research to guide such decisions. Section 6.5.1 presents the views of a group of educators regarding the main challenges in teaching potential community interpreters.

6.5.1   The educators' voices

Six[6] Community Interpreting educators participated in a focus group discussion. Two have professional and teaching experience from Spain, the other four gained their experience in Australia. The language combinations of the educators are Arabic–English, Arabic–Spanish, Chinese–English and Spanish–English. Some of the educators are full-time academics and part-time interpreters, others are full-time interpreters and part-time trainers. This difference in background produced differences in some of the answers, in particular those that related to the usefulness of research. Table 6.1 provides the personal information of each of the respondents.

The participants were asked to discuss the main challenges they faced as Community Interpreting educators. They all agreed on the lack of teaching materials and textbooks to guide them, time limitations and the students' mixed bilingual and bicultural competence as major challenges. A number of related questions were also posed in the course of the discussion.

With regards to teaching materials and textbooks, they commented that as this is a new field, it was difficult to find adequate resources, especially in some rarer language combinations, such as Arabic–Spanish. For this reason, they had to create their own teaching materials, mostly

Table 6.1 Participants' profiles

Respondent #	Language combination	Qualifications	Experience as Community Interpreter	Experience as Community Interpreting educator
1	Spanish–English	BA in Translation, Postgrad. Dip. in Translation, PhD candidate (topic on Community Interpreting)	3 years	2 years
2	Spanish–English	BA, Grad. Dip. Int. & Trans., MA Int. & Trans., NAATI I&T	5 years	3 years
3	Arabic–English	BA in Int. & Trans., PhD in Translation, NAATI I&T	16 years	14 years
4	Arabic–Spanish	BA in English Linguistics, PhD	10 years	5 years
5	Chinese–English	BA, BEd., Dip. Trans. & Int., MA in Trans., M.I.L, TESOL, NAATI I&T	13 years	5 years
6	Chinese–English	BA, Grad.Dip. Int. & Trans.	16 years	9 years

based on their professional experience. They found that even bilingual dictionaries were not always adequate in providing terminological equivalents for vocabulary that is very specific to the Community Interpreting context. One challenge that was highlighted about preparing materials was the difficulty in replicating a spontaneous, real-life situation for students to practise in class. One respondent commented:

> Even when you find materials, I feel they are not appropriate, because they are based on written dialogues. To me, to teach Community Interpreting is to make it as real as possible for the students, that means choosing the right topics, simulating the situation as closely as possible to the real situation, so when we do interpreting exercises based on written materials, in my opinion you're doing something out of context, because it's not the same interpreting spontaneous speech. (Respondent 4)

Although they all attempt to simulate real-life situations as much as possible, it is not easy to achieve. They agreed that every method has its positive and negative points, hence the best option is to use a variety of methods. Scripted dialogues are useful for controlling content, grammatical structures and vocabulary, but unless they contain features of spoken discourse and are well acted out, they will sound stilted and artificial. On the other hand, unscripted dialogues, where actors are provided with a scenario to improvise, can be useful for spontaneity but may lack depth of content and richness of language. Respondent 1 suggested the participation of service providers in classroom role-plays to provide authentic practical experience for both students and providers. (See Ko, 1995, for a discussion on different methods used to teach dialogue interpreting.)

The group members were then asked to comment on what they based their teaching on, considering there is limited published material. This elicited some interesting responses. Their background very much affected their approach to teaching. All agreed that their practical experience was crucial in being able to teach Community Interpreting. However, when considering the usefulness of theory and research, their responses differed. The two full-time practitioners stated that they did not base their teaching on research results much or even at all, although they drew on some theoretical principles. Being full-time practitioners and part-time trainers, they said they did not have the time to conduct research themselves or to read the results of research conducted by others. Most importantly, they did not seem to perceive its usefulness. Respondent 5 said, 'I think the teaching of Community Interpreting should be more focused on actual practice', and Respondent 6 said, 'I don't base my teaching on research at all'. In contrast, another full-time practitioner and part-time trainer, who is a recent graduate, responded very differently:

Quote 6.4   What do you base your teaching on?

I base my teaching on how I was taught and what I considered was effective for me as a student. I also base it on my practice and on the theory. The theory is based on what I learned in my studies, especially theories of pragmatics and discourse analysis, and on the results of published research. I now go back to what I learned as a student with a much deeper understanding of it, which means I can apply it to my practice and my teaching in a much more meaningful way. The more I understand the theory and the practice, the more I can give to my students. It's incremental. My understanding of these issues increases the more I read and the more I practice.

(Respondent 2)

This insightful response demonstrates an ideal situation of an interpreter who received pre-service training where she acquired not only the practical skills but also the theoretical underpinnings to guide her practice. She was also equipped with the tools to continue to learn and develop. Unlike other educators in the group who were pioneers in the training of community interpreters, this respondent had experience as a student of Community Interpreting and was able to assess from a student's point of view, and later from a practitioner's point of view, what were/were not successful teaching strategies and methodologies. By applying successful teaching practices and introducing new ones, she is able to improve on what has been done before.

Respondents 1 and 4 gained their experience in Spain where the field is new. Consequently, they have had to be pioneers in the training of Community Interpreting. Both expressed the view that they had seen a gradual development and evolution in their teaching, which was enriched by their increased knowledge of the literature in the field as well as by their own research.

Quotes 6.5   Evolution of teaching styles

Respondent 4
Yes, well, of course if I compare my teaching during my first year of teaching in 2002 with my teaching last year, you will find a big difference, because there has been some interaction with my past professional experience and literature

and research I've been reading. As a lecturer, I need to keep in touch with the literature and continue learning from new research. There are things you agree with and incorporate and others that you don't find convincing but at least you become aware of them.

Respondent 1
In my case there was a kind of evolution because I started teaching based on my own experience, but then I started reading about register and these kinds of things and to change my practice and what I taught. So the more you read the better you are able to teach, for example the results of your research, the different codes of ethics, and then you're able to see the difference. I can say there was an evolution after reading and doing some research.

Respondent 3, who is the most experienced trainer and one of the most experienced interpreters, stated that he bases his teaching on his experience, theoretical principles and research, but qualifies this:

> ... although, theoretically speaking, we have a long way to go before the settings of Community Interpreting are covered, even marginally. Although the notion of accuracy has been adequately covered in the literature, particularly in the legal and medical fields, areas that affect the very notions of accuracy are still in their fledgling stage. Therefore I find experience quite helpful.

From these responses, we can see that cross-fertilisation takes place between the practice, research and training in the teaching of the academic trainers, whereas this is lacking in the teaching of the practitioner trainers. In most courses, theoretical subjects are taught as plenary lectures to all students by academics, whereas practical tutorials are given by practitioners. However, there needs to be a link between the theory and the practice. For example, different theoretical understandings of the meaning of terms such as accuracy or equivalence will impinge on the way educators teach and assess students.

The participants were asked to comment on the approaches they adopted in assessing students' performance. Respondent 6, who is one of the full-time practitioners, relies heavily on the NAATI assessment guidelines, which are very general in nature. The interpretation of these guidelines differs according to the background and understanding of each assessor. Respondent 4 relies on his academic background in discourse analysis. Interestingly, his statement coincides with the discussion on accuracy presented in chapters 1–3. Respondent 1 agrees with

Respondent 4 and states that due to her lack of professional experience, she has had to rely on what has been written about Community Interpreting by experienced interpreters, educators and researchers. This contrasts with the statement by Respondent 3, who comments that his practice compensates for the gaps in the theory.

Quotes 6.6   On assessment and notions of accuracy

Question: On what do you base your assessment judgements?
Respondent 6: On my own experience as an interpreter and the NAATI guidelines – for example, on accuracy, unjustified omissions, unidiomatic expressions, grammatical errors.

Question: How do you decide what's an unjustified omission, for example?
Respondent 6: If it doesn't affect the meaning and the understanding of the utterance. If it does, then it's a major error.
Respondent 4: In my case, of course, I think everybody takes their background as a starting point. In my case I had specialised in linguistics, especially in fields related to pragmatics and discourse analysis, so that had an important role in defining how to proceed with assessment. Firstly, I'd make a clear distinction between institutional contexts, so for me, there are differences between health care situations or interviews, and legal proceedings, and that difference leads you as a result to establish differences in assessment. So accuracy is understood in a stricter sense in the courtroom than in medical or welfare settings. I don't mean in the case, for example, of interpreting breast cancer for lung cancer, this is as important in the health context as the legal, as the consequences would be as disastrous. What I mean is that interaction in some contexts, such as health care and welfare settings, tends to be more cooperative than in others and, therefore, both the user and the interpreter are given more interactional freedom than, say, in court or police settings. The most important aspect I take into consideration when assessing accuracy is the pragmatic impact, the pragmatic effect in the situation. Accuracy doesn't mean word for word.
Respondent 1: As someone with limited experience as a community interpreter, to me it was important to read the theoretical framework used by scholars from other countries.

The second most common challenge expressed by all was time limitations. This impinged on the way they taught and on the content of the course. Lack of time was a constant source of frustration for these educators, who felt that their students never received enough practice, individual attention, feedback or information to become competent community interpreters.

Quotes 6.7   On time limitations

Respondent 2: There isn't enough time to develop the skills. Students are just beginning to master some of the skills by the time semester is finished. Unfortunately, they don't practise at home, which is what they should be doing.

Respondent 3: Potential settings of Community Interpreting can hardly be touched upon or covered at any length given the time constraints linked to funding and course viability.

Respondent 4: To be honest, before starting teaching in this field I had been working as an English teacher so I had some experience in teaching and tried to adapt that experience to the new context, knowing the situation, the needs of the students and what's expected in order to be a competent interpreter, at the same time being aware of time limitations –aware that 60 hours wasn't enough for a student who had no previous background in the field of Community Interpreting to be able to be a professional interpreter. Of course, we just took it as a kind of basic or introductory course to help the students apply the most basic skills and make them aware of the context in which they were going to work. Given the limitations, our teaching methodology was not very developed, it was a kind of methodology that tried to be as practical as possible considering the time limitations.

The group agreed that due to the complexity of the practice of Community Interpreting, it would be unrealistic to expect any one course to provide students with all the knowledge, skills and competencies needed to become a good interpreter. However, they agreed that training for all community interpreters should be compulsory. Ideally, students would come to the course with excellent bilingual and bicultural competence and a wide general knowledge. They would complete a BA degree first, which would provide them with the theoretical background in interpreting and in linguistics, and then complete postgraduate courses in the different specialisations, such as medical, legal, social welfare or business, to name a few. Alternatively, professionals in those fields with good bilingual skills could train as interpreters at postgraduate level. Failing the ideal, the participants stated that prioritising was necessary in deciding what should be included in the curricula. Dealing with this reality was a source of great frustration to all of them, as they were never sure if they were prioritising correctly. For example, a couple of respondents said that one major challenge was the disparity in the backgrounds, abilities and linguistic competence of the students in the same class. In such a situation it is difficult to cater to every student's needs, and prioritising will be determined by the lowest common denominator, at the risk of wasting the more capable students' time. Respondent 4 stated that he starts teaching the 'basic interpreting skills, to enable them to interpret messages faithfully. Faithfully to me means to maintain the same pragmatic effect.' However, the dilemma is that in order for them to learn to interpret faithfully by maintaining the same pragmatic effect, they need to understand what this means, which requires the teaching of pragmatics. It also requires many skills other than interpreting skills, which they may not possess and may not be able to acquire in a short course. Similarly, when speaking of accuracy, an interesting discussion ensued. The academics in the group viewed accuracy in terms of pragmatic effect and considered features such as hesitations, false starts, discourse markers and register as important aspects to be included when teaching about accuracy. However, due to time limitations, some stated that they did not have time to discuss these features in any detail:

> [H]esitations, register, false starts are all very important, but due to the lack of time, we can't dedicate much time to these things but try to make students aware of the importance of these features. We've had the challenge of having students who come from different backgrounds and have different levels of language competence and interpreting skills, so we had to establish priorities. For example if the student had difficulties with the language or with the basic accuracy of a message, we'd start with that, and leave issues such as register, to the end. (Respondent 4)

In contrast, Respondent 1 said: 'In my case this is something I introduce right from the very beginning, so they get used to it.'

These comments raise the question of when it is best to introduce the most advanced aspects of discourse in the practice of accurate interpreting. According to one of the educators, students need to master the most basic skills first and be able to render the propositional content before being expected to match register and style. The other educator takes the opposite approach, introducing these aspects at the beginning so that students make these features an integral part of their skills development practice. Research into the most effective ways of teaching accurate interpreting would be of great use to educators. Section 6.6 describes the most common content and methodologies of Community Interpreting courses and suggest some innovative practices.

6.6   Content and methodologies of Community Interpreting courses

Box 6.1 presents a summary of the numerous competencies and background knowledge that are commonly deemed necessary for community interpreters. Their number and complexity explain the reason why most of these subject areas and skills can only ever be covered superficially in the curricula of most courses.

Box 6.1   Recognised required knowledge and competencies for community interpreters[7]

1. Knowledge of professional issues: a clear knowledge of the role and ethical requirements of community interpreters (Dueñas Gonzalez et al., 1991; de Jongh, 1992; Edwards, 1995; Mikkelson, 1996).
2. Advanced language competence: advanced bilingual grammatical, semantic and pragmatic competence. Such advanced competence includes a mastery of different registers in both languages, the ability to understand different regional varieties, colloquialisms, idioms and slang; a wide mastery of general and specialised terminology; and adequate pronunciation in both languages (Dueñas Gonzalez et al., 1991; de Jongh, 1992; Colin and Morris, 1996; Benmaman, 1997; Nimrod and Fu, 1997; Hertog and Reunbrouck, 1999).
3. Excellent listening and comprehension skills: the ability to listen actively and analyse text simultaneously in order to comprehend its full meaning and intent. This is a very complex skill, as it depends on many other factors. Chapter 1 discusses these skills in the context of the interpreting process (Giovannini, 1993; Hale and Gibbons, 1999; Sandrelli, 2001; Hale, 2004).
4. Excellent memory skills: good short- and long-term memory (Dueñas Gonzalez et al., 1991; Dunnigan and Downing, 1995; Ginori and Scimone, 1995).
5. Adequate public speaking skills: the ability to speak clearly and audibly in public (Colin and Morris 1996; Hertog and Reunbrouck 1999).
6. Adequate note-taking skills: knowing when and how to take notes to aid memory and ensure completeness (Ginori and Scimone, 1995; Sandrelli, 2001).
7. Advanced interpreting skills: these include short and long consecutive interpreting, simultaneous interpreting and sight translation (Laster and Taylor, 1994; Emerson Crooker, 1996; Gentile et al., 1996).
8. Good management skills: the ability to assess when it is necessary to intervene and how to do it; the ability to coordinate and control the interpreted situation (Gentile et al., 1996; Nimrod and Fu, 1997; Hertog and Reunbrouck, 1999; Sandrelli, 2001).

Box 6.1   (Continued)

9. A knowledge of the context and subject matter: background knowledge of the different settings and main topic areas (Colin and Morris, 1996; Gentile et al., 1996; Benmaman, 1997; Hertog and Reunbrouck, 1999; Sandrelli, 2001).
10. An understanding of the goals of the institutions where the interpreting is taking place, as well as of their discoursal practices (Berk-Seligson, 1990/2002; Roy et al., 1998; Hale, 2004).
11. Cross-cultural awareness (Gentile et al., 1996; Sandrelli, 2001; Chesher et al., 2003).
12. A knowledge of the theories that underpin the practice: knowledge of linguistics, sociolinguistics, pragmatics, discourse analysis, translation theory (Wadensjö, 1992; Hale, 1996; Fowler, 1997; Roy et al., 1998; Petersen, 2000).

The depth with which each of the areas presented in Box 6.1 is covered is determined by the length of the course. As most courses are short, the content is limited in scope and depth, which brings into question their validity and general effectiveness. Research into the optimum length and content of training courses in Community Interpreting would be useful in guiding course developers on how to use limited resources in the most effective way.

The methodologies used in teaching the required areas of competence for Community Interpreting are shared by most interpreting trainers. Table 6.2 presents a summary of the most commonly used methodologies.

The above areas of knowledge and skills are crucial elements in any Community Interpreting course. However, teaching these areas will not be effective if it is not underpinned by a theory of interpreting or informed by the results of research. Roy (2000b: 2) agrees that successful teachers are 'those who base their teaching strategies on theory and research'. Applying theoretical principles in the teaching of the practical skills is essential if students are to understand the reasons why their choices are being assessed as appropriate or inappropriate. The absence of a theoretical basis leads to educators arbitrarily assessing students based on no apparent reason other than their individual choice at the time. Such a teaching style will lead to students' inevitable reliance on the teacher's constant feedback for each rendition. As course time is limited and the main objective of training is to equip students to become independent professionals in the workplace, it becomes clear that such

Table 6.2 Relevant methodologies used to teach Community Interpreting competencies

Area of competence	Methodology	Materials
Language consolidation	Reading, summarising and paraphrasing texts	Material relating to relevant subject matter
Terminology development	• Extracting terminology from different types of texts • Discussing definitions in context • Creating term banks • Providing definitions and asking students to provide the specialist terms • Discussing dialectal differences, especially in languages spoken by different speech communities	• Authentic texts • Transcripts • Background materials • Cloze tests
Memory development	Verbatim repetition of segments in the same language, increasing the length of the utterance gradually	Scripted or unscripted dialogues
Comprehension	• Summarising written texts • Summarising spoken texts • Paraphrasing spoken texts • Answering aural comprehension questions • Answering written comprehension questions • Following oral instructions	Material relating to relevant subject matter
Note-taking	• Teaching note-taking conventions[8] • Having students read a text and create notes for each paragraph	Written texts from a variety of genres and registers, relevant to Community Interpreting contexts and settings

Table 6.2 (Continued)

Area of competence	Methodology	Materials
	• Having students listen to segments, gradually increasing in length, and taking notes • Having students share their notes with the rest of the class on the board and discuss • Having students reproduce the original text from memory and their notes in the same language as the original • Having students swap their notes and reproduce the original text to the class in the same language, from their fellow students' notes • Providing students with short notes and asking them to convert them into a coherent speech.	
Dialogue interpreting	• Role-plays of scripted dialogues, increasing the length of the segments to be interpreted gradually • Role-plays of unscripted dialogues, where students are provided with scenarios on which to base their parts • Laboratory individual practice of dialogue interpreting, where students record themselves and later listen to their performance to self-evaluate it • Use of minimal notes	• Dialogues prepared by the trainer based on personal experience • Scenarios which reflect real-life situations, to provide background for students to ad lib their own dialogues • Authentic transcripts (e.g. court hearings, police interviews)
Interactional management skills	• Class discussion • Video-taping role-plays and analysing performance in class	• Dialogues as above • Commercial and non-commercial audiovisual material

• Appropriate seating arrangements • Introductions, establishing the contract (see Tebble, 2003), explaining role • Asking for repetition or clarification • Knowing when and how to interrupt • Knowing correct protocols (e.g. in the courtroom) • Assessing when to offer cross-cultural insights • Turn management	• Showing videos of other interpreters at work to analyse performance	
Sight translation	• Analysis of authentic texts (structure, register, terminology, content, style) • Making annotations to the text to facilitate delivery, including the use of numbers to guide word-order • Paraphrasing contents of the text in the same language (especially with difficult legal texts) • Sight translating into target language	• Court documents • Police statements • Affidavits • Other legal documents • Consent forms • Application forms • Personal letters
Long consecutive interpreting	• Reading aloud speeches and other texts and allowing students to take notes and deliver the content in the same language. • Reading aloud speeches and other texts and allowing students to take notes and deliver the content in the target language • Increasing the length of speech segments gradually	• Scripted and unscripted speeches • Content that relates to relevant community interpreting settings (e.g. Community Information sessions, judges' rulings, counsel's summations)

Table 6.2   (Continued)

Area of competence	Methodology	Materials
Simultaneous interpreting	• Shadowing exercises using laboratory (repeating content of what is being heard verbatim in the same language) • Copying the intonation, stress and pitch of the speaker • Interpreting into the target language, increasing the speed of the speaker gradually • Having students whisper their simultaneous interpretation to each other and discussing performance from the listener's point of view	• Witness testimonies • Magistrates' and judges' rulings • Counsel's deliberations • Psychiatric patients' consultations
Ethical considerations	• Creating potential ethical dilemmas as part of the dialogue practice • Discussing how such dilemmas would be dealt with in real life • Showing videos with scenarios that present ethical dilemmas and discussing solutions • Analysing and applying the code of ethics to each dilemma	• Materials based on real-life experience • Commercial audio visual material

teaching practices are not only ineffective but also of little long-term value. Rather than attempt to cover every possible interpreting situation in training sessions, a more valuable education would use limited time more wisely by providing students with the necessary tools to assess potential situations and make their own informed choices. This may be best achieved when a discourse-based approach to interpreter education is applied. As Quote 6.8 explains, interpreters need to process meaning at the discourse level in order to understand the whole message and be able to render it accurately into the target language. For this reason, discourse analysis is a very useful theoretical tool.

Quote 6.8   Processing meaning at the discourse level

Discourse analysis is the logical level of processing for interpreters. It is the overall meaning of the discourse that we must convey. Historically, considerable time is spent on the analysis of words, signs, sentences, and sign production which leads to a common complaint about new interpreters: they seem to include the main points and information, but the overall meaning is somehow missing. What is often missing is the coherence of the discourse, the goal of the speaker, the point of the presentation. The features of language that often convey this coherence are not found at the phonological, morphological, or syntactic level, but at the discourse level.

(Winston and Monikowski, 1998: 2)

Some researchers have criticised the superficial nature of most Community Interpreting courses, which tend to concentrate on mechanical skills development and terminology, and do not explore language and interpreting performance beyond the syntactic level (Berk-Seligson, 1990/2002; Hale, 1996; Fowler, 1997; Roy, 2000b; Winston and Monikowski, 2000). Roy (2000b: 2) comments that such courses become 'haphazard strings of exercises and activities that lack a clear purpose'. Although the purpose of every course is to help students achieve a minimum level of professional competence by improving their ability to interpret accurately, the concept of accuracy is far from being clearly understood by those who teach interpreting skills. Different understandings of what accuracy means will lead to different emphases in teaching methods and different assessments of students' performances. As one of the respondents commented (see section 6.5.1), the background of the different trainers will determine the way they teach. If the trainers are practitioners who have not received academic or research training themselves, their perceptions of accuracy will be based on their practical experience and intuition, rather than on the results of research. This was confirmed by two of the participants of the focus group discussion reported in section 6.5.1, and discussed by Gentile (1995) as one of the major difficulties in trying to incorporate theory and practice in training courses, when the theory is taught by full-time academics and the practice is taught by full-time practitioners. Professional practices will vary greatly between different practitioners, as many of the descriptive studies have shown (see Berk-Seligson, 1990/2002; Rigney, 1999; Mason and Stewart, 2001; Angelelli, 2004; Hale, 2004). Much of the descriptive research has found that practising interpreters have very different understandings of what their role entails and of the meaning of accuracy, for example. These studies have revealed that even those interpreters who attempt to be faithful to the source language utterances tend to consider their propositional content only, disregarding many of the discoursal features that impact on the overall pragmatic force and effect of the message. They are also often unaware of the goals, aims and strategies of the speech event in which they are participating, which impinges on their performance as interpreters (see discussion in chapters 2 and 3). Anecdotal evidence also shows that very few interpreters are able to justify their interpreting choices when asked to do so.[9]

Whereas it is crucial for the validity of courses to have the input of practitioners, it is also crucial to ensure that those practitioners who are trainers have the appropriate academic and research background to inform their teaching. As already argued, there needs to be cross-fertilisation between research, training and practice: where the research informs the training and the practice, the training improves the practice and generates research questions, and the practice improves the training and generates research questions. There is very little value in teaching interpreting theory and practice to students as two distinct and unrelated subjects. The practical subjects need to draw on the theory and on research results to achieve an effective approach to interpreter learning. In well-established courses, graduates of the same course who are also practising interpreters are hired as casual trainers. When such highly qualified staff are not available, it becomes the responsibility of the course designers to provide in-service training for staff and to produce detailed teaching materials that incorporate the theory and the results of research in the teaching of practical skills.[10]

6.6.1 A discourse-based approach to interpreter training

Quote 6.9 The role of discourse analysis in interpreting

... what is significant in the process of learning to interpret is understanding the nature of social situations, knowing how language is used, and becoming familiar with discourse processes. Because these processes and the interpreter's role are ineluctably bound to language and patterns of discourse, discourse analysis not only offers a new research framework, but also a new understanding of what aspects are important in the process of teaching interpreting.

(Roy et al., 1998: 1)

Research into Community Interpreting has been largely influenced by discourse studies (see chapter 7). Discourse studies also have important applications for training. Understanding the discourse practices and strategies of the different participants, according to setting, context and situation, allows students to make informed decisions about how to interpret. Chapters 2 and 3 demonstrate how interpreters' unawareness of the importance of many stylistic features in professional discourse, as well as the goals of the relevant institutions and the roles of the participants, lead to inappropriate choices in their interpretations, which carry serious ramifications for the interaction.

6.6.2 An integrated training framework

Table 6.3 presents a Community Interpreting integrated training framework, which attempts to map the knowledge and skills necessary for interpreters, into the three basic steps of the interpreting process. The table is by no means comprehensive. It provides a sample of the fundamental theories necessary for interpreter training and of the way they can be incorporated in the development of different skills, using some suggested exercises.

Although Table 6.3 presents the contents under three specific categories – comprehension, conversion and delivery – the three are interrelated, and exercises for each of the categories will benefit the general interpreting performance. Boxes 6.2 and 6.3 provide two simplified samples of discourse-based training modules in court interpreting. These are only examples of the way theory can be incorporated in the teaching of practical interpreting skills. Much background knowledge is assumed in these samples, which would be covered in previous modules in the course. Modules such as these would need to be repeated for students to consolidate their skills.

Box 6.2   Sample 1

1. Based on studies in forensic linguistics,[11] discuss the discourse of courtroom questions (e.g. question types and their function, discourse strategies used in examination-in-chief and cross-examination, significance of the use of discourse markers to initiate questions).
2. Show a video of courtroom proceedings and ask the students to look for the features discussed above. Discuss how these were used in the video.
3. Provide a transcription of the courtroom questions seen in the video. Separate the class into small groups and ask them to discuss how best to interpret the questions into their target language. Have each group present their findings to the class, commenting on the difficulties they encountered and on the reasons that led them to arrive at their decisions. Issues of terminology can also be discussed here.
4. Based on studies on cross-cultural pragmatics, discuss the students' renditions in terms of politeness conventions, illocutionary force, register and other such concepts. Discuss how these are represented in the structure of each language.

Table 6.3 An integrated training framework

Aspect of the interpreting process that would benefit from the training	Sample theoretical content covered	Sample practical exercises	Sample knowledge, competencies and skills acquired
1. Comprehension	Background information of the different settings (e.g. the legal system, welfare systems, education systems, etc.) and different encounter types within these settings/systems	• Have students research and describe these settings and present to the class in the form of oral presentations for discussion • Have students extract jargon and phrases particular to these settings and create their own glossaries	• Background knowledge of the relevant fields • Language consolidation and terminology building
	Theories of pragmatics, cross-cultural pragmatics, conversation analysis, discourse analysis and critical discourse analysis	• Analyse a variety of texts in class, drawing on the different theoretical models • Have students record interactions and analyse from a conversation analysis perspective • Discuss the way conversation is achieved in the different languages and cultures • Have students analyse relevant texts from a discourse analytical perspective	• Tools necessary to analyse discourse from a number of different perspectives • An understanding of the way language functions (speech act theory) • An understanding of the interaction between context, situation and participants in the comprehension of intended meaning

- Have students analyse relevant texts from a critical discourse analytical perspective

- An understanding of a number of culture- and language-specific discourse norms
- An understanding of the way politeness is expressed in the relevant languages and cultures
- An understanding of the way communication is achieved through a variety of discourse strategies
- An understanding of the pragmatic significance of various discourse features
- An understanding of the rules and conventions of conversation across languages and cultures
- An understanding of socially and culturally appropriate discourse practices
- An understanding of the underlying coherence of different texts
- An understanding of the manifestations of power through the discourse of different participants

Table 6.3 (Continued)

Aspect of the interpreting process that would benefit from the training	Sample theoretical content covered	Sample practical exercises	Sample knowledge, competencies and skills acquired
	Results of research on social psychology and sociolinguistics (e.g. attitudes to and evaluations of speech styles, dialects, notions of receptivity, language and identity)	• Have students study the relevant literature on these topics and draw their application to interpreting • Conduct exercises where students need to identify different speech styles based on the research literature • Conduct experiments with the students whereby they need to hear different speech styles and evaluate them for a number of different character traits and other aspects such as competence and credibility	• Provide students with the analytical skills to evaluate oral speech according to certain parameters • Make students aware of the social relevance of speech styles
	Results of research into the discourse of professional settings in the relevant languages and cultures	• Using relevant texts (e.g. transcriptions of authentic courtroom discourse, doctor-patient discourse, classroom discourse, etc.), analyse the discourse practices relevant to the specific settings	• An understanding of the ways institutional aims and goals are achieved through the different discourse practices of the participants
2. Conversion	Theories of translation	• Have students research and summarise the different translation theories	• Transfer skills • Sight translation skills

Theories of interpreting: Meanings of accuracy according to different settings. Debates on interpreter roles. Ethical codes, dilemmas and considerations according to setting

- Apply the different approaches to translation to different texts
- Discuss the difficulties encountered in attempting to translate into the target language
- Have students role-play different simulated situations. Discuss the students' choices applying the theories already learned
- Record the students' performance, have them transcribe the interpreted interaction and analyse using discourse analysis and conversation analysis. Then have the students present their findings to the class and discuss.
- Role-play situations with overlapping speech, insulting language, the use of the third person and other such difficult occurrences and have students discuss how to deal with such situations, always applying their knowledge of the theory and of research results.
- Present different ethical dilemmas and discuss solutions, making reference to the code of ethics

- Dialogue interpreting techniques
- The ability to assess the appropriateness of interpreting choices
- The ability to analyse their own performance
- The ability to justify and explain their interpreting choices
- The ability to deal with ethical dilemmas
- The ability to manage, coordinate and control interpreted situations when the other participants do not follow standard protocol
- The ability to apply the code of ethics in different situations

Table 6.3 (Continued)

Aspect of the interpreting process that would benefit from the training	Sample theoretical content covered	Sample practical exercises	Sample knowledge, competencies and skills acquired
3. Delivery	Phonology of both languages (segmental and supra-segmental features, intonation patterns, standard pronunciation)	• Have the class listen to different intonations of the same utterances and identify how meaning changes • Discuss the different uses of stress • Show videos of different interactions and ask students to analyse for supra-segmental features • Revise phonemes that may be problematic to speakers of the relevant language combination (e.g. minimal pairs /v/ and /b/ for Spanish speakers)	• Appropriate pronunciation and intonation patterns to achieve the desired effects
	Grammatical structures of both languages	• Compare and contrast different grammatical structures and their functions (e.g. tag questions, the structure of commands, requests, etc. in the different languages)	• Appropriate grammatical structures in students' languages
	Stylistic features (registers, speech styles, speech varieties, dialects)	• Using the different definitions of register already studied, present examples of each and have students identify them.	• Achieve a high level of accuracy of manner as well as content • Master the different registers in both languages

- Give students a text and ask them to reproduce it in different registers
- Have students analyse spoken speech for speaker style, identifying the features discussed in the research literature
- Have students interpret different styles and registers into the target language

- Have students practise the taking of notes to mark style rather than content
- Have students become aware of their own stylistic tendencies by recording themselves and analysing their own speech
- Train students to be in control of their own use of features such as hesitations and fillers

- Become aware of important stylistic features that impact on perceptions formed by listeners
- Learn to transfer the illocutionary point and force of utterances, attempting to achieve a similar perlocutionary act

Table 6.3 (Continued)

Aspect of the interpreting process that would benefit from the training	Sample theoretical content covered	Sample practical exercises	Sample knowledge, competencies and skills acquired
	Public speaking (diction, voice projection, pitch, rhythm, dynamics)	• Use standard public speaking exercises to improve students' diction, voice projection, etc. • Have students practise in a moot court, where acoustics are poor to force them to project their voice so they can be clearly heard • Practise posture and poise	• Ability to speak in public clearly and audibly, projecting a professional image
	Interactional management	• Do exercises where the students need to introduce themselves and their role, interrupt the proceedings or interview to clarify a point, to explain a cultural difference, to ask for a repetition, to control the situation, to educate the participants on how to speak through an interpreter. (See Metzger, 2000, for more ideas.)	• Learn the appropriate protocols for approaching the different participants in the different settings • Gain confidence in having their voice heard as professional interpreters when needed

---

Box 6.3   Sample 2

1. Based on studies on the language of witness testimonies, discuss the significance of presentational style (e.g. powerful versus powerless speech styles, hesitations, register).
2. Have students listen to authentic courtroom tapes of witness testimonies and ask them to analyse each testimony according to the features discussed above. Then have the class share their findings.
3. Play the tapes back to the students and ask them to take notes and then render the segment again in the same language, attempting to maintain the content and the style of the original. Have them practise an innovative type of note-taking, where they note whether the speech is hesitant, whether there are discourse makers or other stylistic features that need to be paid attention to.
4. Show a video of interpreted proceedings and have the students analyze the interpreter's performance. Discuss whether the interpreter succeeded in portraying a similar illocutionary force and presentational style to the original. Discuss the changes that arose due to the mediation of the interpreter and determine which changes were inevitable and which were unjustified.
5. Have the students role-play and interpret the proceedings. Video-record their performance.
6. View the recording and ask the class to discuss their own performance, analysing the appropriateness of their choices based on their knowledge of the theory and highlighting the difficulties. Discuss strategies needed to overcome obstacles.

One aspect of Community Interpreting training that has not been mentioned so far is research training. If research in this field is to be promoted and its results used to inform both training and practice, training in research methods is crucial. Such training, however, can only be possible in university courses, preferably at postgraduate level. Flexible modes of delivery, such as on-line, can be applied for these types of training modules.

6.7   Conclusions

There are numerous issues that present themselves in community interpreter education and training. The first is the incorrect perception that interpreting is an unskilled activity that does not require any professional training. To counter this common misconception, interpreter educators should take on the responsibility of raising awareness among users of interpreting services regarding the complexities of the inter-preting process, the social consequences flowing from incompetent interpreting and the consequent usefulness of interpreter pre-service training and in-service professional development. Such awareness-raising is best accomplished through the pre-service education of the professionals who work with interpreters. Components on working with interpreters would be an ideal addition to legal, medical and other service profession degrees. Educators also have the responsibility of ensuring that the training they offer is effective in improving inter-preters' performance. To accomplish this they need the support of university administrators and of the profession itself. In essence, what is argued for in this chapter and in this book is a united commitment to improve interpreting research, training and practice on the part of all parties involved: service providers, education institutions, policy-makers and interpreters themselves.

Further reading

Corsellis (2005). This chapter offers a useful overview of the major contents of community/public service training courses.

Ko (1995). This chapter presents different ways of teaching dialogue interpreting, with useful comments on the efficacy of each method outlined.

Niska (2005). This chapter provides an overview of interpreting training around the world, with a section dedicated to Community Interpreting.

Roy (2000).This book presents seven chapters with very useful, practical content on how to teach interpreting using a discourse-based approach. It is written by sign language interpreting educators but its content is equally applicable to spoken language interpreting.

Taibi and Martin (2006). This article provides a useful overview of the existing Community Interpreting courses in Spain, with discussions on the issues surrounding them.

Part III

Research into Community Interpreting

Part III
Research into Community Interpreting

7
Main Traditions and Approaches in Community Interpreting Research

This chapter:

- Highlights the benefits of cross-fertilisation between research, training and practice.
- Identifies gaps, weaknesses and concerns in Community Interpreting research.
- Describes the main methodological approaches in Community Interpreting research.
- Presents a number of research studies in Community Interpreting as examples of different research methods.

7.1 Introduction

Research has probably been one of the most neglected areas in Community Interpreting. The limited number of university courses has inevitably impacted on the amount of research conducted in this discipline. Although interest in the complex nature of Community Interpreting has increased in the last 15 years or so, with innovative research publications appearing, there seems to be no consistent link between the results of research, the little training available and the practice of interpreters, with these three dimensions often working in isolation from each other (Benmaman, 1992, 1999). Schäffner agrees that 'advances in research and in training will ultimately also bring benefits to the professional practice' (2004a: 8). However, in order for this to happen, research and training must be accessed by practitioners, and desirably also undertaken by them as co-researchers.

Concept 7.1   The need for a link between research, training and practice

There is a need for productive cross-fertilisation between research, training and the practice of interpreting, where practice generates research questions, research investigates and provides answers to those questions, and training incorporates those answers in their curricula in order to inform practice. Although many of the interpreting educators are also interpreting practitioners and some conduct research, a link does not always exist between these three. First, there may be no connection between training and practice, since training is not a prerequisite for practice. Second, there may be no connection between training and research as many of the existing Community Interpreting training courses are short, practical courses and do not include a research component.

Many of the teaching staff in Interpreting courses are experienced practitioners who have not received academic, research-based training themselves, and base their curricula on practical experience alone. As chapters 5 and 6 show, interpreters and trainers who have received university training are much more aware of the relevance of theory and research in their practice and in their teaching than those who have not been trained and who consequently rely on experience and intuition alone for answers. However, even when such links exist, as is the case in some countries, practitioners need to be convinced that research is relevant to their practice if they are to take notice of it. Gile argues that such is not yet the case in Conference Interpreting and Translation: 'So far, there does not seem to be enough evidence that research has contributed to the translators' and interpreters' know-how to convince them of its usefulness' (2004: 29). This is also true for Community Interpreting, which has an even smaller body of research.

Traditional views of research distinguish between basic and applied research. Basic research aims at testing, refining and expanding on theoretical understandings of principles and phenomena of certain fields: 'The value of a given theory is judged by the extent to which it explains an important phenomenon satisfactorily, organizes knowledge, predicts certain outcomes, focuses research efforts, and excites inquiry' (Frey et al., 2000: 32). Applied research aims at exploring real-life problems and contributing to their solution, seeking to demonstrate the relevance of established theories and, by its focus on experience, to challenge theories whose application may not be evident. Clearly, then, a connection needs to be established between basic and applied research, so that each type of research informs the other. Wood (1995) stresses this interconnection in that 'applied communication research is practising theory and theorizing practice'. As proponents of action research[1] have argued, 'research which produces nothing but books is inadequate' (Cohen et al., 2000: 226, paraphrasing Lewin, a founder of AR). If research is to be of any use to the practice of Community Interpreting, it needs to be both practical and accessible.

Quote 7.1   Practical research

...it would be useful for interpreters to monitor research regarding the most effective strategies for achieving the goals of interpreted encounters... Systematic research regarding the nature of interpreters' strategies and the impact of various strategies in a variety of settings could assist in identifying whether or not certain models of interpreting are best applied or avoided in a given situation, and what types of interpreter strategies are likely to yield desired outcomes.

(Metzger, 1999: 197–8)

The type of practical research Metzger (1999) proposes would be of great benefit to practitioners. As discussed in chapter 5, most practitioners rely on their own experience and that of others to guide their practice, and often wonder if the choices they make are the most appropriate. Candlin makes this very important point when discussing the relevance of applied linguistic research:

> One of the issues articulated in discussion of research studies... relates to the 'so what?' question. This question is often followed by others: What practical application will the research have? How will it impact on the research site? Does it have the potential to improve the situation? (Candlin, 2003: 386)

Along similar lines, Ibrahim (2004) comments that much research has been conducted to tell us 'what' interpreters do in practice, but little (if any) on 'what' interpreters ought to be doing (see discussion in chapter 3). Practitioners may argue that they already know what they are doing, but that they need to know what they should be doing in order to improve their practice. While descriptive research generates much needed and important knowledge about the current state of practice, such research would be of more direct relevance to practitioners if it also investigated the effects of such practices, including aspects such as how different practices and strategies impinge on the goal of the interactions and what strategies and practices are deemed to be appropriate in different settings or circumstances or with different participants. In order for this to be achieved, a combination of research methodologies needs to be applied to the study of Community Interpreting (see section 7.4 below).

However, even when research is practical and relevant, the issue of accessibility remains a challenge. Indeed, much of the research into Community Interpreting has been of a practical nature as it has been mostly conducted by researchers who still work as interpreters part-time or who have had extensive experience as interpreters before becoming academic researchers. However, there is a perception on the part of many practising interpreters that research is of no relevance to them. Such a perception may be due to the fact that they are not reading research material, so the challenge for researchers is to change these negative attitudes by making the results of their research more accessible. Very few practitioners have the time, the know-how or the inclination to search for and read the research literature. If research is to be used to improve practice, other, more accessible forms of dissemination should be used, such as public professional seminars.

7.2 Summary of research studies in Community Interpreting

The first major research studies into Community Interpreting research appeared in the 1980s and concentrated on court and medical interpreting settings (see Berk-Seligson, 1989a and b on court interpreting; Kaufert and Koolage, 1984; Knapp-Potthoff and Knapp, 1987 on medical interpreting). The 1990s saw a dramatic increase in the number of research studies and in the breadth of topics covered, with a continued predominance of data drawn from the courtroom and medical settings. Studies in the medical area covered issues of interpreter-mediated doctor–patient communication, such as interpreter roles and their impact on the interaction (Athorp and Downing, 1996); the loss of crucial information in the medical encounter mediated by unprofessional interpreters; and the disadvantage experienced by minority language-speaking patients (Vásquez and Javier, 1991; Cambridge, 1999); ethical dilemmas for interpreters (Kaufert and Putsch, 1997); patient and doctor satisfaction rates with professional and non-professional interpreters (Kuo and Fagan, 1999); issues of tenor and accuracy analysed from a Hallidayan systemic functional grammar perspective (Tebble, 1998, 1999); and the active involvement of the interpreter in the triadic encounter (Wadensjö, 1992, 1998). In the legal discourse area, the seminal work by Berk-Seligson reported in *The Bilingual Courtroom* (1990) presented one of the first and few large-scale, data-based studies, which looked at the interaction between the interpreter, the legal system and the Spanish-speaking witness from discourse analytical, experimental and ethnographic perspectives. Other linguistic-based research elaborated on Berk-Seligson's (1990/2002) findings and investigated a variety of important issues surrounding the impact of interpreter-induced changes on the pragmatic meaning and force of the original utterances (Hale, 1996; Rigney, 1997; Fraser and Freedgood, 1999). The results of studies on the interpretation of courtroom questions have revealed a tendency on the part of interpreters to interfere unwittingly with lawyers' tactics, introducing strategies of their own (Berk-Seligson, 1999; Hale, 1999; Rigney, 1999). Researchers speculate that such changes may have been brought about by interpreters' lack of awareness of the strategic use of language in the courtroom and of the significance of seemingly superfluous markers, and often also by an inability to achieve such high levels of accuracy (Hale, 1997b; Krouglov, 1999). Other studies have examined the language of the answers of courtroom testimony, paying particular attention to the importance of register in the evaluation of character in the courtroom and its treatment by interpreters (Dueñas González et al., 1991; Hale, 1997a). There have also been studies which investigated the use of interpreter services in the legal system (Downing, 1991; Carroll, 1995) and the role of interpreters in the courtroom and in refugee hearings (Barsky, 1994, 1996; Jansen, 1995).

Studies on the practices and processes of Community Interpreting in general also began to emerge, investigating a range of disparate issues such as impartiality in sign language interpreting (Metzger, 1999); turn-taking and the interpreter's responsibility for the organisation of the interaction (Englund Dimitrova, 1997; Roy, 2000a); on the current state of affairs in Community Interpreting in Australia and the rest of the world (Ozolins, 1991, 1995, 1998); and on the non-English-speaking clients' perceptions and expectations of interpreters (Hale and Luzardo, 1997).

The courtroom and medical settings have maintained their prominence. Recent studies in the medical setting, for example, have investigated the impact and interference of interpreters on the medical consultation (Bolden, 2000; Davidson, 2000; Meyer et al., 2003; Tellechea Sánchez, 2005) and the perception of health care workers, minority language speakers and interpreters themselves of the interpreting process, and of the status, and even usefulness, of interpreters (Lee et al., 2005). In the legal setting, researchers have continued to investigate a number of important questions, including accuracy, cross-cultural pragmatics, the interpreting process, the strategic use of questions and the importance of style (Hale, 2001, 2002, 2004; Mason and Stewart, 2001; Jacobsen, 2002; Fowler, 2003); the ways interpreters deal with cross-cultural differences (Kelly, 2000; Mesa, 2000); and challenges in interpreting for expert witnesses (Miguélez, 2001). A limited number of studies on interpreting for the police have also been published (Berk-Seligson, 2000; Russell, 2000, 2004).

The first decade of the twenty-first century has also seen the emergence of survey studies on issues of quality and service provision from countries where Community Interpreting is in its infancy, such as Austria, Poland or Spain, which report very similar results to those generated previously by studies from countries where Community Interpreting is well established (Kadric, 2000; Pöchhacker, 2000; Valero Garcés, 2003b; Ibrahim, 2004; Tryuk, 2005). Other topics published in this decade include empirical studies on the linguistic coping strategies of sign language interpreters while interpreting in the education setting (Napier, 2002), and on the role of the interpreter, the code of ethics and the feasibility of interpreter neutrality (Davidson, 2001; Rudvin, 2002; Bot, 2003; Chesher et al., 2003; Angelelli, 2004; Mason, 2004; Castillo and Taibi, 2005; Hale, 2005). These studies have outlined the confusion that exists over the interpreter's role, from the perspective of users of interpreting services and interpreting practitioners themselves.

The above summary provides an overview of the main studies on Community Interpreting in the last three and a half decades. For the most part, the aim of research into Community Interpreting has been to find practical answers to improve practice, rather than to advance or refute theories. The underlying premise is that by improving practice, better quality services will be offered to those who are disadvantaged in the community as a consequence of their inability to speak the language of the host country. In the main, Community Interpreting research draws on the results of other discourse studies for information on the discourse practices of the participants in the different institutional contexts; not with the aim of explaining or exposing the political motivations behind them, but to understand better the significance of language features, patterns and trends in the communication process. It is hoped thereby that a greater understanding of the discourse of these contexts will help interpreters make better informed choices in their quest for accuracy. This in turn, it is hoped, will place the minority language speaker in a much more equitable position in comparison with that of the mainstream members of the community.

7.3   Methods used in Community Interpreting research

Community Interpreting research has used multiple research methods, drawn mostly from research methodologies associated with linguistics, sociology and psychology. The use of multiple research methods has also been identified in Conference Interpreting and Translation studies in general (see discussion in Schäffner, 2004b). This multidisciplinary approach can be considered as a positive means of achieving the greater goal of obtaining relevant answers to valid research questions and thereby strengthening the research efforts in the field.

Quote 7.2   Support for interdisciplinary approaches to Interpreting research

Our basic research goal is surely a greater understanding of our subject: this may be reached better through all kinds of cooperative projects and extensions of paradigms rather than by clinging to autonomy.

(Chesterman, 2004: 53)

Individual paradigms within TS and IS* may draw great benefit from research paradigms in other disciplines and rely on 'importing interdisciplinarity' to strengthen the given research model as such and the (sub)discipline as a whole.

(Pöchhacker, 2004b: 114)

*TS = Translation Studies, IS = Interpreting Studies

Gile (2004) comments that the level of scholarship in Interpreting research, which includes Conference Interpreting research, is still low, although improving. One reason he proposes is the lack of research training received by those conducting research.

Quote 7.3   Lack of research training

In Interpreting, the problem is even more salient, as most authors of publications have had no training in research and many take up experimental research with experience only in interpreting and interpreting training, supplemented by whatever ideas and knowledge about research they may have gleaned by reading other publications...The result is methodological weakness in TS.

(Gile, 2004: 29)

The question of research training has been reviewed in chapter 6 with the discussion of Community Interpreting training. It is apparent from the curricula of available courses that research training receives the least consideration in the list of curriculum priorities. The nature of the courses, their goals, together with the limited number of hours and resources available, have led to this situation. Nonetheless, interest in research in Community Interpreting is increasing, and this can only lead to an improvement in the quality of research projects and, it is hoped, to a better understanding of the practice of interpreting generally.

7.3.1 Approaches to research into Community Interpreting

Four main approaches have been adopted by the majority of research studies into Community Interpreting:

1. the discourse analytical approach, using transcriptions of naturally occurring speech for their data;
2. the ethnographic approach, using mostly field observations, interviews and focus groups as elicitation techniques, relying on a number of different theoretical frameworks;
3. survey research, using mostly questionnaires; and
4. the experimental approach using methods from psycholinguistics and psychology.

Although these approaches and methodologies are identified separately here, in practice most Community Interpreting research combines aspects of different methodological and theoretical frameworks, very rarely stating explicitly what approach researchers are adopting. Titscher and colleagues' comment is very germane to studies in Community Interpreting: 'Quite often methods are applied without due reflection and without taking account of ... theoretical roots' (2003: 5). This is not necessarily a negative aspect of Community Interpreting research. By taking a multidisciplinary approach, a new paradigm is created, whereby only the methodologies that are useful to the aims of Community Interpreting research from different disciplines and methodologies are adopted.

7.3.2 Discourse analysis

Nikander describes discourse analysis (DA) as an 'umbrella for various approaches with different theoretical origins and therefore different analytic punctuations and levels of analysis' (1995: 6). Schiffrin also uses DA as the generic term for any approach used to study discourse, and states that discourse studies 'remains a vast and somewhat vague subfield' (1994: viii). As Stubbe and colleagues (in Quote 7.4) propose, the many different discourse analytical approaches captured under the umbrella of DA make it difficult to provide clear and universally acceptable definitions.

Quote 7.4   The meaning of discourse analysis

Any newcomer to the study of conversation or language in use will be bewildered by the array of analytic approaches that exists. Even more seasoned researchers might be challenged to provide comprehensive descriptions of the range of discourse analytical approaches available in disciplines across the humanities and social sciences. These include pragmatics, speech act theory, variation analysis, communication accommodation theory, systemic-functional linguistics, semiotics, proxemics, and various types of rhetorical, stylistic, semantic and narrative analysis.

(Stubbe et al., 2003: 351)

Wooffitt (2005) agrees that the different uses of the term DA have created confusion. This is evident in the attempts by various scholars to define DA, with very different outcomes.

Four main approaches to DA have been applied in one form or another in Community Interpreting research:

1. interactional sociolinguistics (IS) and the ethnography of communication, proposed by Hymes (1962) and Gumperz (1981, 1982);
2. the early micro-linguistic DA, used by scholars such as Brown and Yule (1983) and Coulthard (1985);
3. conversational analysis (CA), originally proposed by Schegloff and Sacks (1973); and
4. critical discourse analysis (CDA), used by Fairclough (1989, 1992) and Wodak (1995).

These can be placed on a continuum. CA, at one extreme, represents the most detailed, micro-analysis of linguistic features and turns in conversation. CDA, at the other extreme, represents the relationship of such micro-analysis to more macro issues of social structure and the distribution of power in institutions and organisations. The other two approaches fall somewhere in between, where the linguistic micro-analysis of interaction is analysed, taking account of the local social context in which it occurs. A short description of these approaches follows.

Quote 7.5   On the fundamental assumptions of conversational analysis

David Silverman (1999), reviewing the work of other CA theorists and researchers, speaks of three fundamental assumptions. First, conversation is a socially structured activity. Like other social structures, it has established rules of behavior. For example, we're expected to take turns, with only one person speaking at a time. In telephone conversations, the person answering the call is expected to speak first (e.g. Hello)... Second... conversations must be understood contextually. The same utterance will have totally different meanings in different contexts... Third, CA aims to understand the structure and meaning of conversation through excruciatingly accurate transcripts of conversations.

(Babbie, 2004: 375)

Conversational analysis emerged in the 1970s within sociology with the work of Harvey Sacks, Gail Jefferson, Emanuel Schegloff and their colleagues. It arose out of the need to study naturally occurring speech, as opposed to artificially constructed sentences, which had been the focus of study in text linguistics. It also offered an alternative to more theoretical orientations towards social structure which was characteristic of the time (see also Coupland et al., 2001). The emergence of CA coincided with the focus on language functions and speech actions, as proposed by pragmatics and speech act theory. CA concentrates on talk in interaction in the form of spoken conversation. Its aim is to determine the patterns and the order produced by individuals in everyday talk. It attempts to discover the taken-for-granted rules of conversation, to see how people interact with each other and make sense of the world in similar ways. It is concerned with the micro-analysis of certain stages of interactions. For example, it can analyse sets of turns, such as

---

Quote 7.6   On the micro-linguistic approach to discourse analysis

The analysis of discourse is, necessarily, the analysis of language in use. As such, it cannot be restricted to the description of linguistic forms independent of the purposes or functions which those forms are designed to serve in human affairs... the discourse analyst is committed to an investigation of what language is used for.

(Brown and Yule, 1983: 1)

---

greetings, closings, turn negotiations or turn projections. The linguistic representations of such units of study are only one aspect of the analysis. Extra-linguistic features, such as gaze, body language, seating arrangements, intonation, are also important.

The micro-linguistic approach to DA described in Quote 7.6 looks at the relationship between form and function in verbal communication and is heavily influenced by pragmatics, and in particular by speech act theory and politeness theory. Mason (2004: 90-5) links Community Interpreting research with three main themes which fall under the interactional pragmatics umbrella: footing, politeness and relevance. Under the theme of footing, as proposed by Goffman (1981), issues such as interpreter–client and interpreter–professional alignment have been studied. Under the theme of politeness, as advanced by Brown and Levinson (1987/1992) and Grice's (1975) work on the cooperative principle, issues of face, mitigation strategies and a pragmatic rendition of appropriate politeness forms in the target language have been researched. The two principles of relevance theory – the cognitive principle and the communicative principle – can be indirectly identified in data-based studies of interpreting performance, which show an adherence to these principles rather than to the underlying objective of faithful translation. In an attempt to maintain relevance in the communicative act, interpreters will often add information to the target language utterances that were not present in the source language utterances, or alternatively omit what they deem to be irrelevant (see discussions in chapters 1–3). Under the umbrella of speech act theory, issues of illocutionary point and force have been prominent in studies into community interpreters' performance.

Quote 7.7   On the ethnography of communication

Ethnography analyses language and text in the context of culture . . . It is uncontested that language exists in a cultural context, but it remains open how the relationship is to be specified: does language function as the expression of culture and is it determined by the non-linguistic features of culture? Are linguistic and non-linguistic components of culture different in principle from one another? Or does language have a determining influence on culture as an organizational principle of the material world? . . . The ethnography of language seeks to describe modes of speech according to the ways in which they construct and reflect social life within particular speech communities.

(Titscher et al., 2003: 90–1)

The terms 'ethnography of communication' and 'ethnography of speaking' were coined by Hymes (1962) to describe both a method and a theory which studies communicative patterns as part of cultural knowledge and behaviour. The ethnography of communication is concerned with what speakers need to know and do in order to communicate appropriately within a particular speech community. Such knowledge and its application constitute what has been referred to as communicative competence (Saville-Troike, 2003).

Quote 7.8 Communicative competence from an ethnography of speaking perspective

Communicative competence involves knowing not only the language code but also what to say to whom, and how to say it appropriately in any given situation. Further, it involves the social and cultural knowledge speakers are presumed to have which enables them to use and interpret linguistic form...Communicative competence extends to both knowledge and expectation of who may or may not speak in certain settings, when to speak and when to remain silent, to whom one may speak, how one may talk to persons of different statuses and roles, what non-verbal behaviours are appropriate in various contexts, what the routines for turn-taking are in conversation, how to ask for and give information, how to request, how to offer or decline and the like – in short, everything involving the use of language and other communicative modalities in particular social settings.

(Saville-Troike, 2003: 18)

The ethnography of communication is very applicable to the study of Community Interpreting. Communicative competence (as described in Quote 7.8) in each language is a prerequisite for interpreters. The inventory proposed by the ethnography of communication (see Box 7.1) to study communicative competence is a very useful tool for studying interpreted interaction, where issues of bilingual competence, interactional skills and cross-cultural knowledge are crucial. Berk-Seligson (1990/2002: 42), for example, claims to have used the ethnography of speaking as one of the methodological concepts that guided her in her research of the bilingual courtroom.

Box 7.1   Inventory for studying communicative competence under an ethnography of communication framework

1. Linguistic knowledge

   Verbal elements
   Non-verbal elements
   Patterns of elements in particular speech events
   Range of possible variants (in all elements and their organisation)
   Meaning of variants in particular situations

2. Interaction skills

   Perception of salient features in communicative situations
   Selection and interpretation of forms appropriate to specific situations, roles
     and relationships (rules for the use of speech)
   Discourse organisation and processes
   Norms of interaction and interpretation
   Strategies for achieving goals

3. Cultural knowledge

   Social structure (status, power, speaking rights)
   Values and attitudes
   Cognitive maps/schemata
   Enculturation processes (transmission of knowledge and skills)

(From Saville-Troike, 2003: 20)

Quote 7.9   On interactional sociolinguistics

Interactional sociolinguistics (IS) has its roots in the ethnography of communication, and analysts using this approach typically focus on linguistic and cultural diversity in communication, and how this impacts on the relationships between different groups in society. IS also represents an approach to discourse analysis which attempts to 'bridge the gap' between 'top-down' theoretical approaches which privilege 'macro-societal conditions' in accounting for communicative practices, and those, such as CA which provide a 'bottom-up' social constructivist account. IS draws heavily on CA techniques in its micro-analytical approach to interactions but unlike CA, an IS analysis explicitly recognizes the wider sociocultural context impacting on interactions.

(Stubbe et al., 2003: 358)

The micro-linguistic approach to DA, the ethnography of speaking and interactional sociolinguistics are perhaps the approaches that best describe the methodology adopted by most Community Interpreting researchers. While analysing the naturally occurring discourse of interpreted interactions, taking account of the syntactic, semantic and pragmatic dimensions of language, Community Interpreting research has generally also considered the function of language and of the sociological context of the interactions. This is true in particular of studies into legal and medical interpreting.

Quotes 7.10   On critical discourse analysis

CDA sees itself as politically involved research with an emancipatory requirement: it seeks to have an effect on social practices and social relationships.

(Titscher et al., 2000: 147)

CDA aims to reveal connections between language, power and ideology, and critical discourse analysts aim to describe the way power and dominance are produced and reproduced in social practice through the discourse structures of generally unremarkable interactions... CDA has its theoretical roots in the work of Marx, Hall, Habermas and Foucault. At its core one finds investigations of the enactment, exploitation, and abuse of social power in everyday interactions. It is therefore particularly useful in analyzing interactions in settings involving a power asymmetry.

(Stubbe et al., 2003: 367)

CDA is concerned with social problems, not with language use *per se*, but with the linguistic character of social and cultural processes and structures. It analyses both the power inherent in discourse and the power exerted over discourse. One basic difference between CDA and other forms of DA is the definition of 'discourse' itself. Within linguistics, this term usually refers to a connected unit of language beyond a single sentence. In CDA, however, discourse means 'different ways of structuring areas of knowledge and social practices and systems of rules implicated in specific kinds of power relations' (Mesthrie, 2000: 323).

CDA is an approach used by some Community Interpreting researchers, especially in the contexts of the Refugee Review Tribunal in Canada (see Barsky, 1994, 1996). Rather than being concerned with the accuracy of the interpreters' performances, these studies have concentrated on the social disadvantage experienced by the minority language speakers and on the need for interpreters to redress this inequality. These researchers suggest that interpreters can help achieve this social goal by deviating from their strict role of interpreter and adopting the role of advocate (see discussion in chapters 2 and 3).

Although each of the different DA methodologies draws on its own distinctive theory and analytical tools, in Community Interpreting research a combination of all the methodologies has been used. As a general rule, there have been two important uses of DA in Community Interpreting research: first, to draw on the results of DA studies to learn about the discourse practices of the institutions in which interpreters operate, and about the conversational patterns and conventions of the speakers of the relevant language communities; and second, to apply similar methods, albeit somewhat eclectically, to the analysis of interpreted discourse in order to describe and analyse the practice of interpreting in context.

Discourse analytical studies in Community Interpreting have mostly been qualitative, although some use a combination of quantitative and qualitative methods (see chapter 8 for an explanation of qualitative and quantitative methods). When both methods are employed, the data are quantitatively analysed first to ascertain the significance of particular discourse occurrences and establish patterns. For instance, if the data show that the interpreters in the sample omit a certain feature of discourse only 1 per cent of the time, then that feature cannot be claimed to be causing any particular difficulties and may not be worth investigating further. If, on the other hand, it is found that such a feature is omitted or misinterpreted 60 per cent of the time, then the quantitative results show that that phenomenon is worthy of investigation. The researcher will then use qualitative methods to provide grounds for understanding the reasons underpinning those results.

Two discourse analytical research studies into different aspects of Community Interpreting are presented below.

Sample Research Study 1

Rosenberg, B. A. (2002). A quantitative discourse analysis of Community Interpreting. *Translation: New Ideas for a New Century* 16 (2002), pp. 222–6.

Summary
This study can be classified as 'action research', as the researcher, who is the interpreter under investigation, is self-analysing his performance. The study analyses eleven transcribed interpreted interviews between physicians and the Spanish-speaking[2] mothers of the patients who were all children. The setting is the paediatric section of a public health care facility in the United States.

Sample Research Study 1   (Continued)

Aim
The aim of the study is to describe the nature of the interpreter-mediated discourse in this setting by expanding on categories proposed by four previous researchers: Wadensjö (1992, 1998), Davidson (1998), Roy (2000) and Metzger (1999). The five categories of interpreter renditions used in this study are: close renditions (those that contain complete interpretations of the original), expanded renditions (those that expand on the content of the original), reduced renditions (those that omit some aspect of the original), zero renditions (those that were entirely uninterpreted) and non-renditions (those contributions that are not interpretations of the original but are the interpreter's own comments).

Methodology and data
The researcher audio recorded eleven interviews, which he later transcribed. Each of the interpreter's renditions (a total of 1,334 utterances) were allocated to one of the above categories and quantified in terms of percentages. The non-renditions category was further analysed and categorised into six groups: 'phatic', 'banter', 'clarifications', 'repetitions', 'understood' and 'off task'. They were also quantified in terms of percentages. All the renditions were also quantitatively analysed according to language. In the discussion section, the researcher makes qualitative speculations as to the reasons behind the different renditions.

Results
The results showed that 40.8 per cent of the renditions fell under the close renditions category, making it the largest single group. Of the rest – over half the renditions (59.2 per cent) – 26.9 per cent came in zero renditions, 19.5 per cent in non-renditions, 9.2 per cent in expanded renditions and 3.6 per cent in reduced renditions. The core of the analysis then concentrates on the non-renditions category. The quantitative breakdown of the sub-categories under non-renditions is as follows: 56.9 per cent phatic, 16.5 per dent clarifications, 7.7 per cent understood, 6.9 per cent off task, 6.2 per cent banter and 5.8 per cent repetitions. Hence the largest sub-category was phatic non-renditions. Phatic expressions are used to keep the communication flow, such as 'Mmmm' or 'Uh ha'. The interpreter uses these expressions to acknowledge the previous speaker or to indicate understanding. The next largest category was clarifications, when the interpreter asked his own questions of either party to clarify what had been said or what he was expected to do. The understood category represents those renditions which both main participants were able to understand without the intervention by the interpreter. As the author states, often the non-English speaker will understand some English and the medical practitioner some Spanish. In those cases, there is no need for the interpreter to interpret. The next category, off task non-renditions, refers to occasions when the interpreter speaks to either party about something that is unrelated to the conversation between the main speakers. The banter category refers to utterances said in jest, especially to children. Finally,

repetitions refer to those instances when the interpreter needs a repetition of some point that has been forgotten (e.g. dates or other numbers).

Commentary
The results of this study demonstrate that in a face-to-face triadic interpreted exchange, the interpreter produces utterances other than direct interpretations in over 50 per cent of the time. Although interpreters themselves may be aware that this is the case, quantifying the different utterances can be illuminating. Phatic expressions, clarifications and repetitions have been identified in other studies as normal aspects of dialogue interpreting. However, banter, off task utterances and understood non-renditions had not been given much previous consideration. As the author comments, it would be interesting to see if banter and off task utterances take place in other, more formal contexts. The understood non-renditions category is one that is also worth investigating further. How much the participants understand without the need for interpretation will depend on the participants themselves. Interpreters are sometimes told that they are there 'just in case the parties do not understand each other' and to interpret only when needed. This can create problems for all parties. First, the main participants may think they understand each other, when in fact they do not. It is difficult for interpreters to know if they should interrupt when they perceive the main participants are not fully understanding each other, even though they may think they are. Secondly, it is difficult for interpreters to maintain concentration if they are to interpret only now and then, rather than consistently. The author argues for further data-based research into these issues and others related to face-to-face interpreted discourse.

Strengths and weaknesses of the study
The study is strong on validity, as the data are drawn from real-life situations. This is a particular strength of DA studies which study authentic discourse. The combination of quantitative and qualitative methods also adds strength to this study. By quantifying the different utterances, the study is able to provide a clearer description of the speech event. The large data base is also a strong point. The fact that only one interpreter was analysed and that the interpreter was the researcher himself can be both a strength and a weakness: a strength in that the researcher is intimately acquainted with the situation and can provide useful insights into the analysis, and it is also useful for him as a practitioner to self-analyse his practice; a weakness in that his judgement may be biased, but also in that the results pertain to his own performance rather than to interpreters' performances in general. In other words, it would not be appropriate to generalise on the basis of one interpreter. The study has great value as a case study and as a starting point to raise issues that can be further analysed with more diverse samples.

Many other questions are raised by this study but are not dealt with by the author and should be further researched. For example, a closer analysis of the instances of banter would be very useful: When did these take place? What was the physician doing at the time? How did all the participants react? To whom were they directed? Did the participants who were left out understand what was happening? Is this a particular feature of interactions with children? These and a number of other questions can be further researched by other studies.

Sample Research Study 2

Wadensjö, C. (1999). Telephone Interpreting and the synchronization of talk in social interaction. In I. Mason (ed.), *Dialogue Interpreting*. Special issue of *The Translator* 5(2): 247–64.

Summary
This study compares two interpreted interactions involving the Swedish police, a Russian-speaking informant and a Russian–Swedish interpreter. One of the interactions was held at the police station, the other was conducted over the telephone.

Aim
The study aims to describe the conversational behaviour of all the participants in each situation and investigate if the different setting and mode have any bearing on those behaviours. In particular, the study looks at how these differences affect the injured party's ability to tell her story.

Methodology and data
The data for the study derive from two recordings of real-life interviews at a police station in Sweden between the three participants mentioned above. The participants and the case were the same for both occasions. The only difference was that on one occasion the interpreter was present at the police station, and on the other, the interpreter was at home, interpreting via the telephone. The telephone interpreted exchange consisted of 4,856 words and was of 38 minutes' duration. The on-site interpreted exchange consisted of 4,277 words and was of 25 minutes' duration. The author states that the study is linked theoretically and methodologically to studies of 'situated social interaction' (Drew and Heritage, 1992; Duranti and Goodwin, 1992) and applies a dialogical view of language and mind, as proposed by Bakhtim (1979). The study analyses the data from the perspectives of the main interlocutors and from the perspective of the interpreter. From the interpreter's perspective, the study looks at issues of confidentiality and involvement and non-verbal communication. From the other participants' perspectives, the study looks at tempo, turn distribution, feedback and overlapping speech.

Results
The study found a number of interesting results. Overall, the on-site interpreted interaction ran much more smoothly than the telephone interpreted interaction. The study found that the interpreter was at an obvious disadvantage when interpreting over the telephone. For example, extra explanations had to be made by the police officer to the interpreter when speaking via the telephone, as the interpreter had no access to the non-verbal communication cues. At times the communication broke down as a result of technical problems, and repetitions had to be made. From the perspective of the informant, some differences were also found. First, she commented that she found it difficult speaking over the telephone, although she could not explain why. A quantitative analysis found that she spoke slightly faster when the interpreter was on site (at an average 2.4 words per second compared to 2.3 words per second over the telephone). There were fewer turns of talk during the telephone interpreted interview, with each turn

also consisting of fewer words for each of the participants. This led the researcher to conclude that the on-site interview seemed to be more fluent. The researcher speculates that the fact that people are more accustomed to speaking face to face may have been the main reason for this. The study also found that there was much more overlap in the on-site interaction, with 155 instances of overlap in the on-site interaction compared with only eleven in the telephone interaction. The overlap in the on-site interaction was adequately timed by the interpreter and did not disturb the flow of the communication.

Commentary
This study investigates an area of Community Interpreting practice that is becoming increasingly popular but has not yet been the subject of much research. This study is very useful in identifying a number of the issues related to this mode of interpreting and in raising many other questions to be further investigated. The study presents some of the anecdotal evidence about this mode of interpreting. Some service providers and clients have expressed a preference for telephone interpreting for reasons of confidentiality and interpreter invisibility. On the other hand, most interpreters seem not to prefer this type of interpreting, not only for the difficulties associated with the interpreting process, but also because of poor working conditions, lack of preparation (both mental and physical) for the job, and for the lack of opportunity to debrief once the interview is over.

Strengths and weaknesses of the study
The strengths of this study lie in the authenticity of the data, the use of the same participants for both sets of data and on the originality of the research question. The fact that the same participants formed part of both interviews and the same topic was discussed produced a controlled environment resembling an experimental study. The study, therefore, scores highly on the authenticity of the data and the situation, making it valid, and on the minimisation of variables, making it more reliable. Had the participants been different, the results may have been attributed to personal differences rather than to differences in mode and setting. Nevertheless, this strength can also be seen as a weakness, as the study can only be taken as a case study and cannot be representative of all telephone interpreted situations. As the researcher states, many more studies of this type need to be conducted to provide further understanding of the complex nature of telephone interpreting and to further investigate the differences, advantages and disadvantages of both modes of interpreting.

7.3.3 Ethnographic studies

Traditional ethnographic studies restricted their scope of investigation to non-Western cultures. Ethnographers would spend time living with communities to learn about and later describe their customs and behaviours. More recent versions of ethnography have included the study of any particular group within any society, such as the courtroom, a hospital or a school. Ethnographic studies in

Community Interpreting have looked at different 'cultures' or 'group-ings' such as the bilingual courtroom or the bilingual hospital (see Berk-Seligson, 2002; Angelelli, 2004). These studies aim at gaining an understanding of the interpreted situation: at discovering how the different participants of interpreted exchanges interact and behave, what their expectations of each other are and the motivations for their choices. The main methods of data collection include interviews, focus groups and annotated observations. Initial ethnographic research can lead to discourse analytical research, which includes the ethno-graphy of speaking, using the discourse recorded during fieldwork as data.

Ethnographic studies in Community Interpreting can be very useful as a way to elicit the views, concerns and needs of the different parties involved in the interpreted encounter. Such research can lead to exper-imental or discourse analytical research that will attempt to answer practical questions posed by the participants of focus groups or ques-tionnaires. Two ethnographic studies into Community Interpreting are showcased below.

Sample Research Study 3

Berk-Seligson, S. (2002). How attention is shifted to the interpreter by the court proceedings and by other parties. in S. Berk-Seligson, *The Bilingual Courtroom* (chapter 5). Chicago: Chicago University Press.

Summary
This study looks at the ethnography of the bilingual courtroom. It specifically explores the verbal behaviour of the court interpreter among the other participants in this highly ritualised setting.

Aim
This study is part of a major ethnographic study. It aims to describe the role played by the interpreter in the courtroom and to demonstrate the ways the interpreter becomes actively involved in the proceedings by having attention shifted to her by the different parties, including herself.

Methodology and data
The researcher spent over seven months during 1982 and 1983 visiting nine courthouses daily. The proceedings involving 18 interpreters were audio-recorded, amounting to a total of 114 hours. The recordings were later transcribed for analysis. The observations and recordings were complemented by detailed notes taken by the researcher as well as by interviews with the interpreters and lawyers involved in the proceedings. The researcher also participated

in a number of interpreter training programmes as an observer to learn more about the issues surrounding court interpreting and the concerns of practitioners.

Results
The study found that the interpreter is far from the unobtrusive figure the court expects her to be. The interpreter's presence is highlighted from the very beginning, through the interpreter's oath. Throughout the proceedings, the various participants direct the court's attention to the interpreter. One way this is done is by judges and lawyers addressing the interpreter rather than the witness directly, in utterances such as 'Ask him...'.

Interpreters also draw attention to themselves when they need to ask for clarification or at times when they make unjustifiable comments. Witnesses also enter into side-conversations with the interpreter. The most important finding is that the interpreter can affect the power and control exerted by the lawyers by inadvertently changing the force and intention of the questions. The interpreter is also found to manifest her own measure of coercion on the witness, sometimes working in favour and sometimes against the efforts of the lawyers.

Commentary
The study highlights a number of important issues. First, it demonstrates that the powerful court participants behave in a way that is inconsistent with their expectations of the role of the interpreter. While they typically believe that the interpreter's role is to interpret all utterances directly without further involvement, in reality they often ask the interpreter to explain, to stop the witness from answering or to make sure that the witness answers relevantly. The study also shows that lawyers are often unaware of the complexities of the interpreting process and do not assist the interpreter in achieving a faithful rendition. On the other hand, it demonstrates that many interpreters are unaware of the significance of certain linguistic features in courtroom discourse and of the effect of many of their choices on the dynamics of the courtroom. They also often seem to act in a haphazard way, guided by their own arbitrary decisions at the time rather than by any systematic code of conduct.

Strengths and weaknesses
The strength of this study lies in the size of the corpus and the diverse nature of the subjects. Whereas the studies mentioned above studied the behaviour of only one interpreter, this study looks at the behaviours of 18 interpreters. Although other aspects of the research reported in Berk-Seligson use both qualitative and quantitative methods, this study is purely qualitative. The qualitative commentary is meticulous, insightful and well informed. However, without any quantification of the occurrences sampled, it is difficult to ascertain whether such behaviours constitute the norm or the exception. Although interviews were conducted with the various participants, and these are reported elsewhere about different issues, it would have been interesting to read the participants' comments on the results of this particular study.

Sample Research Study 4

Angelelli, C. (2004). Interpreters' voices. In C. Angelelli, *Medical Interpreting and Cross-cultural Communication* (Chapter 7). Cambridge: Cambridge University Press.

Summary
This study is part of a larger ethnographic study of the behaviours of the participants in interpreted interactions in a Californian hospital. This study analyses the interpreters' own perceptions of their role.

Aim
The study aims to explore three main issues: the interpreters' perceptions of the parties with whom they work (i.e. the patients and health practitioners); their perception of their own role; and the way they handle stress and tension at work.

Methodology and data
The researcher conducted eleven semi-structured interviews of approximately 45 minutes' duration each. Ten of the subjects were untrained interpreters, the other was their manager. The interviews were later analysed qualitatively. The chapter presents the reader with large excerpts from the interviews followed by the author's commentaries.

Results
The study found that the majority of these interpreters consider their role to go beyond that of interpreting. Some argue that they are there to ensure communication takes place which may involve adding information or changing the original messages. Some argue that they are there as a filter, filtering out what they consider to be irrelevant or offensive. Others believe they are there to help the medical practitioners achieve their goals and others to help the patients present their stories more coherently. As for their perceptions of the other parties, for the most part these interpreters tend to feel frustrated with the patients who, they claim, do not understand the expectations of the health practitioners and offer irrelevant information, and equally with the health practitioners who often do not provide enough information to the patients.

Commentary
The data presented in this study provide very useful insights into the behaviours of these interpreters. Different qualitative assessments of the same data can be made from different perspectives, leaving the reader with an opportunity to analyse the comments for themselves. The author considers the evidence from the interpreters' point of view and from her own observations of their interpreting performance.

Strengths and weaknesses
The strength of this study lies in its large database and in its authenticity. Nevertheless, it cannot be considered to be representative of all interpreting situations. It is a very good case study of the behaviour of interpreted interactions in a

particular hospital, where all the interpreters are untrained and have learned their duties and skills on the job. Similar studies could be conducted with different groups of interpreters from different settings to compare their responses.

7.3.4 Survey research

The aim of survey research is to gather relatively factual information about a set of particular issues from a large number of respondents. Surveys are normally conducted by questionnaires (see chapter 8 for an explanation), but may include interviews or the collection and study of other sources of information, such as official documents. Results of surveys are usually used to make recommendations to policy-makers on issues related to the research. The use of statistics is common in the analysis phase of survey research. The aim of much of this type of research in Community Interpreting has been to canvass the current situation of the profession in a particular country or area. Issues such as working conditions, rates of pay and training requirements have been common points of concern. Surveys have also been used to canvass views, attitudes and perceptions of the participants. An example of a major survey follows.

Sample Research Study 5

Ozolins, U. (2004). Survey of interpreting practitioners. *Report*. Melbourne: VITS.

Summary
This study was undertaken as part of the VITS[3] LanguageLink Good Corporate Citizenship Program. VITS is one of the largest providers of interpreting and translation services in the state of Victoria, Australia. The study surveyed interpreting practitioners working in Melbourne.

Aim
The aim of the survey was to gather detailed information about the interpreting profession in Victoria. The main questions covered include accreditation, training, professional development, working conditions, remuneration, control of the profession and general satisfaction levels with its state.

Methodology and data
The first step of the research study consisted in the establishment of a reference group to advise on the content and conduct of the survey. Representatives from the main stakeholders formed part of the reference group. A questionnaire was then designed taking account of the group's input. This was sent to an external

Sample Research Study 5   (Continued)

research company for feedback, after which refinements were made. The survey aimed at being representative of the interpreting community in metropolitan Melbourne. Practitioners to be surveyed were selected from two I&T agencies. The sample consisted of practitioners with different language combinations, levels of accreditation and training and years of experience. Twenty-four languages were represented and 150 completed questionnaires were returned. The researcher complemented the study with desk research.

Results
The main results can be summarised as follows:

1. There is a significant number of practitioners who do not hold a NAATI accreditation, either because their language is not tested by NAATI or because they have not sat an examination.
2. A significant number of practitioners are highly qualified. No consideration is made to recognise qualifications of any kind or to reward them in their remuneration. This was found to be a disincentive for training and a source of dissatisfaction for the highly educated interpreters.
3. The respondents showed considerable interest in professional development (PD) opportunities. Respondents expressed a preference for formal training institutions to offer PD courses. Respondents also commented on the need for service providers to be trained in how to work with interpreters.
4. Poor remuneration was one of the main sources of dissatisfaction. The survey revealed strong support for pay differentials according to levels of accreditation and training.
5. A high proportion of respondents welcomed the introduction of a regulatory body.

Commentary
The data collected by this survey offer very important information on the state of the profession in Melbourne and on the concerns of practitioners. These results should be followed up in further research and in action through policy. The researcher makes highly pertinent recommendations regarding each of the results.

Strengths and weaknesses
This study provides answers to a wide range of issues. The sample is large, although it is very particular to the situation in the major Australian cities. Although the interpreters were solely from Melbourne, it can be safely assumed that the situation in Sydney would be largely similar. As with most questionnaires, however, the results may be biased, as it is usually the better educated and qualified practitioners who agree to take part. As the researcher comments, very few unaccredited interpreters took part.

7.3.5   Experimental studies

Experimental studies are common in Conference Interpreting research (see Gambier et al., 1997), but have also been used in a limited number of court interpreting research projects (see Berk-Seligson, 1990; Hale, 2004). These studies follow a hypothetico-deductive method, where a hypothesis is tested against the results of controlled experiments. Small experiments are set up to elicit specific types of data. The data are therefore constructed rather than naturally occurring, and thus the variables can be controlled. Psycholinguistics typically employs tight experimental methodology derived from psychology. Such methodology has been extended to some interpreting studies. These studies are mostly concerned with issues related to comprehension, the mental processes of interpreting and the reactions produced by certain utterances, speech styles or other linguistic behaviours on listeners. Experimental studies in Community Interpreting research could be extremely useful to test hypotheses generated by natural data-based research. An example of an experimental study based on the hypotheses generated by a discourse analytical study follows.

Sample Research Study 6

Hale, S. (2004). The style of the Spanish-speaking witnesses' answers and the interpreters' renditions: matched–guise experiments. In S. Hale, *The Discourse of Court Interpreting* (pp. 145-59). Amsterdam and Philadelphia: John Benjamins.

Summary
The experimental research reported in this chapter was conducted as a triangulation technique. The first part of the chapter reports the results of a major discourse analytical study of the witnesses' testimony styles and the interpreters' renditions. Based on the results of the discourse analytical study, and to corroborate the hypotheses raised by such a study, two experiments were conducted.

Aim
The first experiment aimed to discover whether the testimonies of four witnesses would be rated differently in terms of competence, credibility and intelligence, when heard in the original language and when heard in English via the interpreter. The second experiment aimed to discover if it was possible to obtain similar evaluations through an interpreter if the testimony was accurately rendered in terms of both content and style.

Methodology and data
Four chunks of testimony from four Spanish-speaking witnesses were selected from the authentic data of court proceedings. The recordings were played to a class of native Spanish-speaking students who were asked to rank each witness on

Sample Research Study 6   (Continued)

a Likert-type scale. The original recordings of the interpretations of each of these chunks were also played to a class of English-speaking students, who were asked to rank them in the same way as the first group. The results of each of the groups' evaluations were compared and run through an analysis of variance for statistical significance.

For the second experiment, two interpreted versions into English of the chunk of Spanish testimony no. 4 in the previous experiment were produced. One was accurate in terms of content and style, maintaining features such as powerless features as they appeared in the original. This was called the unpolished version. The other version was accurate in content alone, deleting all the powerless features of discourse. This was called the polished version. The two were recorded by a speaker with a native English accent and played to two groups of law students. Both groups were told they were listening to the interpreted version of an original Spanish testimony and asked to rank them on a Likert-type scale. The results of the two groups were then compared and also compared with the previous results achieved for chunk 4 in the first experiment.

Results
The first experiment:
For three of the witnesses, the respondents rated the interpreters' versions more positively than the original witnesses' in all three areas. For one of the witnesses, the respondents rated the original testimony higher than the interpreted testimony. When the different renditions were analysed, it was found that the three witnesses whose evaluations were improved by the interpreters spoke mostly in what O'Barr (1982) calls a powerless speech style, and that many of the powerless features were eliminated by the interpretations. The one witness who was evaluated more positively in his original language was found to have a more powerful speech style. However, the interpreter for this witness added many of the powerless features to the interpretation, changing his original style from powerful to powerless. What this study confirmed is that in both English and Spanish, raters evaluated the powerful style more favourably, and that, by changing the style, interpreters, also change the potential evaluations of the witnesses. It also demonstrated that interpreters do not consistently change speech into the powerful style.

The second experiment:
The polished version was rated as significantly more competent ($p = 0.0000$),[4] more credible ($p = 0.0006$) and more intelligent ($p = 0.0000$). These results showed clearly that the evaluations changed according to style, since the content and the speaker for both versions were the same. When the results of this experiment were compared to the results of the first experiment for the same chunk of testimony, it was found that the unpolished version (the one that was accurate in terms of both content and style) produced very similar rankings to the original Spanish version of the same chunk of testimony. This result showed that it is possible to achieve similar results to the original via an interpreter as long as the rendition is accurate in terms of content and style.[5]

Commentary
The results of this study are significant because they show that it is possible to achieve similar evaluations to the original speaker's if the interpretation is faithful to the original in terms of propositional content and style. A very simple definition of style is used, which refers to O'Barr's distinction between powerful and powerless speech styles. Other aspects of style are not considered, which indicates that even when there are other differences between the interpreter and the original speaker, simply maintaining the few features that form part of the powerless style when they are present, or not adding them when they are not, together with accuracy of content, can demonstrably achieve a very similar evaluation from the listeners.

Strengths and weaknesses
The strength of this study is that the original data are taken from authentic court cases, and the hypotheses raised by the original study are corroborated by the experimental study. The results are also significant for the training and practice of interpreters. The study also has weaknesses and limitations. The volume of data used for the experiment is relatively small and a number of other variables, such as visual stimulation, were not considered. This study should be replicated using different language combinations and different subjects.

This section has provided samples of research projects into Community Interpreting using the main methodologies and approaches. These are further explored in Chapter 8 through the presentation of a number of suggested potential research projects.

Further reading

Frey, Botan and Kreps (2000). This book provides a useful introduction to research methods and concepts used in the study of communication. Beginning researchers will find much needed information that can be applied to the study of Community Interpreting.

Hale (2006). This chapter provides a review of the main research into court interpreting. It describes the different research studies, highlights their strengths and weaknesses, and identifies the gaps that exist in the field, proposing further studies.

Hertog, van Gucht and de Bontridder (2006). This chapter reviews and critiques the most common methodologies used in Community Interpreting research and argues for more rigorous, valid and reliable research.

Pöchhacker (2004). Although this book is not exclusively about Community Interpreting, it provides a very detailed and useful section on interpreting research which covers the field of Community Interpreting.

Schaffner (2004b). This is an edited volume which presents the most recent debates about Interpreting Studies and Interpreting research in general.

Titscher et al. (2003). This article presents the analysis of the same set of data from five discourse analytical approaches. It is very useful in highlighting the different applications and contributions of diverse DA research approaches.

Wadensjö (2001). This chapter provides an excellent introduction to discourse analytical methods into Community Interpreting research. Wadensjö shares her personal experiences relating to researching interpreter-mediated discourse and offers very useful advice to new researchers.

8
Conducting Research in Community Interpreting

This chapter:

- Describes the most widely followed research steps.
- Provides guidelines for conducting research in Community Interpreting.
- Suggests a number of research projects in Community Interpreting.

8.1 Introduction

The principles behind conducting research in Community Interpreting are the same as those which apply to research in the broad area of the social sciences. Many books have been written on how to conduct research and provide detailed information on this topic. This chapter does not attempt to reproduce what has already been written, but provides a summary for new researchers on the main considerations when embarking on research in Community Interpreting. Suggested further readings on general research methods and paradigms, as well as more specific references on Interpreting research, are listed at the end of this chapter.

8.2 Steps to conducting research

> **Quote 8.1   The research process**
>
> A good research study combines scientific methods and theoretical savvy with a creative turn that surprises and interests a community of scholars. As with any creative process, there is no single best way to approach this process. We have

---

Quote 8.1   (Continued)

found that beginning with an explicit research question is often an effective first step, however. A good research question provides a frame for making decisions about data collection and analysis, explains the motivation behind the study, and provides guidance for writing it up. This is not to say that an explicit research question is always required before beginning a study. In fact, some authors even argue against beginning with a theoretical frame at all.

(Phillips and Hardy, 2002: 60)

The most common way of conducting research is by following a logical and clear progression, which consists of a series of steps, such as reviewing the literature, identifying the issues, formulating the research question, selecting the appropriate methods, collecting and analysing the data and writing up the results. As Weir (2004) states, this paradigm is usually attributed to quantitative research. Other paradigms, such as qualitative methodologies, may not necessarily follow these steps, however, it tends to be the most generic and useful approach to take with any research project. Hall (2002) describes the steps in terms of a cycle rather than a linear process, with each step leading to the next, including the results of the project which may lead to further research, thus starting the cycle again. Not all of the steps suggested below will necessarily be taken with every project. The researcher will need to determine which apply to their particular project.

8.2.1   Interest in a topic

The researcher needs to be motivated by curiosity to discover more about a particular subject. An interest in the subject will generate questions about issues surrounding it. There are limitless questions that have not yet been answered by research in the area of Community Interpreting. As a good starting point, the researcher could write a list of all questions of interest and then prioritise them according to limitations of time, resources, usefulness, applicability and ability to carry out the research, utilising the appropriate methods.

Before deciding on the concrete research questions, it is useful to narrow the field of enquiry. The following questions can be used to guide the researcher in deciding on a topic before embarking on a project. These questions are only suggestions; many others could be posed.

1. What is the setting to be studied: medical, legal, welfare, other, or a combination?

2. Why is the setting worth studying? What will be the benefits of the research to the practice or the training of community interpreters?
3. What mode(s) of interpreting will be studied: long consecutive, short consecutive (dialogue), simultaneous, sight translation, or a combination?
4. Why was this mode chosen? Is there a gap in the knowledge of the best strategies used for each of the skills necessary to interpret in the particular mode?
5. What aspect of the interpreting activity will be studied: the process or the product?
6. Will the research be descriptive or deductive? Or will the project use a combination of approaches?
7. Will the research examine linguistic issues such as accuracy, register, lexical gaps, discourse strategies, discourse markers?
8. Will the research examine cross-cultural issues such as describing cross-cultural differences, dealing with cross-cultural pragmatics, bridging cross-cultural gaps?
9. Will the research examine social issues related to Community Interpreting such as participant attitudes, interactional frameworks, interpreter working conditions, ethics, listener perceptions?
10. Will the research examine skill development issues, such as note-taking, study and preparation?
11. Will the research study curriculum issues, such as curriculum design, teaching methods, staff training?
12. Will the research study assessment issues, such as types of tests, reliability and validity of tests, marking systems?
13. How will a better knowledge of these issues lead to improved practice and training?

8.2.2 Reading and reviewing the literature

Once a topic has been decided on, the next step is to review the literature on the chosen topic. In this way the researcher will discover what is already known and what there is yet to learn. It may well be that the questions that are of interest to the researcher have already been adequately answered in research conducted by others, and so a change of focus is needed. Finding a gap in the literature will lead to a justification for new research. The review of the literature will also help the researcher define concrete questions and work out possible hypotheses. The results of research on Community Interpreting have been published in many publications. These include monographs as well as paper and on-line journal articles (see chapter 9 for the main journals in the field). Articles have been published not only in interpreting and translation journals, but also in journals from other fields such as linguistics, sociolinguistics, psychology, forensic linguistics, medicine and law. The researcher is advised to conduct a wide literature search to discover as much as possible what has been published. On-line searches access literature from around the world. Reviewing the reference lists in published works on Community Interpreting is also a good way of ensuring that all major references are covered.

8.2.3　Defining the research question or questions

Based on the researcher's interests, on issues arising out of professional practice and on the findings from the literature review, one or more research questions will be identified. Research questions normally start as very broad, and are later refined and developed into a number of smaller questions that can be adequately addressed by the research project. The research question will guide the researcher in identifying the steps that follow, the data to be collected and the methods to be employed to collect and analyse the data. The significance of the potential results of the study should also be assessed at this stage. The researcher may have a very keen interest in a topic that has not been addressed before. However, if it is of little interest or value to anyone else, it may not be a very useful topic of enquiry.

It is also important to note at this stage that further questions will arise as the project progresses which were not evident to the researcher before the commencement of the project. Such questions can be pursued as part of the same project or in subsequent projects.

8.2.4　Building hypotheses

Hypothesis-building is an essential part of the hypothetical-deductive experimental approach, where a hypothesis is tested against the results of controlled experiments. Non-experimental research can also find speculating on the results of a project useful, although this is not always necessary. As a general rule, a hypothesis is an informed guess about the possible answer to the proposed question. Such a hypothesis can be based on reading the literature, on anecdotal evidence or on personal experience. While reviewing the literature, the researcher may not be convinced about the results of previous research studies that claim to provide answers to a specific question. The researcher may then form the hypothesis, based on personal experience or on anecdotal evidence, that those results are flawed or do not apply generally in other situations. The researcher can then set out to prove or disprove the hypothesis by conducting new research.

8.2.5 Deciding on the approach and the sources of data to be collected

Once the research questions have been refined and a hypothesis proposed, the means by which those questions are to be answered have to be determined. The research question(s) will determine the approach and the type of data to be collected. Other issues, such as the time-frame and the availability of the data, are also considered at this stage. The approaches that are commonly used in Community Interpreting research have been described in chapter 7. These included discourse analysis and ethnographic and experimental studies. The nature of the project will determine if one or a combination of these is to be used.

Data can be collected by different means. The following are the most common:

Interviews: Interviews may be structured or unstructured. Appointments need to be made with the relevant individuals. The researcher may have a structured questionnaire with questions to be read out during the interview, or general questions to guide the flow of the interview but which allow the interviewee to take other directions. The interview can be audio-taped and transcribed later or taken down as the answers are provided in the form of detailed notes.

For examples of the uses of interviews in Community Interpreting research, see project 8.9 below and sample research study 4 in chapter 7.

Questionnaires: Questionnaires can have closed questions asking for specific information or open questions to allow the respondents to provide their own comments. Closed questions are easier to analyse, as the respondents are given multiple-choice answers which are easily coded and quantified. Open questions need to be analysed qualitatively and grouped into categories. They can also be used as verbatim quotations to illustrate the participants' own views. Statistical packages are available to process questionnaire data.[1]

Writing questionnaires is not a simple task. The questions must address the project's research questions. Clarity is essential. Respondents need to be able to understand what is being asked, so that they all interpret the questions in the same way. If not, the questionnaire risks unreliability. A useful first step is to conduct a pilot of the questionnaire to identify any problems with it. If a particular question elicits confusing answers, it is likely that it is ambiguous and needs to be refined. The mode of administration of a questionnaire can be by post, email, tele-phone or personal interview. If the questionnaire is posted, a pre-paid envelope should be enclosed so that the respondent does not have to pay for postage. A standard response rate for questionnaires is approx-imately 20 per cent. This means that in order for the final sample to be large enough to be of any value, the number of questionnaires sent must be much greater than the expected number of responses. For example, if the researcher decides to study 100 questionnaires, then 500 need to be sent out. It is advisable to consult references on questionnaire design before embarking on a survey project.[2]

For examples of uses of questionnaires in Community Interpreting research, see projects 8.2, 8.4, 8.5, 8.6, 8.9, 8.10 and 8.12 below and sample research study 5 in chapter 7.

Focus groups: Focus groups include a facilitator, 8–10 participants and an observer who takes notes. Focus group discussions can also be audio recorded and later transcribed. Focus groups can be held in preparation for a formal questionnaire, to distil ideas and refine ques-tions, or after a questionnaire has been returned and analysed, to clarify issues that were not clear from the results of the questionnaire. Focus groups cannot be representative as the number of participants is small, but they can provide important insights into a topic,[3] espe-cially if the facilitator can engender productive dialogues among the participants.

For examples of the use of focus group discussions in Community Interpreting research see projects 8.4, 8.5 and 8.12 below and chapter 6, where the results of a focus group discussion are reported.

Audio- or video-recordings of interpreted interactions: Authentic or simu-lated interpreted interactions can be audio- or video-recorded to be tran-scribed and analysed later. The detail of the transcription will depend on the research questions and on the approach taken. Some interpreted interactions, such as courtroom proceedings or police records of inter-view, are routinely audio-recorded, which facilitates the data collection process. It also avoids the interference of the presence of the researcher, which can impact on the performance of the interactants. For private interviews, such as lawyer–client, doctor–patient, speech pathologist–patient or any other, the researcher will need to set up the recording equipment in an inconspicuous place, but where it is still capable of producing a good quality recording. Whether the interviews are to be audio- or video-recorded will depend on the purpose of the research. If aspects such as seating arrangements, body language or facial expressions are to be analysed, a video-recording is essential. Video-recordings are also vital in any interaction where sign language interpreting is involved.

See Roy (2000a) for an example of the use of video-recordings in sign language interpreting research. See also projects 8.1, 8.2, 8.4, 8.6 and 8.12 below and sample research studies 1, 2 and 6 in chapter 7 for examples of the use of audio- and video-recordings in Community Interpreting research.

Published material: Published material, such as reports, judgments or transcriptions of oral speech, can also be used. Much of this material can be found on the Web.

See project 8.7 below for an example of the use of these data in Community Interpreting research. See also section 9.9 of chapter 9 for a list of relevant websites which provide publicly available court data.

Observation (fieldwork): There are instances where neither audio- nor video-recordings will be permitted or even possible. In these cases the researcher will need to rely on personal observation to collect the data. This is common in ethnographic research, where the researcher observes the behaviour(s) of a certain group or individual and makes contemporaneous notes.[4]

See projects 8.1 and 8.5 below and sample research study 3 in chapter 7 for examples of the use of observation in Community Interpreting research.

Experiments: Experiments produce very specific data. Experimental designs will differ according to the aims of the experiment. One type of experiment in Community Interpreting involves simulations of interpreted interactions, where all the variables, such as pre-written questions and answers, the setting, length of time allowed and the chosen subjects, are controlled. Such experiments can test results found in naturally occurring situations. For instance, the researcher may want to confirm the ways in which interpreters in a specific language interpret a particular type of question or a politeness marker, for example, and include these features in the simulated text to be interpreted. The same text would be presented to a number of interpreters and the results analysed and compared. Another type of experiment in Community Interpreting involves a control group and an experimental group. The researcher's aim may be to ascertain whether awareness of certain features in the discourse, such as discourse markers, will lead interpreters to keep them in their interpretation, rather than omit them altogether. The control group consists of a group of practising interpreters who are asked to interpret a number of utterances which include discourse markers. The experimental group consists of another group of interpreters who receive a number of classes on the significance and impact of discourse markers and on how to interpret them into the other language. They would then be asked to interpret the same utterances presented to the control group. The results of both groups are later analysed and compared.[5]

See projects 8.3, 8.6 and 8.12 below and sample research project 6 in chapter 7 for examples of the use of experiments in Community Interpreting research.

8.2.6   Conducting ethical research

Ethics is an important part of responsible research. Ethics refers to two main areas: the first relates to obtaining informed consent from the subjects to be studied and permission from the relevant authorities when applicable; the second relates to the integrity of the data and the results the researcher reports in subsequent publications.

In relation to the first issue, the following considerations must be taken into account:

1. *Institutional ethics clearance*: When the data collected for the project are not publicly available and involve human subjects, ethics clearance from the relevant ethics committee must be sought. The institution responsible for clearance may be the university for which the researcher works or in which the researcher is enrolled as a research student, and/or other public organisations, such as the Health Department. It is crucial that ethics clearance be obtained before commencing a research project. Researchers need to anticipate that it may take several months for approval to be obtained. The clearance will be granted if certain conditions are adhered to, which include the points below.
2. *Informed consent*: Adult subjects need to give informed consent to participate in a project. Child subjects require the consent of their parents or guardians. The researcher must provide the subjects with detailed information about the aims and methodology of the project and the nature of their involvement. An information sheet providing the relevant information about the project should accompany a consent form to be signed by the subject. The information sheet and consent form need to be written in the language the participant understands.

In Community Interpreting research, participants may not understand the mainstream language. In those cases, the information sheet and consent form need to be translated into the relevant language.
3. *Confidentiality*: For most projects, an assurance that the subjects' identities will be kept anonymous to maintain confidentiality is also required.

The second aspect of ethical research relates to the integrity of the research project itself and of the results reported by the researcher. The researcher should take every care to ensure that the methods used are reliable, to provide a detailed explanation of the data and methodology as a way of ensuring transparency, and of reporting the results truthfully. The researcher has a moral obligation to the public to conduct responsible research and to disseminate the results in the same manner.

8.2.7   Deciding on the methods of analysis to be employed

The methods adopted will depend on the type of question, on the data and on the orientation of the researcher. (See chapter 7 for the most typical methods in Community Interpreting.)

Some of the questions to be asked before deciding on the method include:

1. Will the study be theoretical or empirical? Empirical research is based on evidence from the real world. Theoretical research is based on ideas that are 'abstract or purely analytical' (McNeill and Chapman, 2004: 2) and not necessarily backed up by evidence. Usually, empirical research informs the theory, so theories can be based on empirical research. On the other hand, the theory informs the type of empirical research that is to be conducted. All data-based research is empirical research.
2. Will the study use qualitative or quantitative methods? Quantitative research derives from the natural sciences and relates to quantifying in statistical terms the results of research. The approach to quantitative research is a positivist one – that the data should be as objective as possible in order to be valid. This means being as free as possible from researcher bias. It is also believed, under this methodology, that the greater and the more random the sample, the more reliable and objective the data will be.
   Qualitative research refers to words rather than numbers and is usually carried out by case studies, interviews, focus groups and/or

single text analysis, where quantification is not seen as important as the analysis of the data by interpretative means. The approach to qualitative research is therefore interpretivist. The researcher's own ideas and opinions are clearly mingled with the analysis. A combination of quantitative and qualitative methods to analyse the data is a very common way to conduct research.

3. Will the study be descriptive or explanatory? Descriptive research aims only to describe a particular situation, strategy or discourse style, for example. The questions descriptive research aims to answer refer to what happens, when, by whom, how many times, etc. Explanatory research aims to explain the reasons behind the what, when or by whom, and attempts to find a solution to the problem. As with the use of quantitative and qualitative methods, a combination of descriptive and explanatory methods is commonly used. McNeill and Chapman comment that 'The distinction between descriptive research and explanatory research is often blurred. Any explanation requires description, and it is difficult, or perhaps impossible, to describe something without at the same time explaining it' (2004: 8).

The need for reliable and valid research methods

Research methods are said to be reliable if other researchers, or the same researcher at a later date, using the same methods, arrive at the same conclusions. There is always the risk that research that is conducted by one researcher in situations that cannot be replicated, with data that cannot be controlled, such as naturally occurring data, is in danger of being considered unreliable. The larger the sample and the greater the frequency of the results, the more reliable the conclusions will be. Many Community Interpreting studies use very small data sets and cannot claim to be representative. They can nevertheless be very useful as case studies. As Phillips and Hardy comment, 'social research does not have to be based on a representative sample . . . case-studies may prompt further, more wide-ranging research, providing ideas to be followed up later' (2002: 120–1). Gile (2004) has criticised translation studies in general for being too subjective, based on theoretical, conceptual arguments alone, rather than on reliable data. Such criticism can be extended to some Community Interpreting research, where a number of studies claim to provide generalisable results of interpreter practices but draw on isolated examples for their conclusions (cf Hertog, Van Gucht and de Bontridder, 2006). Such studies give the reader no indication of the frequency of the occurrence of such practices, making it difficult to ascertain whether the examples presented constitute the norm or the exception in interpreted interaction. It is admittedly very difficult to access large amounts of interpreted data. Most of the studies have been conducted on ad hoc, unprofessional and untrained interpreters. Nevertheless, there has been a tendency to generalise results to apply to all situations and all interpreters. This tendency has led to the very common claim that accurate interpreting is impossible, as is the adherence to the demands of the code of ethics. Although researchers often alert readers to the limitations of their findings, these warnings can often be overlooked when others quote their work.

Triangulation is a common way of ensuring more reliable results. Triangulation refers to the use of a combination of methods to cross-check the reliability of the results. If all the methods lead to the same results, then those results are considered to be reliable.

> A number of writers have used combinations of methods and data as a means of confirming or disconfirming a finding or hypothesis initially produced by the use of one particular method. For example, in-depth interviews may be used to check patterns or findings generated through participant observation, or simple forms of counting may check the generality of a qualitative insight...Thus, if the use of other methods turns up the same finding or result, then it is confirmed. If it does not, then the initial finding may be discarded as an artifact or aberration caused by the method used...(Layder, 1993: 121)

A number of researchers have used triangulation in Community Interpreting research (see Berk-Seligson, 1990/2002; Angelelli, 2004; Hale, 2004). Some research methodologies, such as ethnography, are not as concerned with reliability as much as they are with validity. Validity refers to the authenticity of the data, with whether the data are a true reflection of reality. Naturally occurring data score very highly on the aspect of validity, as they are not manipulated in the same way as experimental data. Experimental data, if constructed by the researcher, can be seen to lack ecological validity.[6] Triangulation, therefore, can help to reduce problems of validity. (See further readings for more information on reliability and validity of research methods.)

8.2.8 Writing up and disseminating the results

In order for any research to be useful to others, its results need to be disseminated. This can be achieved by writing up the results as a report, a thesis or a research paper. As discussed in chapter 7, it is also important to make the results accessible to practitioners, educators and students in oral presentations at conferences, professional seminars and other such venues. The type of paper or presentation will determine the manner in which the results are reported and the detail of its contents. When a research paper is written, it is important to provide all the relevant details of the research methodology, including the methods used to collect and analyse the data as well as a full description of the subjects of the study. By providing a detailed description of these aspects, the project can be adequately assessed by others and even replicated with different data-sets. It is important to point out the study's limitations and to not over-generalise the results or make unsubstantiated claims. When the results are being presented orally, they need to be made accessible to the audience wherever possible, within a limited time period. Usually the best way to present the data is by concentrating on the most important findings and explaining them in language that will be understood by the target audience. The aim of disseminating research results is for others to gain knowledge about the topic which can help them in their practice as interpreters or educators, or can generate more questions for further research.

8.3   Sample research projects

In chapters 1–7, a number of research gaps were identified in different areas of Community Interpreting. Some of these derived from the review of the research literature, some from the analysis of training programmes and some from the responses of practising interpreters themselves. This section provides a number of sample research projects that can be conducted by students of Community Interpreting or other researchers. Each project provides a description of the research question and suggested methods of data collection and analysis.

Research project 8.1

Research question
Is there any difference in the performance of trained and untrained interpreters?

Hypothesis
That trained interpreters perform with a higher level of competence and confidence than untrained interpreters, resulting in a much more satisfactory outcome.

Background
There is still no agreement that training is necessary for community interpreters. This is evident in the fact that compulsory pre-service training is not a reality anywhere in the world (see chapter 6). Proponents of training, however, argue that training is crucial. Little if any research has been conducted to prove this hypothesis empirically. The question is very broad and needs to be narrowed to more manageable questions. The questions posed under step 1 in section 8.2.1 will help the researcher narrow the focus. For this particular project, the aspect of interactional performance has been chosen. This question is not concerned with accuracy of interpretation. The question posed in Project 8.2 looks at accuracy issues.

Revised question
Is there any difference in the interactional performance of trained and untrained court interpreters?

Setting
The courtroom.

Specific issues the study will investigate
a. Observance of courtroom protocol (e.g. knowledge of who to address in which way, bowing when entering the courtroom, knowledge of how to seek leave to speak or ask for clarifications).
b. Appropriate use of grammatical person when interpreting.
c. Number and types of interruptions by interpreter.
d. Ways in which the interpreter ensures all parties are informed if clarifications are necessary.
e. Manner in which the interpreter provides linguistic or cultural explanations to the court.
f. Appropriate use of mode according to phase of the proceedings.

Research methodology
Ethnographic, qualitative and quantitative discourse analytical.

Data collection
- Video-recordings (if permitted) or observation and audio-recordings of interpreted proceedings in the court.
- A minimum of ten court proceedings.
- The profiles of the interpreters to ascertain their level and type of training and their years of experience collected via a short questionnaire administered to the interpreter at the time of consent to participate in the project.

Subjects
Ten interpreters of different language combinations and training backgrounds.

Ethics approval
Ethics clearance will need to be obtained in the form of permission and consent from the Courts Administration, as well as from the participants.

Research project 8.1   (Continued)

Method of analysis
1. The questionnaire results will be collated to establish the differences in education between the interpreters and sort them into two groups. These will be
   used later to correlate the results of the discourse analysis with the interpreters'
   background.
2. The video- and/or audio-recordings will be studied to describe the performances of the different interpreters according to the features stated above.
3. A quantitative analysis of the frequency and percentages of the different findings for each group will be conducted.
4. A qualitative conversational analysis of the interaction will be conducted
   to describe and explain the interpreters' performances according to each
   group.
5. Differences and similarities between the two groups will be noted and
   analysed.

Reflecting on the findings
This stage is crucial for writing up the results. After an objective reporting of the
findings, the author will provide a subjective reading of the results. During this
stage the researcher will reflect and speculate on the possible reasons for the
results, test the stated hypothesis, decide whether further research is needed to
answer the original question, decide whether further questions have arisen from
the research, reflect on the strengths and weaknesses of the study and decide
on a forum for dissemination. The researcher's knowledge of the literature on
related and other relevant research is crucial in reflecting on the reasons for and
significance of the findings.

Writing up the results
Where the results are published will depend on the purpose of the study
and its quality. A useful first forum of dissemination is as a paper at a
conference where feedback from peers can be obtained and further refinements made. The results of this project will be relevant to practitioners, so a
seminar to the relevant professional association would be a good forum for
dissemination.

Research project 8.2

The research question
Are there any differences in the level of accuracy of interpretation achieved by
trained and untrained interpreters when interpreting the question-and-answer
sequence in the courtroom in the consecutive interpreting mode?

Hypothesis
That untrained interpreters will render accurately only the propositional content of the utterances, ignoring stylistic and supra-segmental features that impinge on the pragmatic meaning and force of the discourse.

Background
This is a refined version of the general question presented in Project 8.1 on the differences between trained and untrained interpreters, hence the background is the same. Whereas Project 8.1 looks at the interactional performance of interpreters, this project looks at the level of accuracy achieved by the two groups. These two projects deal with court interpreting. Replications of these projects can be conducted in other settings.

Setting
The courtroom.

Specific issues the study will investigate:
Accuracy of propositional content and of pragmatic force.

a. Omissions and additions to the propositional content of questions and answers.
b. Interpretation of pragmatic markers such as discourse markers, fillers and hedges.
c. Adequate interpretation of the pragmatic force of questions and answers.
d. Interpretation of politeness forms and markers.
e. Accuracy of interpretation of register.
f. Mimicking tone of voice.
g. Use of appropriate intonation patterns.

Research methodology
Ethnographic, qualitative and quantitative discourse analytical.

Data collection
- Audio-recordings of interpreted court proceedings.
- A minimum of ten court proceedings.
- The profiles of the interpreters to ascertain their level and type of training and their years of experience will be collected via a short questionnaire administered to the interpreter at the time of consent to participate in the project.

Subjects
Ten interpreters of the same language combination, five trained and five untrained, with comparable years of experience. The same project can be replicated with different language combinations.

Ethics approval
Ethics clearance will need to be obtained in the form of permission and consent from the Courts Administration, as well as from the participants.

Research project 8.2   (Continued)

Method of analysis
1. The questionnaire results will be collated to establish the differences in education between the interpreters and sort them into two groups. These will be used to correlate the results of the discourse analysis with the background of the interpreters.
2. The audio-recordings will be transcribed and coded for the features outlined above.
3. A quantitative analysis of the frequency and percentages of the different findings for each group will be conducted.
4. A qualitative conversational analysis of the interaction will be conducted to describe and explain the interpreters' performances according to each group.
5. Differences and similarities between the two groups will be noted and analysed.

Reflecting on the findings
As in Project 8.1.

Writing up the results
As in Project 8.1.

Research project 8.3

The research question
Can interpreters be taught to mimic the style of the source speech in their renditions?

Hypothesis
That it is possible for interpreters to obtain a high level of stylistic accuracy once trained to do so.

Background
This study is related to Project 8.2. Whereas in Project 8.2 naturally occurring data are analysed to ascertain whether these features are maintained in the interpreters' renditions, this project uses experimental methods to elicit the data.

Research into speech style has demonstrated that different styles produce different evaluations of the speaker's character, intelligence and trustworthiness from the listener. This is particularly relevant in the legal sector, and to a lesser extent in doctor-patient interactions. Research into interpreted interaction has shown that interpreters rarely maintain stylistic features such as hesitations, fillers, discourse markers, pauses and intonation in their renditions, maintaining the propositional content alone and improving on the coherence of the target language utterances. Such practices may be due to a lack of awareness of the importance of style. This project will attempt to determine whether it is possible, after making interpreters aware of this, to maintain such high level of accuracy.

Setting
Simulated police interviews.

Specific issues the study will investigate
Whether it is possible for interpreters to obtain a high level of stylistic accuracy in their interpretation simply after being made aware of their importance.

The stylistic features that will be analysed are: discourse markers, fillers, hesitations, pauses and appropriate intonation.

Research methodology
Discourse analytical and experimental.

Data collection
- Write simulated dialogues based on authentic oral speech, using discourse markers, fillers, hesitations, pauses and appropriate intonation.
- Form five groups of two interpreters from the same language to act out the parts of minority language speaker and interpreter. If resources permit, have five language combinations.
- If possible, have police officers participate to act out the police role. If not, have mainstream language speakers take the part of the police officer.
- Act out the first interpreted dialogue and audio-record it. The scripted dialogue will only contain the turns in the two languages. The subjects who play the part of the interpreter will interpret each segment without any prior preparation.
- After the first dialogue has been recorded, provide six one-hour classes a week to the group of interpreters on the impact of stylistic features in the evaluation of character and have the interpreters practise a number of dialogues aiming to achieve a high level of stylistic accuracy
- At the completion of the lectures, repeat the original simulated exercise, using the same dialogue and the same interpreters.
- Transcribe the interpreted dialogues, coding the relevant stylistic features (discourse markers, fillers, pauses, etc.).

Subjects
Ten interpreters of five language combinations who have had no prior interpreting training.

Ethics approval
Ethics clearance will need to be obtained from the relevant university. The participants will need to provide informed consent to participate in the project.

Method of analysis
1. The transcriptions will be analysed quantitatively for the occurrences of omissions and rendition of stylistic features in the interpreters' performances, and the results before and after the classes will be compared.

Research project 8.3   (Continued)

2. Qualitative discourse analytical methods will be used for the analysis of the accuracy and effectiveness of the translations. The before and the after performances will be compared.
3. Experts in each of the language combinations will be needed for this project. If the researcher wants to work alone, then only the language combination known to the researcher will be used.

Reflecting on the findings
As in Project 8.1.

Writing up the results
As in Project 8.1.

Research project 8.4

The research question
How consistent are interpreters' evaluations of cultural issues?

Hypothesis
That interpreters will interpret the relevance of culture in different ways depending on their own backgrounds.

Background
The question of whether interpreters should be cultural brokers in the course of their work remains highly controversial (see discussions in chapters 2, 3 and 5). Very little research has been conducted in this area, so a number of questions relating to this would be very useful. The purpose of the proposed question is to ascertain whether cultural issues are easily identified by any interpreter, and whether all interpreters of the same language combination agree on the interpretation of such issues, so as to justify the call for reliable cultural brokerage.

Setting
Simulated doctor-patient consultation.

Specific issues the study will investigate
Whether a group of interpreters working in the same language combination agree on when to offer cultural brokerage and whether their explanations coincide. The researcher will have to identify a number of issues that can be related to cultural differences. This will depend on the language combination studied.

Research methodology
Ethnographic and experimental.

Data collection

- Video-recordings: produce five simulated medical consultations with a patient who speaks the relevant language and an interpreter. Each of these scenarios will present a communication breakdown, despite the accurate interpretation of the interpreter.
- Show the video-recordings independently to each of the ten interpreters and provide them with a short questionnaire asking why the communication breakdowns occurred: Were they due to poor communication skills from the doctor? Lack of understanding of the content? Poor interpretation? Cross-cultural misunderstandings?
- At the conclusion of the evaluation of the videos by all interpreters, invite them to participate in a focus group discussion.

Subjects
Ten interpreters of the same language combination, preferably with different backgrounds, i.e. born in different countries, raised in different countries, different levels of education.

Ethics approval
Ethics clearance will need to be obtained from the relevant university. The participants will need to provide informed consent to participate in the project.

Method of analysis

1. Analyse the results of the questionnaires using both quantitative and qualitative methods.
2. Analyse the focus group discussion.
3. Compare the results from both methods of data collection.

Reflecting on the findings
As in Project 8.1.

Writing up the results
As in Project 8.1.

Research project 8.5

The research question
How often are interpreters confronted with situations that pressure them to breach their code of ethics, in particular concerning matters of accuracy, impartiality and confidentiality, and how do they deal with them?

Hypothesis
That interpreters cannot consistently adhere to their code of ethics due to external pressures beyond their control.

Research project 8.5   (Continued)

Background
Some of the literature claims that interpreters are not able to abide by their code of ethics due to external pressures which lead to ethical dilemmas (see discussion in chapter 4). However, this claim has not been adequately tested empirically. There is ample anecdotal evidence to support the claim that it is difficult for interpreters consistently to abide by their code of ethics, but this does not prove that it is impossible, nor does it specify the types of ethical dilemmas, their frequency, how these pressures impinge on the interpreter's ability to abide by their code of ethics, and how different interpreters deal with such situations. If these questions are adequately answered by empirical research, then steps can be taken to rectify the situation.

Setting
Community Interpreting settings in general.

Specific issues the study will investigate
The types, sources and frequency of ethical dilemmas interpreters face to breach their code of ethics, and their way of dealing with each of them.

Research methodology
Ethnographic.

Data collection

- Questionnaire: a general questionnaire to elicit personal details from inter-preters.
- Observation sheet: an observation sheet for interpreters to take with them to every assignment for a period of six months to document in detail every ethical dilemma they encounter, the speculated reasons for them and their responses to them.
- Have the interpreters return the questionnaire and the observation sheets by a specified date.
- Invite the interpreters to a focus group discussion for debriefing.
- Ethics approval will need to be obtained.

Subjects
Ten interpreters of ten different language combinations with different levels of interpreting training.

Ethics approval
Ethics clearance will need to be obtained from the relevant university. The parti-cipating interpreters will need to provide informed consent to participate in the project. The interpreters who will be making the observation notes after each assignment need to be properly briefed on taking notes anonymously after each assignment.

Method of analysis

- Collect and code the questionnaires.
- Analyse questionnaires quantitatively to describe the background of the interpreters.
- Collect and code the observation sheets. These will need to be qualitatively analysed first to categorise the different ethical dilemmas into groups. A quantitative analysis may be possible to ascertain whether particular dilemmas are more common than others.
- The responses to each dilemma then need to be classified. A quantification of the types of strategies used to deal with each dilemma will be useful.
- The results will then be divided into those dilemmas that are mostly dealt with successfully and those which are not. The researcher will qualitatively analyse the results to speculate on the reasons behind the interpreters' responses, using their questionnaires to take into account each interpreter's background.
- The SPSS package may be used to analyse the data.

Reflecting on the findings
As in Project 8.1.

Writing up the results
As in Project 8.1.

Research project 8.6

The research question
To what extent are renditions of the police caution by different interpreters understood differently by the listeners?

Hypothesis
That different renditions of the caution may influence the way it is understood by the listeners.

Background
Much has been written about the difficulties surrounding the comprehension of the caution when administered by police to English-speaking detainees. These difficulties have been attributed to the syntax and lexis of the caution, as well as to its delivery. The administration of the caution through an interpreter has not received much attention. The few studies that have analysed the interpretation of the caution have looked at case studies and analysed the difficulties encountered by interpreters in achieving an accurate rendition (see discussion in chapter 3). This project will aim to ascertain whether different accurate renditions of the caution will lead to different understandings of it by the listeners and whether the listeners' backgrounds influence their understanding.

Research project 8.6   (Continued)

Setting
Police interviews.

Specific issues the study will investigate
- Linguistic variations in the interpretations of the caution by different interpreters of the same language combination.
- Understanding of the caution by the listeners of the different renditions.

Research methodology
Questionnaire, discourse analysis and experimental.

Data collection
- Questionnaires: Design and administer a questionnaire for the interpreters and one for the minority language speakers to elicit personal details and general answers about the interpretation of the caution.
- Experiment:
  - Have an English speaker read out the caution sentence by sentence and each interpreter interpret it into their target language to three minority language speakers each.
  - At the end of each interpreted sentence, have the interpreter ask the minority language speaker to tell them what they understood by that sentence.
  - Audio-/video-record the interviews.

Subjects
Five interpreters of the same language combination; fifteen minority language speakers. The same project can be replicated using different language combinations.

Ethics approval
Ethics clearance will need to be obtained from the relevant university. The participants will need to provide informed consent to participate in the project.

Method of analysis
1. Code and analyse the questionnaires.
2. Use the results of the questionnaires to inform the qualitative analysis of the results of the experiment.
3. Transcribe the recordings.
4. Compare the renditions of each interpreter using quantitative and qualitative discourse analytical methods.
5. Assess whether the same interpreter interpreted the caution in the same way each time.
6. Compare the responses from each minority language speaker.
7. Analyse whether the differences of understanding of the caution by each minority language speaker relate to the differences found in the interpreters' renditions.

8. Analyse the possible reasons for the differences and ascertain whether they are significant discrepancies.
9. Correlate the results of the minority speakers' questionnaires about their backgrounds, with the results of their answers regarding their understanding of the caution.

Reflecting on the findings
As in Project 8.1.

Writing up the results
As in Project 8.1. The results of this project will be very useful to law enforcement practitioners, the results should therefore be published in legal journals and other publications accessed by police.

Research project 8.7

The research question
Are there any legal appeals on the grounds of incompetent interpreting? If there are, how is incompetent interpreting defined and what have been the outcomes?

Hypothesis
No hypothesis is needed for this project, as it is a purely descriptive study.

Background
Some researchers have speculated that incompetent interpreting can influence the outcome of legal cases. However, for the majority of cases, incompetent interpreting is not detected by any of the other court participants. This project would attempt to ascertain whether there have been cases where lawyers have claimed incompetence as grounds for appeal, on what they have based their claims, whether they have been justified and whether they have been successful. This can be a small study, concentrating on one state or one country, within one jurisdiction, or it can be a major study covering a number of countries and jurisdictions.

Setting
Court interpreting.

- Whether incompetent interpreting is detected at all in this setting.

Specific issues the study will investigate
If so:

- In what jurisdictions?
- In what types of cases?
- On what basis?
- How did the court establish incompetence?
- Have these appeals been successful?
- What were the background, qualifications and language combinations of the interpreters involved?

Research project 8.7   (Continued)

This type of research could lead to practical recommendations for the improvement of interpreting services, the establishment of minimum qualifications for
interpreters working in this field, and the improvement of recruitment procedures.

Research methodology
Descriptive desk research.

Data collection
- The data will comprise published legal judgments. All judgments can be
  accessed on the Web (see a selection of judgments websites in chapter 9).
- Do a search of appeal judgments to look for relevant cases.

Ethics approval
No ethics approval is required for this type of review research, as the data are
publicly available.

Method of analysis
- Sort cases into categories: jurisdiction (civil versus criminal), court tier (e.g.
  District, Supreme), outcome (appeal upheld/dismissed), role of interpreter
  (interpreter for the accused or for one or more witnesses), nature of the appeal
  (type of incompetence quoted as grounds, how were these grounds proven?
  What expert witnesses were called to support such claims?), language of inter-
  preter, qualifications of interpreter.
- Quantify the above categories.
- Qualitatively assess the findings: is there a trend in the types of appeal that were
  upheld? The quantitative results will provide the answer.

Reflecting on the findings
As in Project 8.1.

Writing up the results
As in Project 8.1. The results of this research will be very useful for legal practitioners,
including the judiciary. They should therefore be published in legal journals.

Research project 8.8

The research question
What are the major difficulties encountered by interpreters when interpreting
politeness levels?

Hypothesis
That interpreters may find it difficult to maintain the same levels of politeness
when interpreting unless extra explanations are provided to explain cultural
differences.

Background
Politeness across cultures is expressed through language and through conventional actions. Linguistically, interpreters may need to change the grammatical form of utterances, and at times omit or add certain linguistic markers in order to achieve a pragmatically accurate rendition. For example, a polite indirect request in the form of a question in English may need to be changed into a direct request in the imperative mood in the form of a command, using politeness markers in other languages to achieve the same intention. When politeness is expressed through conventional actions, the interpreter is confronted with further difficulties. Is the interpreter, for example, to explain socio-pragmatic conventions to the different parties to avoid misunderstandings? These can include actions such as avoiding eye contact, personal space, hand shaking or kissing or other greeting conventions, etc.

Setting
Welfare interview (any setting is appropriate).

Specific issues the study will investigate

- Identify the different ways politeness is expressed by participants from different cultures in welfare interviews.
- Identify the linguistic means of expressing politeness.
- Identify the non-linguistic ways of expressing politeness.
- Analyse the way interpreters are able to understand the politeness conventions in one culture and language.
- Analyse the way interpreters are able to convert politeness conventions into pragmatically appropriate practices in the target language and culture, at the same level of politeness.

Research methodology
Ethnographic, discourse analytical (specifically conversation analysis).

Data collection

- Choose a language combination.
- Contact a social security office to obtain permission to video record a number of welfare interviews with interpreters.
- Record at least ten interviews.

Subjects
Welfare worker(s), welfare client(s), interpreter(s).

Ethics approval
Ethics clearance will need to be obtained from the relevant welfare institution and from the relevant university. All the participants will need to provide informed consent to participate in the project.

Method of analysis

- Transcribe interviews and annotate paralinguistic and non-linguistic cues observable on video.

Research project 8.8   (Continued)

- Identify the socio-pragmatic politeness conventions present in the interview (e.g. greetings, request to sit, bows, handshakes, eye contact, etc.).
- Identify the linguistic politeness markers in the speech of both main participants.
- Identify the syntactic and grammatical politeness markers in the speech of both main participants, including the use of indirectness.
- Quantify the frequencies of each type of politeness indicator.
- Analyse the way the interpreter renders the above.
- Qualitatively assess the findings: Can you find any patterns in the way politeness is/is not expressed by the social worker and the welfare recipient? Can you find any patterns in the way interpreters convey those politeness markers and conventions? Do interpreters represent the politeness levels of the main participants or do they use their own politeness conventions regardless of what the other interlocutors do? Do interpreters explain any extra linguistic politeness conventions?

Reflecting on the findings
As in Project 8.1.

Writing up the results
As in Project 8.1.

Research project 8.9

The research question
What are the minority speakers' perceptions and expectations of professional interpreters?

Hypothesis
That most minority speakers who need the services of interpreters have different expectations and perceptions of the role of the interpreter, many of which conflict with the professional interpreter's code of ethics.

Background
The minority language speaker is normally the powerless participant in the interaction. Previous research has found that due to a multiplicity of experiences in speaking through a range of people who act as interpreters - from their own young children, to friends, to ad hoc and professional interpreters - these people may be confused about what to expect from professional interpreters (see discussion in chapter 4). The aim of this study is to ascertain what the general view of minority language speakers is and to propose ways to raise their level of awareness of their entitlements to professional services as well as the professional role of interpreters.

Setting
General community interpreting settings.

Specific issues the study will investigate

- Are service recipients aware of the role of the interpreter?
- What are their perceptions of the role of the interpreter?
- Do they know how to speak through an interpreter?

Research methodology
Ethnographic, questionnaires.

Data collection

- Choose four language pairs.
- Design a questionnaire to be administered to minority language speakers.
- Have the questionnaire translated into the relevant languages.
- Contact ethnic community centres for the relevant languages to obtain permission to administer the questionnaire to their clients.
- Administer the questionnaire in the form of an interview to the different minority language speakers. A number of research assistants with command of the relevant languages will be needed. If this is not possible, the researcher will need to concentrate on the language(s) familiar to them.

Subjects
Twenty speakers of five different community languages. Choose the five community languages that are among the highest languages of demand for interpreter services.

Ethics approval
Ethics clearance will need to be obtained from the relevant university and ethnic community centres. The participants will need to provide informed consent to participate in the project.

Method of analysis

- Codify the questionnaires' answers.
- Quantify the frequencies of each answer.
- Categorise the answers into groups.

Reflecting on the findings
As in Project 8.1.

Writing up the results
As in Project 8.1. The results of this project will be relevant to the community language speakers. The results should therefore be made accessible to them. Publishing an article in the relevant language press can be a good way of disseminating the results.

Research project 8.10

The research question
What are the training requirements, working conditions and pay rates of community interpreters?

Hypothesis
That the majority of employers do not offer higher rates of pay to better qualified interpreters, nor do they provide any training opportunities.

Background
As chapters 5 and 6 have discussed, training is not compulsory in order to practise as an interpreter. Some survey research (e.g. Ozolins, 2004) has found that employers do not pay trained interpreters higher rates, thus providing no incentive to untrained interpreters to acquire any training. Working conditions and remuneration levels are common areas of complaint for practising interpreters. This study should provide empirical data about the extent of the problem in a specific place and area of interpreting. The study can be a narrow study of one state or one country, or it can be a broader study which reviews the situation in more than one country.

Setting
General community interpreting settings.

Specific issues the study will investigate
- The type of interpreting training required by employers of their employees.
- The working conditions and rates of pay employers offer to interpreters with varying training levels.
- The employers' understanding and perception of the practice of Community Interpreting.

Research methodology
Desk research and ethnographic.

Data collection
- Identify the geographical area of the study.
- Choose the major community interpreter employers in the area. These can be found through an internet search or a search on the Yellow Pages directory.
- Design a questionnaire to elicit the appropriate information.
- Administer the questionnaire.

Subjects
At least ten representatives from different employing agencies. The number of agencies will depend on the geographical area covered by the project.

Ethics approval
Ethics clearance will need to be obtained from the relevant university. The participants will need to provide informed consent to participate in the project.

Method of analysis
Qualitative and quantitative. The questionnaire is analysed as proposed for previous projects.

Reflecting on the findings
As in Project 8.1.

Writing up the results
As in Project 8.1. It would be useful for the agencies to receive a report of the results.

Research project 8.11

The research question
How do speech therapists overcome cross-linguistic differences in the speech assessment of speakers of a minority language?

Hypothesis
That very few speech therapists and interpreters are aware of the difficulties associated with speech assessments when an interpreter is involved, which may lead to incorrect assessments.

Background
Patterns of language acquisition are crucial in speech therapists' assessments of their patients' speech. For example, the passive voice in English is believed to be acquired between ages 3 and 4. This may not be the case in other languages, however, where the passive voice may only be used as a highly literary device, such as in Punjabi (see Duncan, 1989). In the case of Spanish, an impersonal third person plural construction such as *Me dijeron que* can be translated as a passive 'I was told' or as 'They told me'. These differences will cause obvious obstacles in the case of an interpreted consultation. The speech therapist will need to be aware of the cross-linguistic differences and the interpreter will also need to be aware of the significance of particular language structures to the therapist's assessment.

Setting
A consultation with a speech therapist where the patient requires the services of an interpreter.

Specific issues the study will investigate

- Whether the speech pathologist has a briefing session with the interpreter prior to the consultation to explain the aims of the consultation and the linguistic features that are important to the assessment.
- Whether the interpreter is equipped to explain cross linguistic differences to the therapist.

Research project 8.11   (Continued)

- Whether the interpreter stops the consultation to address cross linguistic syntactic and semantic differences.
- If so, how frequently and what types of differences are highlighted.
- How the speech pathologist deals with such differences.

Research methodology
Descriptive, using both qualitative and quantitative discourse analytical methods. A descriptive study will be able to identify the issues surrounding this context. Further experimental research can be conducted to investigate specific aspects of the situation.

Data collection

- Choose five language combinations. Alternatively, one language combination can be chosen and the project replicated in other languages.
- Contact a number of speech pathologists to participate in the project
- Video- or audio-record five consultations, including briefings and debriefings if they take place.

Subjects
Five interpreters of different language combination, one or more speech pathologists, five minority language speaking patients.

Ethics approval
Ethics clearance will need to be obtained from the relevant university and the medical institution, if it is not a private practice. The participants will need to provide informed consent to participate in the project.

Method of analysis

- View and transcribe the consultations, briefings and debriefings.
- Identify the issues stated above.
- Quantify each of the occurrences and compare across the different interpreted consultations.
- Qualitatively analyse the ways difficulties were identified and dealt with by the pathologist and by the interpreter.
- Identify further questions to pursue in future experimental studies.

Reflecting on the findings
As in Project 8.1.

Writing up the results
As in Project 8.1. The results of this project will be of relevance to speech pathologists. The results should therefore be published in journals that are relevant to both professions.

Research project 8.12

The format of this project is different from the others, as its focus is on the use of triangulation rather than on the specific research steps. However, the same steps as for the previous projects are also applicable here.

The research question
How do interpreters interpret offensive language and what are the consequences of their choices?

Hypothesis
That interpreters take different approaches to the interpreting of offensive language, from omitting it altogether, to attempting to maintain a pragmatically adequate version of it. It is also hypothesised that the interpreters' choices in this regard will have important consequences on the interaction.

Background
Anecdotal evidence has shown that interpreters disagree about the way they should deal with offensive language in the interaction. Many simply omit it as if it had not been uttered, others will switch to the third person and state that the person has used offensive language, and others will attempt to render the offensive language accurately. Those who fall in the first two categories argue either that it is not necessary to maintain such offensive language or that they do not want to utter it themselves. Those who fall in the third category argue that it is their responsibility to interpret accurately and that not doing so would have consequences on the interaction. However, how to best interpret such language accurately remains an issue. This project will provide an example of triangulation by attempting to answer the research question through the use of different research methods.

Study 1: Discourse analysis
Using a large corpus of naturally occurring interpreted data, identify the instances of offensive language, analyse their use, intention and effect in the source language and describe the way they have been interpreted by the interpreters in the sample. Refer to previous research studies on the use of offensive language in both languages to inform the analysis. Use quantitative methods to reflect the representativeness of the choices, and qualitative methods to speculate on the reasons behind them.

Study 2: Questionnaire
Design a questionnaire for practising interpreters using the results of Study 1. The questionnaire may consist of general questions on how interpreters deal with offensive language and of specific questions on how to interpret offensive language drawing examples from the data used for Study 1. Compare the results of the questionnaire with the results of Study 1.

Research project 8.12   (Continued)

Study 3: Focus group discussion
Invite a group of practising interpreters to participate in a discussion about how to deal with offensive language. Use the results of Studies 1 and 2 to generate questions about the topic. Compare the results of the three studies.

Study 4: Experimental
Choose a small number of segments which contain offensive utterances from the authentic database. Reproduce the situations in simulated settings using a number of different interpreters. Compare the different interpreters' renditions with each others' and with the results of the previous studies.

Study 5: Experimental
Use the recordings of the simulated interpreted interactions produced in Study 4. Assemble two groups of people, one consisting of speakers of the source language and the other consisting of speakers of the target language. Have the two groups listen to the versions they understand. Using a Likert- type scale, have the subjects rate the utterances on a 1–5 scale. The content of the statements will depend on the research questions. If the aim of the research is to ascertain how faithfully interpreters render offensive language into the target language, the statements will relate to the illocutionary force and the perlocutionary act of the offensive language. If the aim of the research is to ascertain how speakers' are perceived differently when heard by those who understand their language and by those who do not through the interpretation, the statements will refer to issues of perception and character. Compare the results from the different groups. While Studies 1–4 relate to the question of what interpreters do, Study 5 relates to the consequences of interpreters' choices and answer the question of what interpreters should be doing in order to achieve greater accuracy.

This chapter has provided the reader with an overview of useful research methods as well as with a number of sample projects that apply those methods. It is hoped that this book in general, and this chapter in particular, will encourage more people to carry out research into different aspects of Community Interpreting that will serve to inform and improve both the training and the practice of interpreters in this field.

Further reading

Boniface (1995). A guide to statistical methods and experimental design in social science research.
Frazer and Lawley (2000). This book provides a practical guide to the design and administration of questionnaires.

Gile (2001). An edited book with contributions from a number of well-known researchers. Although this book's focus is on Conference Interpreting, it is also very useful for those wanting to research into Community Interpreting.

Hertog and van der Veer (2006).This is an edited book consisting of contributions from prominent community interpreting researchers. As the title implies, the contributors review the research into community interpreting that has been conducted thus far and suggest future directions.

Israel and Hay (2006). This book looks at the moral and ethical obligations of social scientists when conducting research.

Krueger and Casey (2000). A guide to conducting focus group interviewing as a method in social science applied research.

Mason (2000). In this chapter, the author provides a summary of the research conducted in dialogue interpreting thus far. It is a useful source of background information for those wanting to do further research into dialogue interpreting.

McNeill and Chapman (2004). This book outlines the various research methods from different paradigms and disciplines. It is a very practical book which provides essential information on how to conduct research in the social sciences.

Penslar (1995). This book looks at the moral and ethical aspects of research.

Taylor (2002). This book looks at different aspects of ethnographic research methodology.

Part IV

Further Resources in Community Interpreting

9
Key Resources

This chapter provides key resources relevant to Community Interpreting. The list is not comprehensive, as new resources are constantly being created, but is a useful starting point for those interested in Community Interpreting research, teaching and practice.

9.1 Bibliographies

The following bibliographies are accessible on the Internet. The reference section to this book is also useful to anyone conducting research. The list below is complementary to that.

Franco Crevati Homepage. Free download of scientific monographs and papers
http://www.sslmit.units.it/crevatin/franco_crevatin_homepage.htm
   Articles and monographs in different disciplines, including linguistics and ethnolinguistics can be downloaded.

Holly Mikkelson's downloadable articles
http://www.acebo.com/papers/pmenu.htm

International Bibliography of Sign Language
http://www.sign-lang.uni-hamburg.de/bibweb/
   A website hosted by the Institute of German Sign Language and Communication of the Deaf, University of Hamburg. It provides an impressive list of articles on sign language from around the world, as well as a list of SL researchers and a useful search engine.

Recommended reference works
http://www.acebo.com/recref.htm

A very useful website with links to reference lists, dictionaries, gloss-aries (e.g. of slang terms) and other very useful references. The site caters mostly for English and Spanish.

Research in Medical Interpretation – Bibliography
http://www.ncihc.org/research.htm
An excellent site on research into Medical Interpreting. This is part of the National Council on Interpreting in Health Care website.

The Critical Link
http://www.criticallink.org/
A number of on-line articles from Critical Link conferences can be accessed. The website is hosted by the Ontario Ministry of Citizenship and Immigration and is in both English and French.

9.2 Journals

Articles on Community Interpreting are published in many journals. These include translation, interpreting, linguistics, social sciences, legal studies and medical studies, to name a few. Below are the most popular and well-established refereed journals in the field. Journals from other disciplines where interpreting articles are sometimes published are also included. Only those whose titles are not self-explanatory are annot-ated. Professional associations publish their own newsletters which are also very useful resources, but are not listed in this section. A list of professional associations is given in section 9.5. Most university libraries subscribe to the journals listed here in paper form. Many journals, however, are also available on-line, and individual articles can often be accessed free of charge or for a fee. Journals other than those below are also quoted in the chapters of this book and referenced in the refer-ence list.

Babel (FIT/John Benjamins, Amsterdam)
http://www.benjamins.nl/cgi-bin/t_seriesview.cgi?series=babel
Dedicated to translation studies.

Forensic Linguistics: The International Journal of Speech, Language and the Law
www.ijsll.bham.ac.uk
Dedicated to the study of language and the law, including legal inter-preting.

Interpretation Studies (Japan Association of Interpretation Studies)
http://www.cl.aoyama.ac.jp/~someya/10-JAIS/

Interpreting (John Benjamins, Amsterdam)
http://www.benjamins.com/cgi-bin/t_seriesview.cgi?series=INTP

Journal of Interpretation (published by the Registry of Interpreters for the Deaf)
http://www.rid.org/pubs/html
Although published by RID, it welcomes articles about spoken language interpreting as well.

Journal of Language and Intercultural Communication (published by Multilingual Matters)
http://www.multilingual-matters.com/multi/journals/journals_laic.asp?TAG=&CID=

Journal of Multicultural Discourses (published by Multilingual Matters)
http://www.multilingual-matters.com/multi/journals/journals_jmd.asp?TAG=&CID

Journal of Pragmatics (published by Elsevier)
http://www.elsevier.com/wps/find/journaldescription.cws_home/505593/description#description

Meta (Presses Universitaires de Montréal)
http://www.erudit.org/en/revue/meta/ (English)
http://www.erudit.org/revue/meta (French)
http://www.erudit.org/es/revue/meta/ (Spanish)
Dedicated to interpreting and translation studies, published in English, French and Spanish.

Perspectives: Studies in Translatology (edited by Multilingual Matters)
http://www.multilingual-matters.com/multi/journals/journals_pst.asp?TAG=&CID=

The Interpreters' Newsletter (Scuola Superiori di Lingue Moderne per Interpreti e Traduttori, Trieste)
http://www.sslmit.units.it/
Published by the Universitá degli studi di Trieste and dedicated mostly to the study of conference interpreting, although it also publishes articles in all types of interpreting and translation.

The Interpreter and Translator Trainer (St Jerome, Manchester)
http://www.stjerome.co.uk/page.php?id=454&doctype=Periodicals&section=1&msg=Periodicals&finds=0&string=

The Sign Language Interpreter and Translator (St Jerome, Manchester)
http://www.stjerome.co.uk/page.php?id=457&doctype=Periodicals&
section=1&msg=Periodicals&finds=0&string=

The Translator: Studies in Intercultural Communication (St Jerome, Manchester)
http://www.stjerome.co.uk/page.php?id=27&doctype=Periodicals&
section=1&msg=Periodicals&finds=0&string=
   An international refereed journal dedicated to the study of interpreting and translation as acts of intercultural communication.

Revista discurso
http://www.revista.discurso.org/
Dedicated to the study of discourse, published in Spanish.

http://www.arabicwata.org
WATA (World Arabic Translator's Association) also publishes electronically previously refereed and non-refereed articles in both Arabic and English. Its focus is on translation but it also publishes articles on generic interpreting issues.

9.3   Useful teaching and learning resources

The following are a selection of practical paper and audiovisual materials.

ACEBO practical materials for interpreting practice in Spanish, Cantonese, Mandarin, Korean, Vietnamese, Polish, Russian, Japanese, Portuguese and Arabic.
http://www.acebo.com/pinfo.htm

Marovich, Neven, Goldman, Sue, Rowan, Magdalena (1998). *Moving towards Meaning.* Adelaide Institute of TAFE. International Languages and Tourism
   A set of three interactive videos and CDs discussing ethical issues relating to the Interpreting profession.

McFall, A. and Sproule, K. (2001). *Interpreting Spanish: Advanced Language Skills.* London: Routledge.

Nolan, J. (2005). *Interpretation: Techniques and Exercises.* Clevedon, Buffalo and Toronto: Multilingual Matters.

Vancouver Community College/Open Learning Agency. *Points of Departure: Ethical Challenges for Court and Community Interpreters.* Video.

9.4   Professional development programmes and courses

The following list is not comprehensive but provides a range of Community Interpreting courses from around the world. The course structures, contents, duration and language combinations can be found on their respective websites.

A list of interpreting and translation courses in the United States
http://www.acebo.com/edinst.htm

9.4.1   Formal Community Interpreting courses

Bachelor of Arts (Interpreting and Translation), University of Western Sydney, Australia
http://handbook.uws.edu.au/hbook/course.asp?course=1519.1

Graduate Certificate in Interpreting and Translation, University of Western Sydney, Australia
http://handbook.uws.edu.au/hbook/course.asp?course=1602.1

Graduate Diploma in Interpreting, University of Western Sydney, Australia
http://handbook.uws.edu.au/hbook/course.asp?course=1637.1

Master of Interpreting and Translation, University of Western Sydney, Australia
http://handbook.uws.edu.au/hbook/course.asp?course=1639.1

Postgraduate Diploma in Translation and Interpreting, Macquarie University, Australia
http://www.ling.mq.edu.au/postgraduate/coursework/tip/pdti.htm

Postgraduate Diploma in Auslan/English Interpreting, Macquarie University, Australia
http://www.ling.mq.edu.au/postgraduate/coursework/tip/pca.htm

Master of Translation and Interpreting, Macquarie University, Australia
http://www.ling.mq.edu.au/postgraduate/coursework/tip/mati.htm

MA in Interpreting and Translation Studies (MAITS), University of New South Wales, Australia
http://languages.arts.unsw.edu.au/MAITS/2006program.htm

Graduate Diploma in Arts in Interpreting and Translation, University of New South Wales, Australia
http://languages.arts.unsw.edu.au/MAITS/2006program.htm

Graduate Certificate in Arts in Interpreting, University of New South Wales, Australia
http://languages.arts.unsw.edu.au/MAITS/2006program.htm

Interpreting LOTE diploma and advanced diploma, NSW and Adelaide TAFE, Australia
http://www.tafensw.edu.au/howex/servlet/Course?Command= GetCourse&CourseNo=3000

http://www.vlepub.sa.edu.au/xml/CarGrpHOSPLANG.aspx
http://www.tafensw.edu.au/howex/servlet/Course?Command= GetCourse&CourseNo=4916

Certificate Programs in Interpreting, Vancouver Community College, Canada
http://continuing.ed.vcc.ca/interpreting/programcourses.htm
BA in Community Interpreting, Germany
http://www.fachkommunikation.hs-magdeburg.de/index/gkbdolm.htm

Diploma in Sign Language Interpreting, Auckland University of Technology, New Zealand
http://www.aut.ac.nz/schools/languages/course_information/sign_ language/di

Certificate in Liaison Interpreting, Auckland University of Technology, New Zealand
http://intouch.aut.ac.nz/intouch/CourseInfo/knowledge_base/kb_sub. php?articleid=397&sectionid=51

MSc/Diploma in Translating and Public Service Interpreting, Heriot Watt University, Scotland.
http://www.postgraduate.hw.ac.uk/course/198/

Master en comunicación intercultural: Traducción e interpretación en los servicios públicos, Universidad de Alcalá, Spain
http://www2.uah.es/aulatraduccion/cursogeneral2004.htm

9.4.2 Short Community Interpreting courses

Community Interpreting and Translation, Macquarie University, Australia
http://www.ling.mq.edu.au/postgraduate/units/trans826/index/htm

Liaison Interpreter qualification, Institut Supérieur d'interpretation et de traduction ISIT, France
http://www.isit.icp.fr/eng/data%20fields/degree_course.htm

Specialist interpreter, Community Interpreting, Sprachen & Dolmetscher institute, Munich, Germany
http://www.sdi-muenchen.de/page3.php?langid=2&content=50&artid=194

Liaison Interpreting CTL5613 elective unit, City University of Hong Kong
http://crl.cityu.edu.hk/prog/prog_mati_ps.asp

Experto universitario en traducción e interpretación para los servicios comunitarios, Universidad de la Laguna, Spain
http://webpages.ull.es/users/experto

Community Interpreting, University of Hawaii (Manoa) for Interpretation and Translation Studies
http://cits.hawaii.edu/current courses.html

Legal, Medical and Community Interpreter courses, Boston University, USA
http://www.butrain.com/cpe/interpreter-translator-overview.asp

9.4.3 Specialist formal Legal Interpreting courses

Master of traduzione e interpretazione giuridica specialistica, Universitá degli studi ferrara
http://www.unife.it/uffici/postlaurea_master_dettaglio-382.htm

Certificate in Advanced Interpreting (Legal), Auckland University of Technology, New Zealand
http://intouch.aut.ac.nz/intouch/CourseInfo/knowledge_base/kb_sub.php?articleid=396&sectionid=51

MA in Bilingual Legal Interpreting, College of Charleston, USA
http://www.cofc.edu/~legalint/

Certificate in Legal Translation and Court Interpreting, Florida International University, USA
http://w3.fiu.edu/translation/images/InterpCert.htm

Certificate in Court Interpreting: Spanish/English, New York University, USA
http://www.scps.nyu.edu/departments/certificate.jsp?certId=155

Certificate in Court Interpreting, San Diego University, USA
http://www-rohan.sdsu.edu/dept/Spanish/contents/court.htm

Certificate in Interpreting with Legal Specialization, University of Minnesota, USA
http://www.cce.umn.edu/certificates/hhs/interpreting/index.html

European professional MA, the Grotius project 98/GR/131
www.legalinttrans.info

BA with specialisation in Court Interpreting, University of South Africa, Pretoria, South Africa
http://www.unisa.ac.za/dept/lng/bacourt.html

9.4.4 Short specialist Legal Interpreting courses

Legal Interpreting unit, University of Western Sydney, Australia
http://handbook.uws.edu.au/hbook/unit.asp?unit=100916.1

Court and Community Interpreting unit (3 credits) Tra 5911, Ottawa University, Canada
http://www.grad.uottawa.ca/programs/masters/translation_interpretation/courses_master_conference_interpreting.html

Introduction to Court Interpretation (general course), Monterey Institute of International Studies, USA
http://www.miis.edu/gsti-course-desc.html

Training in Legal Interpreting, University of Arizona National Center for Court Interpretation, USA
http://nci.Arizona.edu/

Principles of Court Interpretation, University of Hawaii (Manoa) for Interpretation and Translation Studies
http://cits.hawaii.edu/current courses.html

Legal/Court Interpretation (Spanish/English), San Francisco State University, USA
http://www.cel.sfsu.edu/interpretatiom/

9.4.5 Specialist formal Medical Interpreting courses

Certificate in Advanced Interpreting (Health), Auckland University of Technology, New Zealand
http://intouch.aut.ac.nz/intouch/CourseInfo/knowledge_base/kb_sub.php?articleid=395&sectionid=51

Certificate in Interpreting with Health Care Specialisation, University of Minnesota, USA
http://www.cce.umn.edu/certificates/hhs/interpreting/index.html

9.4.6   Short specialist Medical Interpreting courses

Medical Interpreting unit, University of Western Sydney, Australia
http://handbook.uws.edu.au/hbook/unit.asp?unit=100922.1

Training in Medical Interpreting, University of Arizona National Center
for Court Interpretation, USA
http://nci.Arizona.edu/

Medical Interpreter, Southern California School of Interpretation, USA
http://www.interpreting.com/products.htm

9.5   Professional associations and other related professional bodies

The websites hosted by professional associations are excellent resources
for interpreters. They provide much useful information as well as links
to other relevant websites.

AUSIT (Australian Institute of Interpreters and Translators Incorporated)
http://www.ausit.org/eng/showpage.php3?id=646

CHIA (California Healthcare Interpreters Association)
http://www.chia.ws

National Council of Interpreting in Health Care
http://www.ncihc.org/hciaus.aspx

This page provides a list of health care interpreter professional associations in the United States

European Society for Translation Studies
http://est.utu.fi

FIT (International Federation of Translators)
http://www.fit-ift.org

IATIS (International Association for Translation and Intercultural
Studies)
http://www.iatis.org/

IAFL (International Association of Forensic Linguists)
http://www.iafl.org/
Useful as a resource for legal interpreting.

IoL (Institute of Linguists, UK)
http://www.iol.org.uk

MMIA (Massachusetts Medical Interpreters Association)
http://www.mmia.org

NAATI (National Accreditation Authority for Translators and Interpreters, Australia)
http://www.naati.com.au

NAJIT (National Association of Judiciary Interpreters and Translators, USA)
http://www.natij.org

NCIHC (National Council on Interpretation in Health Care, USA)
http://www.ncihc.org

National Council of Interpreting in Health Care (USA)
http://www.ncihc.org/hciaus.aspx

This page provides a list of health care interpreter professional associations in the United States

NRPSI (National Register of Public Service Interpreters)
http://www.iol.org.uk/nrpsi/default.asp

RID (Registry of Interpreters for the Deaf, USA and Canada)
http://www.rid.org

The Critical Link
This is not a professional association, but is included because of the significance of the Critical Link conferences in the development of Community Interpreting. The website promotes the conferences, posts announcements and papers, and acts as a link for anyone interested in Community Interpreting around the world.
http://www.criticallink.org/

A list of interpreting and translation professional associations mostly from the United States, although other countries also feature.
http://www.acebo.com/proforg.htm

9.6   Codes of ethics

Asociación Colombiana de Traductores e Intérpretes (ACTI)
http://www.traductorescolombia.com/codigo.htm

Association of Translators and Interpreters of Alberta (ATIA)
http://www.atia.ab.ca/ethics.htm

AUSIT (1999). *Code of Ethics for Interpreters and Translators.* Sydney: AUSIT.
http://www.ausit.org/eng/showpage.php3?id=650

Austrian Association of Certified Court Interpreters
http://www.gerichtsdolmetscher.at/english/ethics.html

California Rules of Court, Rule 984.4 Professional conduct for interpreters
http://www.courtinfo.ca.gov/rules/titlethree/title3-95.htm

Cross Cultural Health Care Program (CCHCP)
http://www.xculture.org/interpreter/overview/ethics.html

Grupo Trinor
http://www.trinor.com/EN/EN-DOCS/DG10197en.html

Indonesian Translation Service Code of Ethics
http://users.coastal.net.au/bahasa/page3.html

Institute of Translation and Interpreting
www.iti.org.uk/http://iti.org.uk/indexMain.html

International Criminal Tribunal for the former Yugoslavia
http://www.un.org/icty/basic/codeinter/IT144.htm

Irish Translators' and Interpreters' Association
www.translatorsassociation.ie/204.pdf

Society of Translators and Interpreters of British Columbia
http://www.stibc.org/about_code_of_ethics.php

State of Washington Department of Social and Health Services (DSHS)
http://www1.dshs.wa.gov/msa/ltc/ethics.html

The Association of Visual Language interpreters of Canada (AVLIC)
http://www.avlic.ca/Ethics.htm

9.7   Email lists and bulletin boards

ATIBA (Buenos Aires Province (Argentina) Group of Translators and Interpreters)
http://www.onelist.com/group/ATIBA.

AUSIT (Australian Institute of Interpreters and Translators Incorporated)
http://www.ausit.org/eng/showpage.php3?id=646

Forensic Linguistics The discussion list for Language and the Law
http://www.jiscmail.ac.uk/lists/forensic-linguistics.html

IATIS (International Association for Translation & Intercultural Studies)
http://www.iatis.org/

9.8   Web-based glossaries

9.8.1   Medical

www.lexicool.com
A search engine that allows you to choose the kind of glossaries you
would like to find.

www.yourdictionary.com
Medical and legal glossaries.

http://www.medterms.com/Script/Main/art.asp?Articlekey=12914
Information about diseases and a dictionary of medical terms.

http://www.mdchoice.com/ - MDchoice.com
Medical information and a medical dictionary.

http://kidshealth.org/kid/word/index.html
Glossary of medical terms.

http://www.deha.org/Glossary/GlossaryA.htm
Glossary of health care terms.

http://www.meds.com/glossary.html
Medical cancer glossary.

http://www.medterms.com/
Medical monolingual dictionary.

http://www.ifmss.org.uk/glossary/glossary.htm
Multiple sclerosis glossary.

http://www.neuronj.com/glossary.htm
Neurophysiology glossary.

http://www.prk.com/PRK_Glossary.html
Laser eye surgery glossary.

http://www.eclipse.co.uk/moordent/glossary.htm
Glossary of oral physiology

http://www.amconumed.org/glossary.html
Nutritional medicine glossary.

http://pci204.cindoc.csic.es/TESAUROS/Drogas/GlDrogas.htm
Multilingual terminology on drugs.

http://www.whitehousedrugpolicy.gov/streetterms/
The street terms database contains over 2,300 street terms referring to specific drug types or drug activity. The database is used by police officers, parents, treatment providers and others who require a better understanding of drug culture.

http://www.prvademecum.com.ar/
Drugs. Vademécum: Argentina, Brazil, Chile, Colombia, Mexico, Paraguay, Peru, Uruguay, Venezuela

9.8.2 Legal

http://www.autoaccident.com/glossary.htm
Glossary of personal injury law terms.

http://www.prisonwall.org/lingo.htm
Prison slang. Glossary of terms that relate to prison culture.

http://www.law.nyu.edu/library/foreign_intl/
Law glossaries and encyclopaedias.

http://www.ssa.gov/espanol/glossintro.html
Social security Spanish-English glossary.

http://www.willworks.com/glossary.htm
Will Works legal glossary.

9.8.3 General topics

http://www.geocities.com/bible_translation/glossary.htm
Glossary of translation theory terms.
http://www.uta.fi/FAST/GC/gc.html
Links to glossaries on any topic, e.g. European Union abbreviations, Catholic encyclopaedia, musical, political, rhetorical or medical.

http://www.lenguaje.com/enlaces/jergas/venezolanismos.htm
General, IT and miscellaneous glossaries.

http://www.encyberpedia.com/glossary.htm
Dictionaries, encyclopaedias, glossaries, languages, thesauruses.

http://orbita.starmedia.com/~startra/glosterminos.htm
Spanish taboo words.

http://www.admin.ch/ch/f/bk/sp/dicos/biling.html
Bilingual electronic dictionaries.

http://www.imf.org/external/np/term/index.asp
IMF web page. Institutional terms.

http://www.egroups.com/group/GlossPost
All topics. GlossPost is a list for translators, interpreters, terminologists and technical writers. Here you can post the URLs of any interesting glossaries or dictionaries found on the Internet, whether monolingual, bilingual or multilingual.

http://deafness.about.com/cs/signfeats2/a/signdictionary.htm
A general website providing a list of sign language dictionaries on line.

9.9 Useful research resources

The following websites are all court-related sites and transcripts of judgments from different courts. These are useful for discourse analysis and other types of research: see sample research projects in chapter 8.

Her Majesty's court service
http://www.hmcourts-service.gov.uk/judgments.htm

Family Court of Australia
http://www.familycourt.gov.au/presence/connect/www/home/judgments/newjudgments/

Public record search
http://gov-records.com/landingpages/public_record_search.html

Court records and criminal search
http://court.documentsdot.com/?gclid=COi8reKjkYkCFQxgYAodcErd4g

World judgment records
http://www.worldlii.org/catalog/2574.html

Supreme Court of Western Australia judgments
http://decisions.justice.wa.gov.au/supreme/supdcsn.nsf

Judgments of the Supreme Court of Canada – Decisions
http://scc.lexum.umontreal.ca/en/index.html

House of Lords' judgments
http://www.publications.parliament.uk/pa/ld/ldjudgmt.htm

Supreme Court of India judgments
http://www.scjudgments.com/

Judgments and legal reference from Hong Kong
http://www.judiciary.gov.hk/en/legal_ref/judgments.htm

Violence against women in war – network Japan
http://www1.jca.apc.org/vaww-net-japan/english/
womenstribunal2000/judgement.html

Court of International Justice decisions
http://www.worldcourts.com/pcij/eng/decisions.htm

European Court of Human Rights
http://www.echr.coe.int/ECHR/EN/Header/Case-
Law/HUDOC/HUDOC+database/

Judgments and court transcripts
http://www.manitobacourts.mb.ca/judgements_transcripts.html

German judgments
http://www.iuscomp.org/gla/judgments/judgments.htm

Courts of New Zealand decisions
http://www.courtsofnz.govt.nz/from/decisions/judgments-supreme-
06.html

USA public record search
http://www.usatrace.com/judgmentsliens.html

9.10   Other useful websites

Information on Community Interpreting in Sweden
http://lisa.tolk.su.se/SA-QUEST.HTM

Forensic linguistics website
http://www.flrchina.com/en/website/fllinguistics/01.htm#Back2
This is a very useful website which provides links to other sites related
to language and the law, including legal interpreting.

Notes

1 Overview of the field of interpreting and main theoretical concepts

1. Translation with a capital letter will be used to refer to the practice of written translation, whereas translation with lower case will be used to refer to the overarching term used by many to include both the written and the oral modes.
2. See Austin (1962) for a full explanation on speech acts. Speech acts are utterances that perform an 'act'. The example here represents a legal speech act, which acts as a command to plead either guilty or not guilty.
3. Speech acts may need to adhere to 'felicity conditions' to be effective. In this case, the setting of the courtroom requires that the defendant state his/her innocence or guilt in a certain way, using a specific structure in the language.
4. Bente Jacobsen, Aarhus School of Business, private communication.
5. AUSIT, the Australian national professional association for interpreters and translators.

2 Interdisciplinarity: Community interpreting in the medical context

1. Note that the use of the term 'professional' here refers to paid staff interpreters, rather than university-trained medical interpreters.

3 Interdisciplinarity: Community interpreting in the legal context

1. A recent appeal case on the grounds of poor interpreting in Western Australia revealed that the police interview was conducted with the assistance of a bilingual police officer. The appeal case, however, was against the unprofessional interpreter whose services were used in court.
2. Anecdotal evidence has shown that it is not uncommon for detainees to threaten interpreters.
3. The term used in British Commonwealth countries.
4. The term used in the United States.
5. Such exercises are standard in the Legal Interpreting courses at the University of Western Sydney, which form part of the degrees in Interpreting and Translation.
6. www.rrt.gov.au.
7. Direct examination is the term used in the United States.

4 Analysing the interpreter's code of ethics

1. Turkish interpreter with NAATI professional accreditation, no formal interpreter training, with 5–10 years' experience as an interpreter.
2. Spanish interpreter with NAATI professional accreditation, with a BA in Interpreting and Translation and 10–20 years' experience.
3. Japanese interpreter with no NAATI accreditation, no interpreting training and between 10–20 years' experience.
4. The Australian Institute for Interpreters and Translators, the national professional association.
5. The National Accreditation Authority for Translators and Interpreters, the Australian accreditation body which sets examinations and approves courses.
6. College of Technical and Further Education. These colleges conduct training courses for the trades and some professions up to advanced diploma level.
7. Auslan (Australian sign language) interpreter with NAATI para-professional accreditation, with an Interpreting Certificate from a TAFE and 5–10 years' experience.
8. I routinely conduct sessions for magistrates on working with interpreters. The evaluations consistently comment on how little they knew about the complexity of the interpreting process before the session and on how their eyes were opened.
9. Spanish interpreter with NAATI professional accreditation, with a BA (I&T), Graduate Diploma (I&T) and an MA (I & T), with less than five years' experience.
10. Arabic interpreter with NAATI professional accreditation, with no interpreting qualifications but with an MA level qualification in another field, and with 10–20 years' experience.
11. Australian sign language.

6 Community interpreting training

1. Throughout this chapter I use 'training' as a generic term to refer to preservice education. I will not enter into a debate on the meanings of 'education' and 'training'. The term 'professional development' is used to mean 'in-service' education.
2. The debate on this issue was held on the AUSIT e-bulletin during 2006.
3. One such example is the BA in Interpreting and Translation, which focuses on Community Interpreting and Translation. It is a three-year, full-time, NAATI-approved programme, consisting of 24 units: Introduction to Interpreting, Interpreting Skills, Medical Interpreting, Legal Interpreting, Introduction to Translation, Translation Skills, Community Translation, Specialised Translation, Interpreting and Translation Professional Practicum, Accreditation Studies, Linguistics, Sociolinguistics: An Introduction to Language and Culture, Bilingualism and Biculturalism, Second Language Acquisition, English Semantics and Pragmatics, Text and Discourse in English, six units in the language other than English in a variety of topics and two free electives. This course is the oldest Community Interpreting and

Translation degree in Australia, dating back to 1984. Details can be accessed at http://handbook.uws.edu.au/HBOOK/course.asp?course=1519.2.
4. It would be impossible to provide a detailed overview of every Community Interpreting course that is available. Chapter 9 lists the web addresses of a number of such courses from around the world.
5. Examples include: BA (Interpreting and Translation) and MA I&T, both with NAATI accreditation from the University of Western Sydney, Australia; the BA in Public Service in Germany; the BA with specialisation in Court Interpreting from the University of South Africa; the MA in Intercultural Communication, and Public Service Translation and Interpreting from Universidad de Alcala de Henares, Spain; the MA in Bilingual Legal Interpreting at the University of Charleston; and degrees in Community Interpreting offered in Sweden.
6. A special thank you goes to the participants of the focus group: Howard Lam, practising interpreter and casual tutor at the University of Western Sydney (UWS); David Huang, practising interpreter and casual tutor at UWS; Raymond Chakhachiro, full-time lecturer at UWS; Mustapha Taibi, full-time lecturer at UWS, formerly lecturer at Universidad de Alcala de Henares, Spain; Erika González, lecturer at Universidad del País Vasco in Spain and Endeavour Award recipient at UWS; Elizabeth Friedman, practising interpreter and casual tutor at UWS.
7. I acknowledge with thanks the input of Erika González regarding the range of skills and competencies required of community interpreters.
8. See, for example, Gillies (2005).
9. One common comment from participants of a professional development course for practising interpreters I conducted was that the course had given them the knowledge to be able to justify their choices.
10. At the University of Western Sydney, for example, casual part-time staff receive 'staff manuals' which have been written by full-time staff, for each unit that is taught multilingually. These staff manuals provide not only the unit outline (with objectives and contents), but also detailed suggestions on how to teach each practical class. These manuals aim at ensuring that there is uniformity across the different tutors and languages.
11. The study of language and the law.

7   Main traditions and approaches in community interpreting research

1. Action research is 'a form of self-reflective enquiry undertaken by participants in social situations in order to improve the rationality and justice of their own practices, their understanding of these practices, and the situations in which the practices are carried out' (Carr and Kemmis, 1986: 162).
2. A large proportion of the Community Interpreting studies have analysed Spanish–English interpreted data. This, however, does not limit their relevance to that language combination. The same studies can be replicated in other language combinations.
3. Victorian Interpreting and Translation Service.
4. For a result to be statistically significant, it needs to score at < 0.05.

5. Style included only those features of discourse identified by O'Barr (1982) as features of powerless discourse. Other features that could determine style were not considered.

8 Conducting research in community interpreting

1. Packages such as SPSS, ACCESS or EXCEL are all adequate statistical programs. ACCESS and EXCEL are standard packages in Micosoft software. SPSS, which is a more advanced package, is a separate program.
2. See further reading for references on questionnaire design and administration.
3. See further reading for references on focus group interview techniques.
4. See further reading for references on ethnographic research methods.
5. See further reading for references on experimental research methods.
6. Ecological validity refers to how much the experimental setting, situation and subjects resemble the real-life activity the research project is attempting to emulate. See Hall (2005) for a discussion of the need for ecological validity.

References

AACCI (Austrian Association of Certified Court Interpreters). *Code of Ethics*, http://www.gerichtsdolmetscher.at/english/ethics.html.

ACTI (Asociación Colombiana de Traductores e Intérpretes). *Código de ética del traductor*, http://www.traductorescolombia.com/codigo.htm

Adler, H. (2002). The sociophysiology of caring in the doctor-patient relationship. *Journal of General Internal Medicine* 17, 874–81.

Ainsworth-Vaughn, N. (1998). *Claiming Power in Doctor–Patient Talk*. New York and Oxford: Oxford University Press.

Ainsworth-Vaughn, N. (2001). The discourse of medical encounters. In D. Schiffrin, D. Tannen and H. Hamilton (eds), *The Handbook of Discourse Analysis* (pp. 453–69). Malden, MA and Oxford: Blackwell.

Alcaraz, E. (1996). Translation and pragmatics. In R. Álvarez and M. C. A. Vidal (eds), *Translation, Power, Subversion* (pp. 99–115). Clevedon: Multilingual Matters.

Alexieva, B. (1997). A typology of interpreter-mediated events. *The Translator* 3(2), 153–74.

Anderson, R. B. W. (2002). Perspectives on the role of interpreter. In F. Pöchhacker and M. Shlesinger (eds), *The Interpreting Studies Reader* (pp. 209–17). London: Routledge.

Angelelli, C. (2004). *Medical Interpreting and Cross-cultural Communication*. Cambridge: Cambridge University Press.

Arrojo, R. (1998). The revision of the traditional gap between theory and practice and the empowerment of translation in postmodern times. *The Translator* 4, 25–48.

Athorp, C. and Downing, B. (1996). Modes of doctor–patient communication: How interpreter roles influence discourse. Paper presented at the 1996 Annual Conference of the American Association for Applied Linguistics, Chicago.

ATIA (Association of Translators and Interpreters of Alberta). *Code of Ethics*, http://www.atia.ab.ca/ethics.htm.

Attorney General's Department (1991). *Commonwealth Attorney General's Department's Access to Interpreters in the Australian Legal System Report*. Canberra: AGPS.

AUSIT (1999). *Code of Ethics for Interpreters and Translators*. Sydney: AUSIT.

Austin, J. (1962). *How to Do Things with Words*. Oxford: Oxford University Press.

Australian Law Reform Commission. (1992). *Multiculturalism and the Law Report* (No. 57). Sydney: ALRC.

AVLIC (The Association of Visual Language Interpreters of Canada). *Code of Ethics and Guidelines for Professional Conduct*, http://www.avlic.ca/Ethics.htm.

Babbie, E. (2004). *The Practice of Social Research*. Belmont, CA: Wadsworth.

Baker, M. (1992). *In Other Words: A Coursebook on Translation*. London: Routledge.

Bakhtim, M. (1979). *Estetika Slovesnogo Tvorchestva*. Moscow: Isskusstvo.

Bakhtin, M. (1981). *The Dialogic Imagination: Four Essays*. Austin: University of Texas Press.

Barnett, S. (1989). Working with interpreter. In D. Duncan (ed.), *Working with Bilingual Language Disability* (pp. 91–112). London and New York: Chapman and Hall.

Barsky, R. (1994). *Constructing a Productive Other*. Amsterdam and Philadelphia: John Benjamins.

Barsky, R. (1996). The interpreter as intercultural agent in convention refugee hearings. *The Translator* 2(1), 45–63.

Barsky, R. (2000). *Arguing and Justifying: Assessing the Convention Refugees' Choice of Moment, Motive and Host Country*. Aldershot and Burlington, VT: Ashgate.

Bazzanella, C. and Damiano, R. (1999). The interactional handling of misunderstanding in everyday conversations. *Journal of Pragmatics* 31, 817–36.

Benmaman, V. (1992). Legal interpreting: an emerging profession. *The Modern Language Journal* 76(4) (Winter), 445–53.

Benmaman, V. (1997). Legal Interpreting by any other name is still Legal Interpreting. In S. E. Carr, R. Roberts, A. Dufour and D. Steyn (eds), *The Critical Link: Interpreters in the Community* (pp. 179–90). Amsterdam and Philadelphia: John Benjamins.

Benmaman, V. (1999). Bilingual legal interpreter education. *Forensic Linguistics* 6(1), 109–14.

Bergmann, J. (1992). Veiled morality: notes on discretion in psychiatry. In P. Drew and J. Heritage (eds), *Talk at Work: Interaction in Institutional Settings* (pp. 137–62). Cambridge: Cambridge University Press.

Berk-Seligson, S. (1989a). The role of register in the bilingual courtroom: evaluative reactions to interpreted testimony. *International Journal of the Sociology of Language* 79, 79–91.

Berk-Seligson, S. (1989b). The impact of politeness in witness testimony: the influence of the court interpreter. *Multilingua* 7(4), 441–39.

Berk-Seligson, S. (1990/2002). *The Bilingual Courtroom. Court Interpreters in the Judicial Process*. Chicago: The University of Chicago Press.

Berk-Seligson, S. (1999). The impact of court interpreting on the coerciveness of leading questions. *Forensic Linguistics* 6(1), 30–56.

Berk-Seligson, S. (2000). Interpreting for the police: issues in pre-trial phases of the judicial process. *Forensic Linguistics* 7(2), 212–37.

Berk-Seligson, S. (2004). The Miranda warnings and linguistic coercion: the role of footing in the interrogation of a limited English-speaking murder suspect. In J. Cotterill (ed.), *Language in the Legal Process* (pp. 127–43). New York: Palgrave Macmillan.

Bogoch, B. (1994). Power, distance and solidarity: models of professional-client interaction in an Israeli legal aid setting. *Discourse & Society* 5(1), 65–88.

Bolden, G. (2000). Toward understanding practices of medical interpreting: interpreters' involvement in history taking. *Discourse Studies* 2(4), 387–419.

Boniface, D. R. (1995). *Experiment Design and Statistical Methods for Behavioural and Social Research*. London: Chapman and Hall.

Bot, H. (2003). The myth of the uninvolved interpreter interpreting in mental health and the development of a three-person psychology. In L. Brunette, G. Bastin, I. Hemlin and H. Clarke (eds), *The Critical Link 3* (pp. 27–35). Amsterdam: John Benjamins.

Bowen, S. and Kaufert, J. (2003). Assessing the 'costs' of health interpreter programs: the risks and the promise. In L. Brunette, G. Bastin, I. Hemlin and

H. Clarke (eds), *The Critical Link 3: Interpreters in the Community* (pp. 261–72). Amsterdam: John Benjamins.

Brennan, M. (1999). Signs of injustice. *The Translator* 5(2), 221–46.

Brown, G. and Yule, G. (1983). *Discourse Analysis*. Cambridge: Cambridge University Press.

Brown, P. and Levinson, S. (1987/1992). *Politeness: Some Universals in Language Usage*. Cambridge: Cambridge University Press.

Byrne, P. and Long, B. (1976). *Doctors Talking to Patients*. London: Her Majesty's Stationery Office.

California Rules of Court. Rule 984.4 Professional Conduct for Interpreters, http://www.courtinfo.ca.gov/rules/titlethree/title3-95.htm

Cambridge, J. (1999). Information loss in bilingual medical interviews through an untrained interpreters. *The Translator* 5(2), 201–19.

Cambridge, J. (2004). Public service interpreting: practice and scope for research. In C. Schäffer (ed.), *Translation Research and Interpreting Research: Traditions, Gaps and Synergies* (pp. 49–51). Clevedon, Buffalo and Toronto: Multilingual Matters.

Campbell, S. (2001). *Interpreting in the courtroom. National Judicial Orientation Programme*. Sydney: University of Western Sydney.

Candib, L. (1995). *Medicine and the Family: A Feminist Perspective*. New York: Basic Books.

Candlin, C. and Candlin, S. (2003). Health care communication: a problematic site for applied linguistics research. *Annual Review of Applied Linguistics* 23, 134–54.

Candlin, S. (2003). Issues arising when the professional workplace is the site of applied linguistic research. *Applied Linguistics* 24(3), 386–94.

Carr, W. and Kemmis, S. (1986). *Becoming Critical: Knowing through Action Research*. Victoria, NSW: Deakin University Press.

Carr, S., Roberts, R., Dufour, A. and Steyn, D. (eds) (1997). *The Critical Link: Interpreters in the Community*. Amsterdam and Philadelphia: John Benjamins.

Carroll, J. (1995). The use of interpreters in court. *Forensic Linguistics* 2(1), 65–73.

Castillo, G. and Taibi, M. (2005). El papel del intérprete en el ámbito sanitario: reflexiones desde la experiencia. In C. Valero Garcés (ed.), *Traducción como mediación entre lenguas y culturas* (pp. 108–13). Alcalá de Henares: Universidad de Alcalá.

Catford, J. C. (1965). *A Linguistic Theory of Translation*. London: Oxford University Press.

CCHCP (Cross-Cultural Health Care Program). Code of Ethics, http://www.xculture.org/interpreter/overview/ethics.html.

Chan, S. (1992). Families with Asian roots. In E. W. Lynch and M. J. Hanson (eds), *Developing Cross-cultural Competence: A Guide for Working with Young Children and Their Families* (pp. 181–257). Baltimore, MD: PH Brookes.

Chesher, T. (1997). Rhetoric and reality: two decades of community interpreting and translating in Australia. In S. E. Carr, R. Roberts, A. Dufour and D. Steyn (eds), *The Critical Link: Interpreters in the Community* (pp. 277–89). Amsterdam and Philadelphia: John Benjamins.

Chesher, T., Slatyer, H., Doubine, V., Jaric, L. and Lazzari, R. (2003). Community-based interpreting: the interpreters' perspective. In L. Brunette, G. Bastin, I. Hemlin and H. Clarke (eds), *The Critical Link 3* (pp. 273–91). Amsterdam and Philadelphia: John Benjamins.

Chesterman, A. (2004). Paradigm problems? In C. Schäffner (ed.), *Translation Research and Interpreting Research: Traditions, Gaps and Synergies* (pp. 52–6). Clevedon, Buffalo and Toronto: Multilingual Matters.

Cicourel, A. (1999). The interaction of cognitive and cultural models in health care delivery. In S. Sarangi and C. Roberts (eds), *Talk, Work and Institutional Order* (pp. 183–224). Berlin and New York: Mouton de Gruyter.

Cohen, L., Manion, L. and Morrison, K. (2000). *Research Methods Education* (5th edition). London and New York: Routledge.

Colin, J. and Morris, R. (1996). *Interpreters and the Legal Process.* Winchester: Waterside Press.

Conley, J. and O'Barr, W. M. (1990). *Rules versus Relationships. The Ethnography of Legal Discourse.* Chicago and London: The University of Chicago Press.

Cook, M., Eades, D. and Hale, S. (eds) (1999). *Forensic Linguistics* 6(1). Special issue on Legal Interpreting.

Cordella, M. (2004). *The Dynamic Consultation: A Discourse Analytical Study of Doctor–Patient Communication.* Amsterdam and Philadelphia: John Benjamins.

Corsellis, A. (2005). Training interpreters to work in the public services. In M. Tennent (ed.), *Training for the New Millennium* (pp. 153–73). Amsterdam and Philadelphia: John Benjamins.

Cotterill, J. (2000). Reading the rights: a cautionary tale of comprehension and comprehensibility. *Forensic Linguistics* 7(1), 4–25.

Cotterill, J. (2004). 'Just one more time...': Aspects of intertextuality in the trial of O. J. Simpson. In J. Cotterill (ed.), *Language in the Legal Process* (pp. 147–61). New York: Palgrave Macmillan.

Coulthard, M. (1985). *An Introduction to Discourse Analysis.* London: Longman.

Coulthard, M. (2004). Whose voice is it? Invented and concealed dialogue in written records of verbal evidence produced by police. In J. Cotterill (ed.), *Language in the Legal Process* (pp. 19–34). New York: Palgrave Macmillan.

Coupland, J., Robinson, J. and Coupland, N. (1994). Frame negotiation in doctor–elderly patient consultations. *Discourse and Society* 5, 8–124.

Coupland, N., Sarangi, S. and Candlin, C. N. (eds) (2001). *Sociolinguistics and Social Theory* Harlow and New York: Longman.

Coupland, N., Wiemann, J. M. and Giles, H. (1991). Talk as 'problem' and communication as 'miscommunication': an integrative analysis. In N. Coupland, H. Giles and J. M. Wieman (eds), *Miscommunication and Problematic Talk* (pp. 1–17). London: Sage.

Dam, H. (1993). Text condensing in consecutive interpreting. In G. Y. and J. Tommola (eds), *Translation and Knowledge: SSOTT IV* (pp. 297–313). Turku: University of Turku, Centre for Translation and Interpreting.

Dam, H. (1998). Lexical similarity vs lexical dissimilarity in consecutive interpreting: a product-oriented study of form-based vs meaning based interpreting. *The Translator* 4(1), 49–68.

Danet, B. and Bogoch, B. (1980). Fixed fight or free for all? An empirical study of combativeness in the adversary system of justice. *British Journal of Law and Society* 7(36), 36–60.

Davidson, B. (2000). The interpreter as institutional gatekeeper: the social-linguistic role of interpreters in Spanish-English medical discourse. *Journal of Sociolinguistics* 4(3), 379–405.

Davidson, B. (2001). Questions in cross-linguistic medical encounters: the role of the hospital interpreter. *Anthropological Quarterly* 74(4), 170–8.

Davidson, D. (1984). *Inquiries into Truth and Interpretation*. New York: Oxford University Press.

De Jongh, M. E. (1992). *An Introduction to Court Interpreting, Theory and Practice*. New York and London: University Press of America.

Dirks, G. (1977). *Canada's Refugee Policy: Indifference or Opportunism?* Montreal: McGill-Queens University Press.

Dobinson, I. and Chiu, T. (2005). Access and equity: the New South Wales court interpreter service. Current issues in criminal justice. *Journal of the Institute of Criminology* 17(1), 30–46.

Downing, B. (1991). Professional interpretation: ensuring access of refugee and immigrant patients, Paper presented at the National Conference on the Health and Mental Health of Soviet Refugees. Chicago.

Drew, P. (1992). Contested evidence in courtroom cross-examination: the case of a trial for rape. In P. Drew and J. Heritage (eds), *Talk at Work: Interaction in Institutional Settings* (pp. 470–520). Cambridge: Cambridge University Press.

Drew, P. and Heritage, J. (eds) (1992). *Talk at Work: Interaction in Institutional Settings*. Cambridge: University of Cambridge Press.

DSHS (State of Washington Department of Social and Health Services). *Interpreter Code of Ethics*, http://www1.dshs.wa.gov /msa/ltc/ethics.html.

Du Cann, R. (1986). *The Art of the Advocate*. New York: Penguin Books.

Dueñas González, R., Vásquez, V. and Mikkelson, H. (1991). *Fundamentals of Court Interpretation*. North Carolina: Carolina Academic Press.

Duncan, D. (ed.) (1989). *Working with Bilingual Language Disability*. London and New York: Chapman and Hall.

Dunnigan, T. and Downing, B. T. (1995). Legal interpretation on trial. In M. Morris (ed.), *Language and the Law*, ATA Scholarly Monograph Series (Vol. 3, pp. 93–113). Amsterdam and Philadelphia: John Benjamins

Duranti, A. and Goodwin, C. (eds) (1992). *Rethinking Context – Language as an Interactive Phenomenon*. Studies in Social and Cultural Foundation of Language. Cambridge: Cambridge University Press.

Eades, D. (1994). A case of communicative clash: Aboriginal English and the legal system. In J. Gibbons (ed.), *Language and the Law* (pp. 234–64). London and New York: Longman.

Ede, R. and Shepherd, E. (2000). In *Active Defence* (p. 141). London: The Law Society.

Edwards, A. (1995). *The Practice of Court Interpreting*. Amsterdam: John Benjamins.

Emerson Crooker, C. (1996). *The Art of Legal Interpretation: A Guide for Court Interpreters*. Portland, OR: Portland State University, Continuing Education Press.

Englund Dimitrova, B. (1997). Degree of interpreter responsibility in the interaction process in community interpreting. In S. Carr, R. Roberts, A. Dufour and D. Steyn (eds), *The Critical Link: Interpreters in the Community* (pp. 147–64). Amsterdam and Philadelphia: John Benjamins.

Erasmus, M. (2000). Community Interpreting in South Africa: current trends and future prospects. In R. Roberts, S. Carr, D. Abraham and A. Dufour (eds), *The Critical Link 2: Interpreters in the Community* (pp. 191–206). Amsterdam and Philadelphia: John Benjamins.

Fairclough, N. (1989). *Language and Power*. London and New York: Longman.

Fairclough, N. (1992). *Discourse and Social Change*. Oxford: Polity Press.

Felstiner, W. and Sarat, A. (1986). Law and strategy in the divorce lawyer's office. *Law and Society Review* 20(1), 93–134.

Ferguson, W. J. and Candib, L. M. (2002). Culture, language and the doctor–patient relationship. *Family Medicine* 34(5), 353–61.

Foley, T. (2006). Lawyers and legal interpreters: different clients, different culture. *Interpreting* 8(1), 97–104.

Foley, W. A. (1997). *Anthropological Linguistics: An Introduction*. Malden, MA and Oxford: Blackwell.

Fowler, Y. (1997). The courtroom interpreter: paragon and intruder? In S. Carr, R. Roberts, A. Dufour and D. Steyn (eds), *The Critical Link: Interpreters in the Community* (pp. 191–200). Amsterdam and Philadelphia: John Benjamins.

Fowler, Y. (2003). What did the witness actually say? In L. Brunette, G. Bastin, I. Hemlin and H. Clarke (eds), *The Critical Link 3: Interpreters in the Community*. (pp. 195–209). Selected papers in legal, health and social service settings, Montreal, Canada 22–26 May 2001. Amsterdam and Philadelphia: John Benjamins.

Frankel, R. (1979). Talking in interviews: a dispreference for patient-initiated questions in physician-patient encounters. In G. Psathas (ed.), *Everyday Language: Studies in Ethnomethodology* (pp. 231–62). New York: Irvington.

Fraser, B. and Freedgood, L. (1999). Interpreter alterations to pragmatic features in trial testimony, Paper presented at the annual meeting of the American Association for Applied Linguistics 21. Stanford, CA.

Frazer, L. and Lawley, M. (2000). *Questionnaire Design and Administration: A Practical Guide*. Brisbane: John Wiley & Sons Australia.

Frey, J. (1998). The clinical philosophy of family medicine. *American Journal of Medicine* 104, 327–29.

Frey, L., Botan, C. and Kreps, G. (2000). *Investigating Communication: An Introduction to Research Methods* (2nd edition). Boston, London, Toronto, Sydney, Tokyo and Singapore: Allyn and Bacon, www.iti.org.uk/http://iti.org.uk/indexMain.html.

Gambier, Y., Gile, D. and Taylor, C. (eds) (1997). *Conference Interpreting: Current Trends in Research*. Amsterdam and Philadelphia: John Benjamins.

Garber, N. (2000). Community Interpretation: a personal view. In R. Roberts, S. Carr, D. Abraham and A. Dufour (eds), *The Critical link 2: Interpreters in the Community* (pp. 9–20). Amsterdam and Philadelphia: John Benjamins.

Gehrke, M. (1993). Community interpreting. In C. Picken (ed.), *Translation – The Vital Link: Proceedings of the XIII the World Congress of FIT* (Vol. 1, pp. 417–21). London: Institute of Translation and Interpreting.

Gentile, A. (1995). Translation theory teaching: connecting theory to practice. In C. Dollerup and V. Appel (eds), *Teaching Translation and Interpreting* (Vol. 3, pp. 55–62). Amsterdam and Philadelphia: John Benjamins.

Gentile, A. (1997). Community interpreting or not? Practices, standards and accreditation. In S. Carr, R. Roberts, A. Dufour and D. Steyn (eds), *The Critical Link: Interpreters in the Community* (pp. 109–18). Amsterdam and Philadelphia: John Benjamins.

Gentile, A., Ozolins, U. and Vasilakakos, M. (1996). *Liaison Interpreting*. Melbourne: Melbourne University Press.

Gibbons, J. (1990). Applied linguistics in court. *Applied Linguistics* 11, 229–37.

Gibbons, J. (1995). What got lost? The place of electronic recording and interpreters in police interviews. In D. Eades (ed.), *Language in Evidence: Linguistic and Legal Perspectives in Multicultural Australia* (pp. 202–15). Sydney: University of New South Wales Press.

Gibbons, J. (1996). Distortions of the police interview process revealed by video-tape. *Forensic Linguistics* 3(2), 289–98.

Gibbons, J. (2003). *Forensic Linguistics*. Malden, MA and Oxford: Blackwell.

Gibbons, P., Busch, J. and Bradac, J. (1991). Powerful versus powerless language: consequences for persuasion, impression formation, and cognitive response. *Journal of Language and Social Psychology* 10(2), 115–32.

Gile, D. (1995). *Basic Concepts and Models for Interpreter and Translator Training.* Amsterdam and Philadelphia: John Benjamins.

Gile, D. (1998). Norms in research on conference interpreting: a response to Theo Hermans and Gideon Toury. *Current Issues in Language and Society* 5(1 and 2), 99–106.

Gile, D. (2004). Translation research versus interpreting research: kinship, differences and prospects for partnership. In C. Schäffner (ed.), *Translation Research and Interpreting research: Traditions, Gaps and Synergies* (pp. 10–34). Clevedon, Buffalo and Toronto: Multilingual Matters.

Gile, D. (ed.) (2001). *Getting Started in Interpreting Research.* Amsterdam and Philadelphia: John Benjamins.

Gile, D. (forthcoming). Research and training at the service of professionalism and ethics in public service interpreting. In Z. Ibrahim and R. Bell (eds), *Issues in Translation and Interpreting: Perspectives on Professionalism.*

Giles, H. and Sasoon, C. (1983). The effect of speaker's accent, social class background and message style on British listeners' social judgments. *Language and Communication* 3, 305–13.

Gillies, A. (2005). *Note-taking for Consecutive Interpreting – A Short Course.* Manchester: St Jerome.

Ginori, L. and Scimone, E. (1995). *Introduction to Interpreting.* Sydney: Lantern.

Giovannini, M. (1993). *Report on the Development of English Language Assessment Tools for Use in Ministry Supported Cultural Interpreting Services for the Settlement and Integration Section.* Toronto: Ministry of Citizenship.

Goffman, E. (1981). *Forms of Talk.* Oxford: Basil Blackwell.

Greatbatch, D. and Dingwall, R. (1999). Professional neutralism in family mediation. In C. Roberts and S. Sarangi (eds), *Talk, Work and Institutional Order. Discourse in Medical, Mediation and Management Settings* (pp. 271–92). Berlin and New York: Mouton de Gruyter.

Grice, P. (1975). Logic and conversation. In P. Cole and J. Morgan (eds), *Speech Acts: Syntax and Semantics* (Vol. 3, pp. 41–58). New York: Academic Press.

Grice, P. (1975). Logic and conversation. In P. Cole and J. Morgan (eds), *Syntax and Semantics* (Vol. 3, pp. 41–58). New York: Academic Press.

Griffiths, J. (1984). What do Dutch lawyers actually do in divorce cases? Paper presented at the workshop on the study of interaction between lawyer and client. University of Groningen, Netherlands.

GT (Grupo Trinor). Code of Professional Conduct. http://www.trinor.com/EN/EN-DOCS/DG10197en.html

Gumperz, J. J. (1981). The linguistic bases of comunicative competence. In D. Tannen (ed.), *Analyzing Discourse: Text and Talk* (pp. 323–34). Washington, DC: Georgetown University Press.

Gumperz, J. J. (1982). *Discourse Strategies.* Cambridge: Cambridge University Press.

Hale, S. (1996). Pragmatic considerations in court interpreting. *Australian Review of Applied Linguistics* 19(1), 61–72.

Hale, S. (1997a). The treatment of register in court interpreting. *The Translator* 3(1), 39–54.

Hale, S. (1997b). Interpreting politeness in court. A study of Spanish-English interpreted proceedings. In S. Campbell and S. Hale (eds), *Proceedings of the 2nd Annual Macarthur Interpreting and Translation Conference 'Research, Training and Practice'* (pp. 37–45). Milperra: UWS Macarthur/LARC.

Hale, S. (1999). The interpreter's treatment of discourse markers in courtroom questions. *Forensic Linguistics: The International Journal of Speech, Language and the Law* 6(1), 57–82.

Hale, S. (2001). How are courtroom questions interpreted? An analysis of Spanish interpreters' practices. In I. Mason (ed.), *Triadic Exchanges: Studies in Dialogue Interpreting* (pp. 21–50). Manchester: St Jerome.

Hale, S. (2002). How faithfully do court interpreters render the style of non-English-speaking witnesses' testimonies? A data-based study of Spanish-English bilingual proceedings. *Discourse Studies* 4(1), 25–47.

Hale, S. (2004). *The Discourse of Court Interpreting: Discourse Practices of the Law, the Witness and the Interpreter.* Amsterdam and Philadelphia: John Benjamins.

Hale, S. (2005). The interpreter's identity crisis. In J. House, M. R. Martín Ruano and N. Baumgarten (eds), *Translation and the Construction of Identity* (pp. 14–29). Seoul: International Association for Translation and Intercultural Studies.

Hale, S. (2006). Themes and methodological issues in Court Interpreting research. In E. Hertog and B. van der Veer (eds), *Linguistica Antverpiensa. Taking Stock: Research and Methodology in Community Interpreting* (5/2006). (205–228). Antwerp: Hoger Instituut voor Vertalers & Tolken.

Hale, S. and Gibbons, J. (1999). Varying realities: patterned changes in the interpreter's representation of courtroom and external realities. *Applied Linguistics* 20(1), 203–20.

Hale, S. and Luzardo, C. (1997). What am I expected to do? The interpreter's ethical dilemma. A study of Arabic, Spanish and Vietnamese speakers' perceptions and expectations of interpreters. *Antipodean: The Australian Translation Journal* 1 (October), 10–16.

Hall, J. K. (2002). *Teaching and Researching Language and Culture.* London: Longman Pearson.

Harres, A. (1998). But basically you're feeling well, are you? Tag questions in medical consultations. *Health Communication* 10, 111–23.

Harris, B. (1977). The importance of natural translation. *Working Papers on Bilingualism* 12, 96–114.

Harris, B. (1983). There's more to interpreting than conference interpreting. *Information* 11(3), 4–5.

Harris, B. and Sherwood, B. (1978). Translating as an innate skill. In D. Gerver and H. W. Sinaiko (eds), *Language Interpretation and Communication* (pp. 155–70). New York and London: Plenum Press.

Harris, S. (1984). Questions as a mode of control in magistrates' courts. *International Journal of the Sociology of Language* 49, 5–27.

Hatim, B. (2001). *Teaching and Researching Translation.* Harlow: Longman Pearson.

Hatim, B. and Mason, I. (1990). *Discourse and the Translator.* London and New York: Longman.

Heath, C. (1992). The delivery and reception of diagnosis in the general-practice consultation. In P. Drew and J. Heritage (eds), *Talk at Work. Interaction in Institutional Settings* (p. 580). Cambridge: University of Cambridge Press.

Herbert, J. (1952). *The Interpreter's Handbook: How to Become a Conference Interpreter.* Geneva: Georg.

Hermans, J. (1978). The future of translation theory: a handful of theses. Paper presented at the International Symposium on Achievements in the Theory of Translation, Moscow.

Hermans, T. (1995). Disciplinary objectives. The shifting grounds of translation studies. In P. Fernandez Nistal and J. M. Bravo Gonzalo (eds), *Perspectivas de la traduccion ingles-espanol* (pp. 9–26). Valladolid: Universidad de Valladolid.

Hertog, E. and Reunbrouck, D. (1999). Building bridges between conference interpreters and liaison interpreters. In M. Erasmus (ed.), *Liaison Interpreting in the Community* (pp. 263–77). Pretoria: Van Schaik.

Hertog, E. and B. van der Veer (eds) (2006). *Linguistica Antverpiensa. Taking Stock: Research and Methodology in Community Interpreting* (5/2006). Antwerp: Hoger Instituut voor Vertalers & Tolken.

Hertog, E., van Gucht, J. and de Bontridder, L. (2006) Musings on methodology. In E. Hertog. and B. van der Veer (eds), *Linguistica Antverpiensa. Taking Stock: Research and Methodology in Community Interpreting* (pp. 121–34). Antwerp: Hoger Instituut voor Vertalers & Tolken.

Hervey, S. G. J., Higgins, I. and Haywood, L. M. (1995). *Thinking Spanish Translation: A Course in Translation Method, Spanish to English.* London and New York: Routledge.

Holmes, J. (1978). The future of translation theory: a handful of theses. Paper presented at the International Symposium on Achievements in the Theory of Translation, Moscow.

House, J. (1977). *A Model for Translation Quality Assessment.* Tubingen: Gunter Narr Verlag.

House, J., Kasper, G. and Ross, S. (2003). Misunderstanding talk. In J. House, G. Kasper and S. Ross (eds), *Misunderstanding in Social Life* (pp. 1–21). London: Longman Pearson.

Hymes, D. (1962). The ethnography of speaking. In T. Gladwin and W. C. Sturtevant (eds), *Anthropology and Human Behavior* (pp. 13–53). Washington, DC: Anthropology Society of Washington.

Ibrahim, Z. (2004). Clashes of perception in the Malaysian court. In Z. Ibrahim, A. R. Mohd Zid, F. Kamaruddin, L. Baskaran and R. Appacutty (eds), *Language, Linguistics and the Real World. Vol. 2: Language Practices in the Workplace* (pp. 247–80). Kuala Lumpur: University of Malaya.

International Criminal Tribunal for the Former Yugoslavia. *The Code of Ethics for Interpreters and Translators Employed by the International Criminal Tribunal for the Former Yugoslavia,* http://www.un.org/icty/legaldoc-e/index.htm.

Isaacs, K. (2002). *Speech Pathology in Cultural and Linguistic Diversity.* London and Philadelphia: Whurr.

Israel, M. and Hay, I. (2006). *Research Ethics for Social Scientists: Between Ethical Conduct and Regulatory Compliance.* London and Thousand Oaks, CA: Sage.

ITI (Institute of Translation and Interpreting). *Code of Ethics.* www.iti.org.uk.

ITIA *(Irish Translators' and Interpreters' Association). Code of Practice and Professional Ethics,* http://www.translatorsassociation.ie.

ITS (Indonesian Translation Service). *Code of Ethics.* http://users.coastal.net.au/bahasa/page3.html

Jacobsen, B. (2002). Pragmatic meaning in court interpreting: an empirical study or additions in consecutively interpreted question-answer dialogues. Unpublished PhD thesis. Netherlands: Aarhus School of Business.

Jansen, P. (1995). The role of the interpreter in Dutch courtroom interaction: The impact of the situation on translational norms. In J. Tommola (ed.), *Topics in Interpreting Research* (pp. 11–36). Turku: University of Turku. Centre for Translation and Interpreting.

Johnson, A. (2004). So...? Pragmatic implications of so-prefaced questions in formal police interviews. In J. Cotterill (ed.), *Language in the Legal Process* (pp. 91–110). New York: Palgrave Macmillan.

Kadric, M. (2000). Interpreting in the Austrian courtroom. In R. Roberts, S. Carr, D. Abraham and A. Dufour (eds), *The Critical Link 2: Interpreters in the Community* (pp. 153–64). Amsterdam and Philadelphia: John Benjamins.

Kalin, W. (1986). Troubled communication: cross-cultural misunderstandings in the asylum hearing. *International Migration Review* XX(2), 230–41.

Kaufert, J. and Koolage, W. (1984). Role conflict among 'culture brokers': the experience of native Canadian medical interpreters. *Social Science and Medicine* 18(3), 283–6.

Kaufert, J. and Putsch, R. (1997). Communication through interpreters in healthcare: ethical dilemmas arising from differences in class, culture, language and power. *The Journal of Clinical Ethics* 8(1), 71–87.

Kelly, A. (2000). Cultural parameters for interpreters in the courtroom. In R. Roberts, S. Carr, D. Abraham and A. Dufour (eds), *The Critical Link 2: Interpreters in the Community* (pp. 131–52). Amsterdam and Philadelphia: John Benjamins.

Knapp-Potthoff, A. and Knapp, K. (1987). The man (or woman) in the middle: discoursal aspects of non-professional interpreting. In K. Knapp and W. Enninger (eds), *Analysing Intercultural Communication* (pp. 181–211). The Hague: Mouton.

Ko, L. (1995). Teaching dialogue interpreting. In C. Dollerup and V. Appel (eds), *Teaching Translation and Interpreting 3* (pp. 119–28). Amsterdam and Philadelphia: John Benjamins.

Koller, W. (1995). The concept of equivalence and the object of translation studies. *Target* 7(2), 191–222.

Krouglov, A. (1999). Police interpreting: politeness and sociocultural context. *The Translator* 5(2), 285–302.

Krueger, R. A. and Casey, M. A. (2000). *Focus Groups: A Practical Guide for Applied Research* (3rd edition). Thousand Oaks, CA: Sage.

Kuo, D. and Fagan, M. (1999). Satisfaction with methods of Spanish interpretation in an ambulatory care clinic. *Journal of General and Internal Medicine* 14, 547–50.

Kurz, I. (2001). Quality from the user perspective. Plenary presentation at the first international conference on quality in conference interpreting 2001. University of Granada, Almuñécar, 19–21 April.

Kurzon, D. (1996). To speak or not to speak: the comprehensibility of the revised police caution (PACE). *International Journal for the Semiotics of Law* IX (25), 3–16.

Laster, K. and Taylor, V. (1994). *Interpreters and the Legal System*. Sydney: The Federation Press.

Layder, D. (1993). *Strategies in Social Research*. Cambridge: Polity Press.

Lee, T., Lansbury, G. and Sullivan, G. (2005). Health care interpreters: a physiotherapy perspective. *Australian Journal of Physiotherapy* 51, 161–5.

Linell, P. (1996). Approaching dialogue: on monological and dialogical models of talk and interaction. In *Working Papers from the Department of Communication Studies* (Vol. 7). Linköping: Department of Communication Studies.

Maley, Y. and Fahey, R. (1991). Presenting the evidence: constructions of reality in court. *International Journal for the Semiotics of Law* V(10), 3–17.

Maley, Y., Candlin, C., Crichton, J. and Koster, P. (1995). Orientations in lawyer–client interviews. *Forensic Linguistics* 2(1), 42–55.

Mason, I. (1999). Introduction. *The Translator* 5(2), 147–60.

Mason, I. (2000). Models and methods in dialogue interpreting research. In M. Olohan (ed.), *Intercultural Fault Lines: Research Models in Translation Studies I. Textual and Cognitive Aspects* (pp. 215–32). Manchester: St Jerome.

Mason, I. (2001). Introduction to I. Mason (ed.), *Triadic Exchanges: Studies in Dialogue Interpreting* (pp. i-vi). Manchester: St Jerome.

Mason, I. (2004). Conduits, mediators, spokespersons: Investigating translator/interpreter behaviour. In C. Schäffner (ed.), *Translation Research and Interpreting Research: Traditions, Gaps and Synergies* (pp. 88–97). Clevedon, Buffalo and Toronto: Multilingual Matters.

Mason, I. and Stewart, M. (2001). Interactional pragmatics, face and the dialogue interpreter. In I. Mason (ed.), *Triadic Exchanges: Studies in Dialogue Interpreting* (pp. 51–70). Manchester: St Jerome.

McNeill, P. and Chapman, S. (2004). *Research Methods*. London and New York: Routledge.

Mesa, A. M. (2000). The cultural interpreter: an appreciated professional. Results of a study on interpreting services: client, health care worker and interpreter points of view. In R. Roberts, S. Carr, D. Abraham and A. Dufour (eds), *The Critical Link: Interpreters in the Community* (pp. 67–79). Amsterdam and Philadelphia: John Benjamins.

Mesthrie, R. (2000). Critical sociolinguistics: approaches to language and power. In R. Mesthrie, J. Swann, A. Deumert and W. L. Leap (eds), *Introducing Sociolinguistics* (pp. 316–53). Amsterdam and Philadelphia: John Benjamins.

Metzger, M. (1999). *Sign Language Interpreting. Deconstructing the Myth of Neutrality*. Washington, DC: Gallaudet University Press.

Meyer, B., Apfelbaum, B., Pöchhacker, F. and Bischoff, A. (2003). Analysing interpreted doctor–patient communication from the perspective of linguistics, interpreting studies and health sciences. In L. Brunette, G. Bastin, I. Hemlin and H. Clarke (eds), *The Critical Link 3* (pp. 67–79). Amsterdam: John Benjamins.

Miguélez, C. (2001). Interpreting expert witness testimony: challenges and strategies. In I. Mason (ed.), *Triadic Exchanges: Studies in Dialogue Interpreting* (pp. 3–20). Manchester: St Jerome.

Miguélez, C. (2003). Traducción e interpretación en los servicios públicos en la Unión Europea. In C. Valero Garcés (ed.), *Traducción e interpretación en los servicios públicos. Contextualización, actualidad y futuro* (pp. 35–50). Granada: Editorial Comares.

Mikkelson, H. (1996). Community Interpreting: an emerging profession. *Interpreting* 1(1), 125–9.

Mikkelson, H. (1998). Towards a redefinition of the role of the court interpreter. *Interpreting* 3(1), 21–45.

Mikkelson, H. (nd). Interpreting is interpreting – or is it?http://www.acebo.com/papers/interp.1htm.

Mishler, E. (1984). *The Discourse of Medicine: Dialects of Medical Interviews.* Norwood, NJ: Ablex.

Moeketsi, R. H. (1998). Statements about Sesotho questions used in the South African courtroom. *South African Journal of African Languages* 18(3), 72–7.

Moeketsi, R. H. (1999). *Discourse in a Multicultural and Multilingual Courtroom: A Court Interpreter's Guide.* Pretoria: JL van Schaik.

Moeketsi, R. H. and Wallmach, K. (2005). From sphaza to makoya! A BA degree for court interpreters in South Africa. *Speech, Language and the Law* 12(1): 77–108.

Morris, R. (1999). The gum syndrome: predicaments in court interpreting. *Forensic Linguistics* 6(1), 6–29.

Morris, R. (2000). Plus ça change...? Community interpreters at the end of the twentieth century. In R. Roberts, S. Carr, D. Abraham and A. Dufour (eds), *The Critical Link 2: Interpreters in the Community* (pp. 243–64). Amsterdam and Philadelphia: John Benjamins.

NAJIT (National Association of Judicial Interpreters and Translators). *Code of Ethics and Professional Responsibilities,* http://www.najit.org/ethics.html.

Napier, J. (2002). *Sign Language Interpreting. Linguistic Coping Strategies.* Coleford: Douglas McLean.

Neumann Solow, S. (1981). *Sign Language Interpreting: A Basic Resource Book.* Silver Spring, MD: National Association of the Deaf.

Nicholls, L. (1992). The challenges of interpreting and translating in Australia. *Ausit Journal* 2(1), 18–26.

Nida, E. (1964). *Towards a Science of Translation.* Leiden: Brill.

Nieto García, P. (2005). La interpretación social en la policía nacional, guardia civil y policía local de Segovia. In C. Valero Garcés (ed.), *Traducción como mediación entre lenguas y culturas* (pp. 193–201). Alcalá de Henares: Universidad de Alcalá.

Nikander, P. (1995). The turn to the text: the critical potential of discourse social psychology. *Nordiske Udkast* 2, 3–15.

Nimrod, N. and Fu, C. (1997). *Community and Cultural Interpretation Techniques Program: Resource Guide for Service Providers.* Algonquin, Ontario: Algonquin College.

Niska, H. (1998). *Community Interpreting in Sweden.* Stockholm: Stockholm University.

Niska, H. (2005). Training interpreters. Programs, curricula, practices. In M. Tennent (ed.), *Training for the New Millennium* (pp. 34–64). Amsterdam and Philadelphia: John Benjamins.

Nord, C. (1997). *Translating as a Purposeful Activity: Functionalist Approaches Explained.* Manchester: St Jerome.

O'Barr, W. M. (1982). *Linguistics Evidence: Language, Power, and Strategy in the Courtroom.* New York: Academic Press.

O'Barr, W. and Conley, J. (1990). Litigant satisfaction versus legal adequacy in small claims court narratives. In J. N. Levi and A. G. Walker (eds), *Language in the Judicial Process,* (pp. 97–129). New York: Plenum.

Obenaus, G. (1994). The legal translator as information broker. In M. Morris (ed.), *Translation and the Law.* American Translators Association Scholarly Monograph Series (Vol. VIII, pp. 247–59). Amsterdam and Philadelphia: John Benjamins.

Ong, L., De Haes, J., Hoos, A. and Lammes, F. (1995). Doctor–patient communication: a review of the literature. *Social Science and Medicine* 40(7), 903–18.

Ozolins, U. (1991). *Interpreting Translating and Language Policy*. Melbourne: National Languages Institute of Australia.

Ozolins, U. (1995). Liaison interpreting: theoretical challenges and practical problems around the world. *Perspectives: Studies in Translatology* 2, 153–60.

Ozolins, U. (1998). *Interpreting and Translating in Australia: Current Issues and International Comparisons*. Melbourne: Language Australia.

Ozolins, U. (2004). *Survey of Interpreting Practitioners: Report*. Melbourne: VITS.

Penslar, R. L. (ed.) (1995). *Research Ethics: Cases and Materials*. Bloomington, IN: Indiana University Press.

Petersen, R. (2000). Metacognition and recall protocols in the interpreting classroom. In C. Roy (ed.), *Innovative Practices for Teaching Sign Language Interpreters* (pp. 132–52). Washington, DC: Gallaudet University Press.

Phillips, N. and Hardy, C. (2002). *Discourse Analysis: Investigating Processes of Social Construction*. London and New Delhi: Sage.

Pöchhacker, F. (1999). The evolution of community interpreting. *Interpreting* 4(1), 125–40.

Pöchhacker, F. (2000). The community interpreter's task: self-perception and provider views. In R. Roberts, S. Carr, D. Abraham and A. Dufour (eds), *The Critical Link 2: Interpreters in the Community* (pp. 49–66). Amsterdam and Philadelphia: John Benjamins.

Pöchhacker, F. (2004a). *Introducing Interpreting Studies*. London and New York: Routledge.

Pöchhacker, F. (2004b). I in TS: On partnership in Translation Studies. In C. Schaffner (ed.), *Translation Research and Interpreting Research: Traditions, Gaps and Synergies* (pp. 104–15). Clevedon, Buffalo and Toronto: Multilingual Matters.

Rabin, C. (ed.) (1958). *The Linguistics of Translation*. London: Secker and Warburg for the Communication Research Centre, University College.

Rigney, A. (1997). The pragmatics of question/answer structures in a bilingual courtroom. Paper presented at the Conference of the National Association of Judiciary Interpreters and Translators. Seattle, USA.

Rigney, A. (1999). Questioning in interpreted testimony. *Forensic Linguistics* 6(1), 83–108.

Ríos, C. (1997). Hedges and all that: is vagueness translatable? *Babel* 43(1), 1–13.

Roberts, R. (1997). Overview of community interpreting. In S. Carr, R. Roberts, A. Dufour and D. Steyn (eds), *The Critical Link: Interpreters in the Community* (pp. 127–38). Amsterdam and Philadelphia: John Benjamins.

Roberts, R., Carr, S., Abraham, D. and Dufour, A. (eds). (2000). *Critical Link 2: Interpreters in the Community. Papers from the Second International Conference on Interpreting in the Legal, Health and Social Service Settings*. Amsterdam and Philadelphia: John Benjamins.

Rosenberg, B. A. (2002). A quantitative discourse analysis of community interpreting. translation. *New Ideas for a New Century* 16, 222–6.

Rosenthal, D. E. (1974). *Lawyer and Client. Who's in Charge?* New York: Russell Sage Foundation.

Roter, D. L. (1984). Patient question asking in physician-patient interaction. *Health Psychology* 3, 395–409.

Roter, D. L., Hall, J. A. and Katz, N. R. (1988). Patient-physician communication: a descriptive summary of the literature. *Patient Education and Counselling* 12(2), 99–119.

Roy, C. (2000a). *Interpreting as a Discourse Process.* New York and Oxford: Oxford University Press.

Roy, C. (2000b). Training interpreters – past, present, and future. In C. Roy (ed.), *Innovative Practices for Teaching Sign Language Interpreters* (pp. 1–14). Washington, DC: Gallaudet University Press.

Roy, C. (ed.) (2000). *Innovative Practices for Teaching Sign Language Interpreters.* Washington, DC: Gallaudet University Press.

Roy, C., Winston, E., Monikowski, C., Pollitt, K., Peterson, R., Davis, J. et al. (1998). *The Critical Link: Innovative Theory and Practice for Educating Interpreters.* Papers presented at the Critical Link 2 conference, 'Standards and Ethics in Community Interpreting: Recent developments', http://www.criticallink.org/English/criticallink2_papers.htm#3.

RRT (2003a). *Refugee Review Tribunal Annual Report 2002–2003.* Sydney and Melbourne: Refugee Review Tribunal.

RRT (2003b). *Interpreter's Handbook.* Sydney and Melbourne: Refugee Review Tribunal.

Rudvin, M. (2002). How neutral is neutral? Issues in interaction and participation in Community Interpreting. In G. Garzone (ed.), *Perspectives on Interpreting* (Vol. 33, pp. 217–33). Bologna: CLUEB.

Russell, S. (2000). Let me put it simply...: the case for a standard translation of the police caution and its explanation. *Forensic Linguistics* 7(1), 26–48.

Russell, S. (2004). Three's a crowd: shifting dynamics in the interpreted interview. In J. Cotterill (ed.), *Language in the Legal Process* (pp. 111–26). New York: Palgrave Macmillan.

Sacks, H. S. E. and Jefferson, G. (1974). A simplest systematics for the organisation of turn-taking for conversation. *Language and Communication* 50, 696–736.

Sandrelli, A. (2001). Teaching Liaison Interpreting. Combining tradition and innovation. In I. Mason (ed.), *Triadic Exchanges: Studies in Dialogue Interpreting* (pp. 173–96). Manchester: St Jerome.

Sapir, E. (1949). *Selected Writings.* Berkeley, CA: University of California Press.

Saville-Troike, M. (2003). *The Ethnography of Communication* (3rd edition). Malden, MA: Blackwell.

Schäffner, C. (2004a). Researching translation and interpreting. In C. Schaffner (ed.), *Translation Research and Interpreting Research: Traditions, Gaps and Synergies* (pp. 1–9). Clevedon, Buffalo and Toronto: Multilingual Matters.

Schäffner, C. (ed.) (2004b). *Translation Research and Interpreting Research: Traditions, Gaps and Synergies.* Clevedon, Buffalo and Toronto: Multilingual Matters.

Schegloff, E. (1987). Some source of misunderstanding in talk-in-interaction. *Linguistics* 25, 201–18.

Schegloff, E. and Sacks, H. (1973). Opening up closings. *Semiotica* 8, 289–327.

Schiffrin, D. (1994). *Approaches to Discourse.* Oxford and Malden, MA: Blackwell.

Schweda Nicholson, N. (1994). Training for refugee mental health interpreters. In M. Tennent (ed.), *Training for the New Millennium* (pp. 209–15). Amsterdam and Philadelphia: John Benjamins.

Searle, J. R. (1975). Indirect speech acts. In J. Cole and J. Morgan (eds), *Speech Acts: Syntax and Semantics* (Vol. 3, pp. 59–82). New York: Academic Press.

Serle, G. (1973). Recreating an era: Victoria in the 50's and 80's. In D. Duffy, G. Harman and K. Swan (eds), *Historians at Work: Investigating and Recreating the Past* (pp. 49–60). Sydney: Hicks Smith & Sons.

Shlesinger, M. (2000). Interpreting as a cognitive process: how can we know what really happens? In S. Tirkkonen-Condit and R. Jääskeläinen (eds), *Tapping and Mapping the Processes of Translation and Interpreting: Outlooks on Empirical Research* (pp. 3–15). Amsterdam and Philadelphia: John Benjamins.

Shuy, R. (1976). The medical interview: problems in communication. *Primary Care* 3(3), 365–86.

Shuy, R. (1997). Ten unanswered language questions about Miranda. *Forensic Linguistics* 4(2), 175–96.

Silverman, D. (1999). *Doing Qualitative Research: A Practical Handbook.* Thousand Oaks, CA: Sage.

Singelis, T. (1994). Nonverbal communication in intercultural interactions. In R. W. Brislin and T. Yoshida (eds), *Improving Intercultural Interactions: Modules for Cross-cultural Training Programmes* (pp. 268–94). London: Sage.

Slevsky, H. (1982). Teoreticheskie problemi klassifikatzii vidov perevoda [Theoretical problems of the classifications of types of translation]. *Fremdsprachen* 26(2), 80–6.

Smirnov, S. (1997). An overview of liaison interpreting. *Perspectives: Studies in Translatology* 5(2), 211–26.

Snell-Hornby, M. (1988). *Translation Studies: An Integrated Approach.* Amsterdam and Philadelphia: John Benjamins.

STIBC (Society of Translators and Interpreters of British Columbia). *Code of Ethics,* http://www.stibc.org/about_code_of_ethics.php.

Straker, J. and Watts, H. (2003). Fit for purpose? Interpreter training for students from refugee backgrounds. In L. Brunnette, G. Bastin, I. Hemlin and H. Clarke (eds), *The Critical Link 3* (pp. 163–76). Amsterdam and Philadelphia: John Benjamins.

Stubbe, M. L. C., Hilder, J., Vine, E., Vine, B., Marra, M., Holmes, J. and Weatherall, A. (2003). Multiple discourse analyses of a workplace interaction. *Discourse Studies* 5(3), 351–88.

Stygall, G. (1994). *Trial Language: Differential Discourse Processing and Discursive Formation.* Amsterdam and Philadelphia: John Benjamins.

Taibi, M. and Martin, A. (2006). Training public service translators and interpreters: difficulties in an uncharted field. In J. Kearns (ed.), *Translation Ireland* 17:1. Special Issue: *New Vistas in Translator and Interpreter Training* (pp. 93–107). Dublin: Irish Translators' and Interpreters' Association.

Taylor, S. (ed.) (2002). *Ethnographic Research: A Reader.* London and Thousand Oaks, CA: Sage.

Tebble, H. (1998). Medical Interpreting. Improving communication with your patients. Canberra and Geelong: Language Australia/Deakin University.

Tebble, H. (1999). The tenor of consultant physicians. Implications for medical interpreting. *The Translator* 5(2), 179–99.

Tebble, H. (2003). Training doctors to work effectively with interpreters. In L. Brunnette, G. Bastin, I. Hemlin and H. Clarke (eds), *The Critical Link 3. Interpreters in the Community. Selected Papers in Legal, Health and Social Service Settings.* Montreal, Canada, 22–26 May 2001 (pp. 81–98). Amsterdam and Philadelphia: John Benjamins.

Tellechea Sánchez, M. T. (2005). El intérprete como obstáculo: fortalecimiento y emancipación del usuario para superarlo. In C. Valero Garcés (ed.), *Traducción como mediación entre lenguas y culturas* (pp. 114–22). Alcalá de Henares: Universidad de Alcalá.

Thomas, J. (1983). Cross-cultural pragmatic failure. *Applied Linguistics* 4(2) (Summer), 91–111.

Titscher, S., Meyer, M., Wodak, R. and Vetter, E. (2003). *Methods of Text and Discourse Analysis*. London: Sage.

Todd, A. (1983). A diagnosis of doctor–patient discourse in the prescription of contraception. In S. Fisher and A. Todd (eds), *The Social Organization of Doctor–Patient Communication* (pp. 159–88). Washington, DC: Center for Applied Linguistics.

Toury, G. (1980). *In Search of a Theory of Translation*. Tel Aviv: Porter Institute.

Toury, G. (1995). *Descriptive Translation Studies and Beyond*. Amsterdam and Philadelphia: John Benjamins.

Tryuk, M. (2005). Community interpreting: an emerging profession in Poland. Myth and reality. In C. Valero Garcés (ed.), *Traducción como mediación entre lenguas y culturas* (pp. 27–34). Alcalá de Henares: Universidad de Alcalá.

Tseng, J. (1992). Interpreting as an Emerging Profession in Taiwan – A Sociological Model. Unpublished MA, Fu Jen Catholic University.

Valero Garcés, C. (2003a). *Una visión general de la evolución de la Traducción e Interpretación en los Servicios Públicos.Traducción e interpretación en los servicios públicos. Contextualización, actualidad y futuro*. Granada: Editorial Comares.

Valero-Garcés, C. (2003b). Responding to communication needs. Current issues and challenges in community interpreting and translation in Spain. In L. Brunette, G. Bastin, I. Hemlin and H. Clarke (eds), *The Critical Link 3* (pp. 175–92). Amsterdam and Philadelphia: John Benjamins.

Vásquez, C. and Javier, R. A. (1991). The problem with interpreters: communication with Spanish-speaking patients. *Hospital and Community Psychiatry* 42(2), 163–5.

Viaggio, S. (2004). *Teoría general de la mediación interlingüe*. San Vicente: Publicaciones Universidad de Alicante.

Wadensjö, C. (1992). *Interpreting as Interaction. On Dialogue Interpreting in Immigration Hearings and Medical Encounters*. Linkoping: Linkoping University.

Wadensjö, C. (1998). *Interpreting as Interaction*. London and New York: Longman.

Wadensjö, C. (1999). Telephone interpreting and the synchronization of talk in social interaction. *The Translator* 5(2), 247–64.

Wadensjö, C. (2001). Approaching interpreting through discourse analysis. In D. Gile, H. Dam, F. Dubslaff, B. Martinsen and A. Schjoldager (eds), *Getting Started in Interpreting Research: Methodological Reflections, Personal Accounts and Advice for Beginners* (pp. 185–98). Amsterdam and Philadelphia: John Benjamins.

Waitzkin, H. (1991). *The Politics of Medical Encounters: How Patients and Doctors Deal with Social Problems*. New Haven, CT and London: Yale University Press.

Wallmach, K. (2002). 'Seizing the surge of language by its soft, bare skull': simultaneous interpreting, the Truth Commission and country of my skull. *Current Writing*. Special issue on Translation and Power, 14(2), 64–82.

Weir, C. (2004). *Language Testing and Validation: An Evidence-based Approach*. Basingstoke: Palgrave Macmillan.

Wells, W. (1991). *An Introduction to the Law of Evidence*. South Australia: A. B. Caudell.

Whitney, M. S. (1986). *Spanish/English Contrasts: A Course in Spanish Linguistics*. Washington, DC: Georgetown University Press.

Winston, E. and Monikowski, C. (1998). Discourse mapping: developing textual coherence skills. In C. Roy et al., 'The Critical Link: Innovative Theory and

Practice for Educating Interpreters'. Paper presented at the Critical Link 2 conference, Vancouver, Canada. http://www.criticallink.org/journalscl2/3.pdf.

Winston, E. and Monikowski, C. (2000). Discourse mapping: developing textual coherence skills in interpreters. In C. Roy (ed.), *Innovative Practices for Teaching Sign Language Interpreters* (pp. 15–66). Washington, DC: Gallaudet University Press.

Wodak, R. (1995). Power, discourse, and styles of female leadership in school committee meetings. In D. Corson (ed.), *Discourse and Power in Educational Organizations* (pp. 31–54). Cresskill, NJ: Hampton Press.

Wodak, R. (1997). Critical discourse analysis and the study of doctor-patient interaction. In B.-L. Gunnarsson, P. Linell and B. Nordberg (eds), *The Construction of Professional Discourse* (pp. 173–200). London and New York: Longman.

Wood, J. T. (1995). Theorizing practice, practicing theory. In K. N. Cissna (ed.), *Applied Communication in the 21st Century* (pp. 181–92). Mahwah, NJ: Lawrence Erlbaum.

Wooffitt, R. (2005). *Conversation Analysis and Discourse Analysis: A Comparative and Critical Introduction*. London: Sage.

Zoppi, K. and Epstein, R. M. (2002). Is communication a skill? Communication behaviours and being in relation. *Family Medicine* 34(5), 319–24.

Index

Accessible research   236, 251
Accreditation   60, 146, 156, 162, 165, 168, 219, 220
Accuracy   26, 31, 32, 33, 42, 48, 49, 51, 59, 60, 63, 74, 85, 86, 87, 88, 93, 96, 140, 149, 151, 152, 153, 154, 158, 173, 174, 176, 183, 189, 190, 200, 201, 202, 210, 223, 227, 237, 238, 239, 240, 241, 242, 243
Action research   199, 211
Actors   13, 171
Ad hoc interpreters   27, 28, 47, 57, 63, 68, 104, 124, 126, 164, 165, 167
Adversarial   41, 46, 62, 66, 85, 90, 91, 120
Advocate   43, 45, 51, 54, 58, 70, 73, 85, 86, 122, 126, 131, 132, 144, 211
Applied research   198
Attitude   11, 27, 50, 60, 73, 102, 132, 138, 142, 145, 149, 159, 161, 164, 166, 188, 200, 209, 219, 227
Audio recording   80, 237, 238, 239, 240

Backtracking   10, 11, 25
Basic research   198, 203
Briefing   43, 61, 76, 141, 145, 244, 253, 254

Case studies   233, 234
Certification   68, 168
Co-construction of discourse   49
Coerciveness   71
Coherence   17, 19, 20, 91, 147, 148, 152, 153, 183, 187, 240
Communication   7, 14, 15, 16, 30, 36, 37, 39, 40, 43, 44, 51, 55, 58, 59, 62, 73, 84, 88, 110, 119, 120, 124, 125, 126, 127, 128, 138, 139, 151, 154, 155, 159, 187, 199, 200, 202, 205, 207, 208, 209, 212, 214, 215, 218, 223, 243
Communicative competence   208, 209
Compulsory training   35, 51, 79, 92, 162, 163, 166
Conflict   34, 40, 45, 70, 97, 104, 108, 115, 117, 118, 119, 120, 121, 129, 250
Conflict of interest   70, 117, 118, 119, 120, 121, 129
Consecutive interpreting   9, 10, 11, 14, 22, 24, 25, 28, 31, 32, 177, 181, 238
Consequence   11, 26, 31, 32, 41, 43, 45, 46, 48, 49, 62, 63, 65, 72, 86, 92, 104, 105, 133, 161, 166, 174, 194, 202, 255, 256
Content, propositional   9, 10, 11, 15, 24, 25, 32, 33, 42, 49, 59, 60, 61, 65, 74, 91, 92, 96, 110, 111, 115, 120, 126, 141, 152, 155, 176, 181, 182, 184, 185, 190, 193, 212, 219, 221, 222, 223, 239, 240
Context   4, 7, 8, 10, 12, 14, 16, 17, 20, 21, 23, 28, 30, 34, 39, 45, 48, 65, 71, 75, 76, 79, 85, 87, 88, 116, 117, 127, 132, 152, 159, 160, 162, 171, 174, 175, 177, 178, 179, 184, 186, 202, 205, 206, 207, 208, 209, 210, 211, 213
Control   35, 37, 38, 57, 58, 62, 67, 71, 74, 76, 79, 104, 113, 121, 135, 146, 158, 177, 189, 191, 192, 217, 219, 243
Conversational analysis   94, 205, 206, 238, 240
Cooperative Principle   15, 18, 207
Credibility   93, 96, 85, 86, 91, 92, 131, 188, 221
Critical Discourse analysis   205, 210

Cross-cultural   42, 43, 83, 88, 89, 111, 112, 119, 125, 126, 129, 132, 134, 138, 141, 144, 178, 181, 185, 186, 202, 208, 218, 227, 243
Cross-examination   91, 185
Cultural   7, 9, 16, 28, 30, 45, 49, 61, 62, 76, 83, 84, 85, 88, 110, 111, 119, 127, 128, 131, 132, 133, 134, 138, 139, 141, 142, 143, 144, 151, 155, 169, 170, 175, 187, 192, 207, 208, 209, 210, 237, 242, 248
   Cultural broker   45, 131, 134, 242

Data-based research   213, 221, 233
Debriefing   43, 141, 244, 254
Definitions of Community Interpreting   27
Definitions of translation   4, 6, 13
Descriptive research   126, 199, 234
Desk research   220, 248, 252
Dialogue interpreting   9, 10, 11, 12, 13, 24, 25, 28, 32, 171, 180, 189, 213, 214
Dilemma   57, 62, 76, 122, 129, 130, 131, 133, 135, 136, 142, 143, 158, 176, 182, 189, 189, 200, 244, 245
Direct interpreting approach   49, 61
Discourse analysis   94, 126, 172, 173, 174, 178, 182, 183, 184, 186, 189, 204, 205, 206, 209, 210, 211, 229, 238, 240, 246, 255
Discourse markers   10, 11, 60, 95, 96, 176, 185, 227, 232, 239, 240, 241
Discourse strategies   13, 73, 80, 95, 185, 187, 227
Discourse style   11, 17, 234, 240, 241

Empirical   126, 159, 202, 233, 237, 244, 252
Equivalence   4, 5, 6, 7, 20, 113, 123, 160, 173
Ethical   26, 34, 40, 48, 61, 62, 91, 103, 106, 107, 113, 114, 115, 116, 121, 122, 123, 128, 129, 130, 131, 133, 135, 136, 144, 150, 151, 154, 177, 182, 189, 200, 232, 233, 244, 245
Ethnography of communication   106, 114, 126, 205, 207, 208, 209

Evidence   19, 65, 66, 67, 70, 74, 75, 77, 82, 83, 84, 85, 91, 142, 184, 198, 215, 218, 228, 233, 244, 255
Evolution in teaching   172, 173
Examination-in-chief   91, 185
Expectation   24, 35, 41, 61, 65, 84, 97, 129, 131, 104, 114, 137, 145, 159, 160, 201, 208, 216, 217, 218, 250
Experiments   11, 164, 221, 228, 229, 231, 232, 235, 241, 242, 246, 254, 256
Explanatory research   234

Face   58, 97, 207, 213
Faithfulness   5, 6, 93, 106, 123, 142, 153, 176, 183 256,
Fidelity   5, 109, 110, 112, 115
Fieldwork   216, 231
Focus groups   169, 183, 204, 216, 230, 233

Hedges   23, 74, 111, 113, 239
Hesitation   10, 11, 96, 117, 176, 191, 193, 240, 241
Hypothesis   104, 221, 228, 229, 235, 239, 255
Hypothetico-deductive method   221

Illocutionary force   11, 74, 140, 185, 191, 193, 256
Illocutionary point   11, 13, 20, 23, 207
Impartiality   26, 41, 45, 46, 48, 49, 70, 73, 84, 85, 105, 108, 117, 118, 119, 120, 121, 122, 123, 124, 125, 126, 127, 129, 131, 134, 149, 150, 151, 158, 210, 243
Implications   65, 76, 77, 88, 140, 145, 160, 165
Inquisitorial   66, 82, 91
Interactional sociolinguistics   205, 209, 210
Interpreter choices   56, 63, 75, 104, 161, 164, 178, 182, 184, 185, 189, 193, 255, 256
Interpreter's aim   11, 12, 120, 127
Interpreters as barrier   51

Interpreting labels, liaison, ad hoc, cultural, public service, community-based   14, 27, 28, 104, 124, 126, 128, 131, 127
Interpreting modes   10, 22, 24, 28, 31, 35
Introductions   43, 73, 181

Language barrier   11, 40, 69, 85, 124, 125, 155
Legal domains   65, 66, 88, 113, 117, 119, 120, 123, 129
Likert-type scale   222, 256
Literal   5, 7, 16, 22, 42, 58, 105, 106, 107, 109, 110, 112, 113, 116, 152, 174
Literal translation   7, 23, 92, 93, 105, 106, 110, 112, 116
Literature review   228

Manner   11, 15, 16, 25, 33, 41, 52, 60, 62, 74, 91, 107, 111, 112, 152, 153, 190, 233
Meaning   4, 5, 6, 7, 12, 14, 15, 16, 18, 19, 25, 28, 33, 42, 45, 54, 60, 74, 76, 78, 89, 92, 93, 96, 104, 106, 107, 109, 110, 111, 112, 113, 117, 128, 132, 134, 152, 156, 174, 177, 182, 183, 186, 189, 190, 201, 205, 206, 209, 239
Mediated   42, 51, 105, 200, 212, 224
Mediated approach   41, 42, 62
Memory   8, 22, 75, 76, 160, 177, 179, 180
Misconceptions   92, 93, 145, 147, 193, 164
Misunderstanding   12, 16, 17, 18, 19, 20, 21, 35, 39, 46, 54, 72, 73, 92, 119, 126, 134, 138, 141, 152, 156, 157, 243, 249
Mutual understanding   14, 15, 61, 64

NAATI   83, 102, 104, 116, 124, 146, 156, 165, 170, 173, 174, 220
Natural   21, 23, 35, 46, 111, 140, 164, 204
Natural interpreters   23, 164
Normative role   45

Observation   204, 216, 218, 244, 245, 231, 235, 237
Overlapping speech   57, 58, 61, 62, 75, 96, 129, 45, 189, 214

Perception   35, 63, 79, 90, 143, 145, 146, 147, 156, 158, 159, 162, 183, 191, 193, 200, 201, 209, 218, 219, 227, 250, 251, 252, 256
Performance   23, 48, 54, 55, 59, 91, 94, 105, 106, 107, 108, 109, 114, 116, 120, 123, 126, 134, 135, 145, 147, 159, 160, 162, 165, 173, 180, 181, 182, 183, 184, 185, 189, 193, 194, 207, 210, 211, 213, 218, 236, 237, 238, 239, 240, 241, 242
Perlocutionary act   11, 13, 20, 140, 191, 256
Police   12, 26, 32, 65, 66, 67, 68, 69, 70, 71, 72, 73, 74, 75, 76, 77, 78, 79, 81, 89, 202, 214, 230, 241, 245, 246, 247
Politeness   16, 20, 53, 97, 132, 141, 143, 174, 180, 181, 185, 187, 207, 231, 239, 248, 249, 250
Power   11, 27, 37, 38, 39, 40, 46, 50, 51, 53, 58, 75, 79, 95, 96, 71, 73, 75, 79, 95, 96, 113, 122, 193, 167, 187, 205, 209, 210, 250
Pragmalinguistic transfer   23
Pragmatic   4, 6, 7, 12, 15, 16, 18, 20, 22, 23, 24, 40, 42, 74, 78, 128, 132, 138, 141, 160, 161, 174, 176, 177, 184, 187, 201, 202, 205, 206, 207, 210, 239, 249, 250, 255
Pragmatics   12, 94, 161, 172, 174, 176, 178, 185, 186, 202, 205, 206, 207, 227
Pressures on interpreters   35, 53, 71, 72, 73, 130, 131, 162, 243, 244
Professional   15, 26, 27, 29, 31, 32, 33, 34, 35, 36, 43, 46, 47, 51, 53, 54, 57, 58, 61, 62, 65, 69, 70, 75, 79, 80, 81, 83, 84, 88, 91, 92, 93, 101, 102, 103, 104, 105, 108, 111, 114, 115, 116, 118, 119, 120, 122, 123, 125, 126, 128, 129, 130, 131, 134, 135, 136, 138, 143, 146, 147, 148, 149, 150, 151, 156, 157, 158,

Professional – *continued*
159, 160, 161, 162, 193, 165, 167,
171, 172, 174, 175, 185, 192, 197,
200, 207, 219, 220, 250
Professional development   102,
108, 114, 135, 158, 165, 194,
219, 220
Professional identity   35, 167
Professionalism   47, 146, 148, 149,
151, 158
Propositional content   9, 11, 24, 25,
96, 176, 184, 239, 223, 240
Public service   28, 29, 127, 139, 167,
168
Public trust   104, 105

Qualifications   69, 117, 146, 147,
148, 149, 164, 167, 220, 247,
248, 231
Qualitative methods   211, 213, 233,
234
Quantitative methods   211, 217, 226,
233, 234, 237, 238, 245, 248, 255
Questionnaires   204, 216, 219, 220,
243, 245, 246, 247, 251, 229, 230

Rapport-building   40, 41, 43, 59, 72,
226, 229, 235, 237, 238, 239, 240,
242, 243, 245, 246, 248
Recognition   161, 163, 164, 166
Refugee   27, 201, 210
Register   11, 18, 19, 22, 25, 31, 32,
39, 47, 60, 71, 74, 77, 78, 81, 91,
93, 96, 97, 110, 111, 113, 119,
139, 140, 173, 176, 177, 179, 181,
185, 190, 191, 193, 201, 227, 239
Relations orientation   80, 82, 83
Relationship   4, 6, 12, 15, 28, 31, 37,
38, 39, 40, 46, 47, 49, 53, 58, 60,
65, 66, 71, 82, 122, 205, 207, 209,
210
Reliability   227, 229, 235
Remuneration/pay rates   63, 83, 86,
108, 138, 146, 148, 149, 157, 158,
161, 162, 165, 169
Repercussions   41, 105
Repetitions   10, 11, 111, 113, 117,
212, 213, 214, 252

Representativeness   230, 234, 252,
255
Research training   183, 193, 197,
198, 203
Robotic performance – machine,
literal renditions   134, 109
Rules of evidence   66, 82, 91
Rules orientation   80, 82

Satisfaction levels   35, 36, 47, 82,
219
Semantic   4, 6, 7, 16, 19, 22, 23, 24,
78, 111, 138, 177, 205, 210, 254
Sight translation   9, 13, 14, 22, 31,
32, 89, 177, 181, 188
Simultaneous interpreting   9, 10, 11,
13, 14, 19, 22, 24, 25, 28, 31, 32,
75, 94, 177, 182, 227
Source text   4, 5, 6, 9, 11, 13, 106,
109, 112
Source text-oriented   9
Sources of misunderstanding   16, 17,
92, 134
Speech style, powerful/powerless
222, 223
Speaker's intentions   7, 72, 95
Speech Act theory   186, 205, 206,
207
Strategic use of language   41, 90, 91,
149, 201
Stress   87, 88, 135, 182, 190, 218
Style   8, 11, 12, 13, 17, 24, 25, 37, 49,
82, 83, 85, 86, 87, 91, 95, 96, 97,
110, 111, 113, 117, 140, 141, 176,
181, 188, 190, 191, 193, 202, 221,
222, 223, 234, 240, 241
Subjective interpretation   7
Subtitling   9, 13, 14

Target audience-oriented   9
Target text   6, 7, 13
Teaching materials   170, 171, 179,
180, 182, 184
Text condensing   9, 10
Transcriptions   188, 204, 231, 241
Translation machine   42
Translation norms   6
Translation process   4, 5, 8, 21, 22
Triangulation   221, 235, 255

Trust   26, 49, 145, 146, 149, 150, 153, 157, 240
Turn-taking   57, 58, 76, 145, 208

Understanding, misunderstanding   5, 7, 8, 9, 11, 13, 14, 15, 17, 22, 23, 28, 33, 35, 36, 37, 38, 39, 41, 44, 46, 54, 61, 64, 65, 69, 72, 73, 79, 83, 85, 90, 95, 138, 141, 143, 145, 146, 148, 151, 152, 154, 155, 156, 157, 158, 159, 160, 164, 173, 183, 184, 198, 202, 203, 204, 211, 212, 213, 215, 216

Validity   227, 235

Working conditions   35, 44, 84, 94, 138, 144, 157, 158, 162, 215, 219, 227, 252
Working with interpreters   35, 59, 94